Fentanyl

Fentanyl

Fighting the Mass Poisoning of America and the Cartel Behind It

Jake Braun

BLOOMSBURY ACADEMIC

NEW YORK • LONDON • OXFORD • NEW DELHI • SYDNEY

BLOOMSBURY ACADEMIC
Bloomsbury Publishing Inc, 1359 Broadway, 12th Floor, New York, NY 10018, USA
Bloomsbury Publishing Plc, 50 Bedford Square, London, WC1B 3DP, UK
Bloomsbury Publishing Ireland, 29 Earlsfort Terrace, Dublin 2, D02 AY28, Ireland

BLOOMSBURY, BLOOMSBURY ACADEMIC and the Diana logo are trademarks of
Bloomsbury Publishing Plc

First published in the United States of America 2025

A catalog record for this book is available from the Library of Congress.

Library of Congress Cataloging-in-Publication Data
Names: Braun, Jake author
Title: Fentanyl : fighting the mass poisoning of America and the cartel behind it /
Jake Braun.
Description: New York : Bloomsbury Academic, 2025. | Includes bibliographical
references and index.
Identifiers: LCCN 2025020158 (print) | LCCN 2025020159 (ebook) |
ISBN 9798881808471 hardback | ISBN 9798881808488 epub |
ISBN 9798881867478 adobe pdf
Subjects: LCSH: Drug control—United States | Drug traffic—Mexico |
Fentanyl—United States | Opioid abuse—Government policy—United States
Classification: LCC HV5825 .B7195 2025 (print) | LCC HV5825 (ebook)
LC record available at https://lccn.loc.gov/2025020158
LC ebook record available at https://lccn.loc.gov/2025020159

ISBN: HB: 979-8-8818-0847-1
ePDF: 979-8-8818-6747-8
eBook: 979-8-8818-0848-8

Typeset by Deanta Global Publishing Services, Chennai, India
Printed and bound in the United States of America

For product safety–related questions contact productsafety@bloomsbury.com.

To find out more about our authors and books visit www.bloomsbury.com and sign up
for our newsletters.

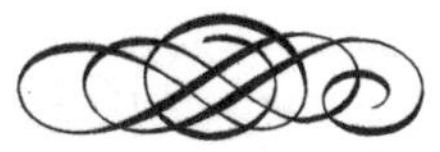

Contents

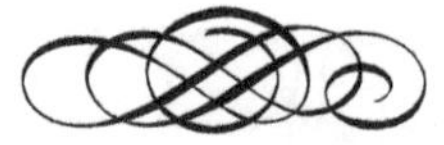

Acknowledgments

I would like to thank the following people without whose support I would not be able to have completed this book, or honestly much else in life:

My mother Teresa, father Denny, and brothers Mike and Joe. I want to thank Joe in particular for his in-depth research and technical review and editing of the book. As well as Alex, Cordi and, of course, Jena. Morgan Ryan, Jane Holl Lute, Doug Lute, Ali Mayorkas, John Tien, Mary Ellen Callahan, PJ Lechleitner, Troy Miller, Ken Wainstein, Tom Bush, Matthew Swenson, Janene Corrado, Eric Hysen, Fernando Lujan, Jorge Comas, Coqui Baez, Katie Tobin, Karson Stevenson, Frank Taylor, Hafsah Lak, John Cohen, Phil Groven, Mary Pat Bonner, Bob Fenton, Liz Sherwood-Randall, and Ambassador Cathy Russell

Those, along with Joe, who spent countless hours reviewing and editing the book like Mathew Brodman, Maya Worman, Marsha Espinosa, and Admiral Brian Penoyer

The crew that came up the ranks with me at DHS, the White House and many other fascets of my life like Chloe Himmel, Nate Snyder, Fayrouz Saad, Chris Derusha, Jake Heller, Phil Stupak, Jason Houser, Jaclyn Houser, Mike Garcia, Ben Rohrbaugh, Becca Sharp, Jon Carson, Jay Rowell, Bill Doerrer and Claudia Chavez.

Preface

Fentanyl is my insider account of how the fentanyl crisis took center stage in the Joe Biden Administration amid a series of other national security emergencies. It then follows our scramble to respond to the epidemic as Mexican cartels went through their most radical transformation in fifty years. As a senior official in the Biden administration, I worked at both the White House and, separately, the Department of Homeland Security (DHS). At DHS, I worked with the team that established and oversaw the counterfentanyl strategy for DHS. I was also part of the White House National Security Council (NSC) working group that developed the Biden administration's government-wide strategic plan for combating fentanyl. The NSC fentanyl strategy was the first of its kind for any administration.

In the first year of the administration, my colleagues and I rarely slept as the Colonial Pipeline cyberattack, the migrant surges at the border, the Haitian presidential assassination, and, most significantly, the withdrawal from Afghanistan crushed us day in and day out. As I caught my breath in late 2021, we got word that the United States had just passed the grim milestone of nearly one hundred thousand Americans dying from fentanyl-related causes that year, ten times more overdose fatalities than the most deadly narcotics in the early 2000s, when DHS was created. Consequently, I was tasked to work with the West Wing and seniormost leadership in other agencies to develop a fentanyl strategy.

I spent the next year working with a team to coerce and cajole the bureaucracy at DHS and elsewhere into action. That effort brought me to Mexico to meet with Mexican agents on our payroll who kick down cartel doors for the United States there. I also spent time with Artificial Intelligence wizards hidden in nondescript offices in Virginia suburbs who hunt down Chinese fentanyl precursor chemicals online, and I even met with Russian migrants in U.S. detention facilities who migrated through cartel-controlled areas of Mexico. In the process, I came to understand the remarkable transformation the cartels in Mexico have gone through in the last fifty years. They went from entities the size of Fortune 50 companies specializing in a marijuana and cocaine distribution business to one specializing in migration and, separately, fentanyl.

To this day, some senior officials misunderstand the epidemic and think that fatalities are so incredibly high from fentanyl because drug use, particularly of hard drugs like cocaine, has increased over time. With the exception of legalized marijuana, that couldn't be further from the truth in the United States. While cocaine use is still strong in Europe and other places with a burgeoning middle class, like Brazil, it has plummeted in the United States. In fact, cocaine use is at an all-time low. The reason narcotics fatalities have skyrocketed is not because of increased drug use. Rather, fatalities are driven by the increased lethality of the drugs. More specifically, it's driven by the lethality of fentanyl cut into nearly all illicit drugs.

My team went round and round with agents, intelligence analysts, White House officials, leaders in Mexico, journalists, and many others on the most effective strategy to stop fentanyl from killing Americans. It became clear that, to beat the cartels, we should employ the same counternetwork strategy used against al-Qaeda and the Islamic State of Iraq and Syria (ISIS) to win the war on terror. The typical "kingpin" strategy wouldn't work. This was not the old "Chicago Outfit" that could be imperiled by confining Al Capone behind bars. We knew for certain this was true because just a few years earlier, in one of the greatest real-life cops-and-robbers sagas in history, U.S. and Mexican law enforcement *had* deposited the most notorious kingpin of all cartels, Joaquín "El Chapo" Guzmán, in a Supermax penitentiary in Florence, Colorado. Yet, fentanyl still flowed. Nearly all experts I spoke with agreed executing a counternetwork strategy against the cartels was paramount to degrading the organization and thwarting fentanyl. So that's what we set out to do.

After much painstaking effort, we successfully executed the most sweeping takedown of cartel leadership and infrastructure related to fentanyl since the crisis began. Due to the efforts of heroic agents, intelligence officers, and national security experts, the leviathan U.S. government is now marshaled against the Chinese chemical companies and cartels propagating the fentanyl epidemic in ways never before imagined. Further, this strategy seems to be working. Just a year after it was kicked off, 2024 fentanyl fatalities are down an astonishing 37 percent.[1] That means tens of thousands of those who would have otherwise found themselves in an early grave in 2024 are still alive today. In fact, 2023, the year the effort was launched, witnessed the first year-over-year drop in overdose deaths in over a decade since the crisis began. Then in 2024, after the counter-fentanyl campaign impacts could be fully realized, overdose deaths dropped a full 37 percent.[2] These drops are unprecedented. Enforcement can not claim sole ownership of the decline. Public awareness and broader distribution of antidotes like naloxone certainly have had an impact. That being said, it is also true that the decline began at nearly the exact same time as the campaign was launched. That being said, we have in no way solved the problem yet. The book ends with where we need to go from here to win the battle against the cartels and the Chinese chemical companies and once and for all end the fentanyl crisis in America.

Much of this book is my firsthand account of what happened as we ramped up the counterfentanyl effort to combat the Chinese chemical companies and cartels responsible for the fentanyl epidemic. Thus, there are fewer citations in sections that relate to what we experienced at that moment as there are few news reports and no books or scholarly papers on these events yet as far as I can find. However, my accounts of what happened in the book went through thorough review from more than a dozen current and former senior officials, many of whom were physically present at the events discussed or had direct knowledge of the events. Hopefully this firsthand account will spur journalists, other authors, and academics to delve into this issue in the future.

Notes

1 Garnett, Matthew F., and Arialdi M. Miniño. 2024. "Drug Overdose Deaths in the United States, 2003-2023." https://doi.org/10.15620/cdc/170565.
2 CDC, National Center for Health Statistics, Office of Communication. May, 2025. "U.S. Overdose Deaths Decrease Almost 27% in 2024." https://www.cdc.gov/nchs/pressroom/nchs_press_releases/2025/20250514.htm.

1

Tyranny of the Urgent

"They keep talking about a 'NEO' on these calls. What the hell is a NEO?"

"NEO is a noncombatant evacuation operation. Basically, if the Taliban routs the Afghan army, we are going to evacuate the embassy and then get out as many Afghans as we can who helped us during the war."

"Wait, what? So, like what we did in Saigon at the end of Vietnam?"

"I hope it will be more organized than that. But, yeah."

"Well, I don't know much about Afghanistan, but despite Taliban advances, all our experts predict the Afghan national forces will hold off the Taliban. Maybe indefinitely. So, we likely won't need a NEO, right?"

"Eh, I give the national forces a week, maybe two before they are overrun."

"A week? Where in God's name are we going to put all these people in a week?"

"Great question. Any idea what they did with the people after the NEO in Saigon?"

"That happened five months before I was born. So, no."

"Well, we better figure it out because this is going to come faster than people are expecting."

"Ugh. OK. I will start making calls."

These are snippets of multiple conversations I had with Department of Homeland Security (DHS) Deputy Secretary John Tien in his second month on the job. Besides being the chief operating officer of DHS, he acted as the DHS Front Office's unofficial resident expert on all things Afghanistan. Tien served as senior director for the Iraq and Afghan wars in the White House National Security Council during the George W. Bush and Barack Obama administrations.

Colonial Cyberattack

It had been a crushing two months since he took office in June 2021, coinciding with my start in March. DHS grappled with the fallout from the Colonial Pipeline cyberattack that left thousands of people without fuel for weeks.[1] Maybe more disturbing, though, the attack laid bare the glaring vulnerabilities of our critical infrastructure to cyberattacks. Colonial proved our critical infrastructure was not only vulnerable to nation-states but even common cybercriminals seeking to extort money from private firms operating our nation's essential services like petroleum distribution, electrical grid, water utilities, voting systems, and more.

These systems were often built more than a century ago and largely analog. The steady march of technology throughout the last decade connected these old systems to the internet. Those connections made our critical infrastructure vulnerable to cyberattack in ways impossible just twenty years earlier. After the Colonial attack, our cyber ninjas at DHS's Cybersecurity and Infrastructure Security Agency (CISA) and the Federal Bureau of Investigation (FBI) sprang into action. They immediately coordinated with the company to turn the fuel pumps back on and hunt down the thieves who launched the ransomware attack.

Fortunately, the FBI, assisted by other three-letter agencies, swooped in and pulled back ransom the hackers extorted from Colonial.[2]

As with the NEO in Afghanistan, this was yet another crisis where DHS found itself with a leading role but no playbook. The department responded to ransomware attacks on critical infrastructure daily and maintained well-trodden playbooks for dealing with such attacks. However, it had yet to write a playbook on alleviating miles-long lines of cars waiting for gas as a result of a cyber attack. The country had not seen a fuel crisis like this since the

1970s. Our emergency responders did not train for this like we do hurricanes or terrorist attacks. Playbook or not, DHS was thrust into a national crisis affecting millions of people's daily lives. Any crisis that far reaching becomes deeply political and, consequently, all consuming. One may assume this particular crisis solely affected CISA as it was a cyberattack. Thus, the crisis could be compartmentalized into just one of the twenty-three subcomponents of DHS. While partially true, crises that unfold on a national scale are ultimately managed in the Front Office of the department.

The DHS "Front Office" occupies a T-shaped suite on the second floor of the old St. Elizabeths Hospital in Southeast Washington, DC. That T-shaped office on the second floor houses the Secretary's Office, the Deputy Secretary and their top advisors.

The people working in those corridors are presented with every major domestic crisis happening at a given moment all at once. During this summer of 2021, I mentioned to Tien in passing that "DHS operates in a state of emergency as its standard operating procedure." Those of us who wander the halls of the Front Office careening from crisis to crisis often joke that St. Elizabeths may have had a new coat of paint slapped on it, but it has not shed its original charge as the first federally operated psychiatric hospital in the United States. Aside from the highest-ranking officials at DHS, other notable previous residents were John Hinckley Jr., who shot President Ronald Reagan, and poet Ezra Pound, who was a fascist collaborator during World War II.[3]

Haitian Assassination

Tien and I reflected on the history of St. Elizabeths amid another unforeseen crisis just a few weeks after the Colonial Pipeline attack. Masked gunmen assassinated Jovenel Moïse, president of Haiti, around 1:00 a.m. on July 7, 2021.[4] Just as the fallout from the Colonial Pipeline cyberattack seemed to ebb, we got word of the assassination. Initial reports contend the conspirators mowed down the president over a dispute over contracts with the Haitian government and possibly his alleged relation to drug traffickers.

One may assume that the assassination of a foreign leader would fall to the State Department. It is indeed true that diplomatic relations with Haiti are managed by the State Department. Haiti, however, lies just a few hundred miles from Miami. Millions of Haitians live in the United States, and conversely, U.S. citizens live in Haiti. So, crises originating there, like the massive earthquake in 2010 that decimated parts of the island or this presidential assassination, have ripple effects across the ocean felt on the homeland as intensely as they are in Haiti.

When I heard about the assassination, I initially thought, "Huh, well, the weekend plans of the Caribbean desk folks at the National Security Council (NSC) and State Department just went out the window. They are going to be stuck in windowless classified offices all weekend."

Shortly after the news broke, we were notified that the Haitian First Lady survived the attack and was evacuated to a hospital in the United States.[5] DHS played a role in the evacuation. Still, evacuating someone to the United States for medical attention is something DHS staff can do in their sleep. No Front Office attention is required for such an operation. Then we find out that the assailants were employed by a security front company in Miami.[6] Then we are told a Homeland Security Investigations (HSI) unit has been investigating a conspiracy related to the president and his assailants for months. Then news outlets reported that basic services broke down, and order devolved to chaos. The interim government requested assistance restoring law and order and basic services. The interim government's ability to facilitate the takeoff and landing of flights for humanitarian aid diminished. Even mundane responsibilities like managing the airport were in dire need of attention. Thus, DHS's Transportation Security Administration (TSA) experts were deployed to Haiti.[7]

It looked like the DHS Front Office would be sucked into the Haitian crisis after all. Fallout from the Haitian presidential assassination was the next major crisis handed to Tien. As Senior Counselor to the Secretary, I was assigned to advise Tien on major assignments. He was an incredibly competent and wickedly smart leader but had no background in Homeland Security. I had worked at the department for more than a decade. President Obama appointed me to be his White House Liaison to the Department, and later I was hired as a consultant in DHS Headquarters. I was assigned to Tien to help him see around corners at DHS and fix problems.

A looming crisis all too easy to envisage was the chaos in Haiti leading to a massive migration crisis in the United States. I paced around the T-shaped corridors of St. Elizabeths squawking into one phone while dialing someone else on another. We wrangled a team of experts from the TSA, CISA, Customs and Border Protection (CBP), and the Federal Emergency Management Agency (FEMA) to deploy to Haiti and help the interim government restore order. If the Haitian government didn't act fast to restore basic services and order, thousands of Haitian refugees would show up on the shores of the Florida and Southwest Border of the United States within weeks.

Despite its best efforts, the interim government failed to gain a grip on the situation. Living conditions in Haiti had been trending in the wrong direction for some time. The assassination was not the sole reason public order devolved. However, living standards plummeted in the months and years that followed.[8] Thousands of Haitians every week launched from Port-au-Prince to brave the perilous eight-hundred-mile voyage to Florida.[9] The glorified dinghies that passed for seafaring ships were often intercepted by the U.S. Coast Guard (USCG), which is also a component of DHS.

Once interdicted by the USCG, people would often throw their children overboard, knowing that the heroic men and women of the USCG would dive into the ocean to save the children. Once aboard the USCG ship, the child would be granted asylum and become a U.S. citizen. Migrants would also do unconscionable acts of self-mutilation like swallowing batteries because they knew the USCG staff was required by law to get them medical attention in the United States. Once admitted to the hospital, they could apply for asylum. It is impossible to imagine how desperate these refugees were to escape the squalid conditions in Haiti.

Hearing these tales of desperation erased any doubt in our minds of just how dire conditions were in Haiti. Consequently, we expected legions of Haitians to strike out for a better life in the United States. As predicted, shortly after the assassination, nearly fifteen thousand Haitian migrants appeared under a bridge in Del Rio, Texas.[10] We had been monitoring several caravans of mostly Haitian migrants entering southern Mexico for weeks; however, they seemed to dissipate into the general population in Mexico. Then, out of nowhere, they reappeared on Mexico's northern border.

The task at hand escalated from emergency response after the assassination in Haiti to a humanitarian and border security crisis for CBP in Del Rio. Overnight we surged hundreds of staff from across DHS to provide humanitarian assistance while at the same time screening migrants for security threats like potential terrorists obfuscating themselves in the deluge of migrants under the bridge. One might assume this crisis response could be walled off from the rest of DHS and isolated to CBP, much like the migration crisis on the high seas seemed confined to the USCG. It is true that some components of DHS, such as the Secret Service, were not affected much by these disasters; however, all emergencies of this magnitude ultimately claim residence in the DHS Front Office. The twenty or so senior officials toiling there juggle these emergencies all at once.

The Border

Amid the fallout from the chaos in Haiti, another crisis had been unfolding in slow motion at the southern border and on Fox News every day since sometime in February 2021. Upward of ten thousand migrants were arriving every day across the Southwest Border. The Border Patrol had not encountered such high numbers since before 9/11, when a sprawling security infrastructure was first installed along the border. Gone were the days when thousands of migrants could just sprint across the border during harvest season. They often traveled back home after the farmwork was complete. Many did it all over again the following year in a cyclical migration pattern that went on for decades before 9/11. Some migrants still venture undetected across the treacherous Sonoran Desert. The notorious reputation of that deadly route, however, dissuades most migrants from crossing there. Consequently, migrants hire illicit guides colloquially referred to as "coyotes" to guarantee passage to the United States. Coyotes coach migrants not to evade Border Patrol but, rather, present themselves to the Border Patrol agents and "claim fear." By claiming fear— or, more precisely, fear of persecution in their home country[11]—migrants are designated asylum seekers and granted a right by U.S. law to have their case heard in a U.S. court.

The problem the asylum procedure presents, of course, is that the courts are overflowing with cases. The wait time to have one's case heard can be three to five years.[12] Thus, the challenge arises of what to do with these migrants between the time they present themselves to the Border Patrol agent and their distant court date. Families and children cannot be sent back to their country of origin until the case is heard. This rule may seem counterintuitive in theory, but in practice it makes sense. For example, if a Jewish refugee from Nazi Germany found his way to the United States, claimed fear of persecution, and petitioned for asylum, he should not have been sent back to Nazi Germany to await a decision on his application. He waits here.

So while awaiting a court date, refugees are processed into an immigrant database. They are screened for any derogatory information such as questionable foreign travel and links to terrorist groups, gangs, or cartels. At the time some single males, who make up the majority of the migrants, could just be sent back due to a law the Donald Trump administration invoked during the COVID-19 lockdown that enables the United States to deny entry to anyone during a pandemic.[13] Every day around ten thousand people showed up. The border stations were not equipped to deal with volume even a third of that. So everything from processing lines to detention facilities to buses and child housing backed up day-in and day-out until the system was overrun. Even after the system was overrun, though, the waves of people did not ebb. No matter how backed up the border infrastructure was, around ten thousand new people showed up the next day, and the day after that, and the day after that.

All these crises occurred in the summer of 2021 during the COVID-19 pandemic. The pandemic was raging and was particularly deadly in Latin America at the time. This was, in part, what was driving the surge in migrants, along with violent crime and low economic standards in some countries, some extreme weather incidents, and especially the booming U.S. economy. Unemployment had reached a historic low. And 2021 was the summer we all ventured outside after getting vaccinated. Outside we found our favorite bars and restaurants barely operational due to staffing shortages. Those staffing shortages were a magnet that no amount of enforcement could overcome.

In fairness to right-wing criticism of the Joe Biden administration, coyotes also drove migrant demand by using misinformation—advertising Biden's short-term ban on deportations and reversal of Trump-era practices of separating families and detaining children in cages.[14] The coyotes also told migrants that the time was right to travel to the United States after a court decision to shutter makeshift refugee camps on the Mexican side of the border. These camps were another creation of the Trump administration that were believed to deter migrants. Once the courts banned the camps, the coyotes marketed the decision as further evidence that the summer of 2021 was an opportune time to migrate to the United States.

All these drivers of migration amounted to border patrol facilities overflowing with migrants. DHS transformed into a logistics operation coordinating massive new facilities to house the migrants overnight. It bought tens of thousands of beds and rented hundreds of bus services to move migrants from facilities that were over capacity to those with space until those too ran out of space. The facilities became everything from likely the largest child day care in the country to mass vaccination staging locations and everything in between. Everyone from Secretary Alejandro Mayorkas to Deputy Secretary Tien, Domestic Policy Council Director Susan Rice, and the director of U.S. Immigration and Customs Enforcement (ICE) and the commissioner of CBP were on an endless series of calls to stem the tide of migrants and humanely and securely process those who had arrived. Hundreds of thousands of lives hung in the balance of the sprawling migrant processing and housing operation. Particularly because COVID-19 contorted the already intricate logistics of the massive operation, we were forced to deploy the government's top logistician at FEMA to manage it.

So in the summer of 2021 the twenty-five or so souls scrambling around the T-shaped Front Office of DHS were managing the largest surge of migrants on the Southwest Border in at least twenty years. Those same twenty-five people were responding to an unprecedented cyberattack and resulting national fuel shortage on the Colonial Pipeline system. The same people were sucked into dealing with the Haitian presidential assassination and resulting Haitian migration crisis. As FEMA is part of DHS, there were also multiple extreme weather events we mitigated that summer. For example, I haven't even gone through our response to Hurricane Ida, which is tied as the strongest hurricane to hit Louisiana and only bested by Hurricane Katrina in terms of devastation caused to the state.[15] So when Tien told me the NEO was coming and we may have to resettle tens of thousands of Afghans in the midst of all this, I didn't know whether to laugh or cry.

NEO

Tien's prediction that the Taliban would quickly trounce the Afghan army proved prescient. The date he anticipated the NEO evacuation also proved accurate within a few days. We looked on with trepidation as television cameras beamed the chaos around the globe. Like everyone else in the United States, we watched CNN in stunned silence as people climbed over each other to get on the huge C-17 military transport planes out of Kabul. The scene was reminiscent of the desperate Hattians throwing children overboard so the USCG would save them. Here, too, we all stared aghast as Afghans handed their babies over the fence to total strangers at the Kabul airport. Those total strangers passed the children to American soldiers in hopes the children would escape to a better life in the United States.[16] These images beamed around the globe and elicited sympathy from every parent on the planet. Yet few but the Haitians could empathize with the extreme desperation these parents must have felt as they handed their babies over to strangers, likely never to be seen again.

In the weeks leading up to the evacuation, there were heated interagency debates on what to do with the Afghans. Initially, we were most concerned for those who helped us during the war and faced retribution when the Taliban gained control. In between dealing with the aforementioned myriad crises, a key question arose regarding where the Afghans would be housed. They required security screening and immigration documents before they could live as U.S. citizens. We all hoped for an orderly process where our allies in Afghanistan could be properly vetted before they came to the United States.

At DHS, our primary goal for the evacuation was to ensure no terrorists erroneously snuck on to the planes with those headed for the United States. However, DHS rarely is dealt a hand that includes an orderly process. The hand we are typically dealt, instead, is chaos during a state of emergency that we need to wrangle and transform into order. So we plan for the worst. Like everyone else in the federal government, we thought we had a lot more time to plan. Tien was alone in his accurate prediction that Kabul would fall fast.[17]

The Department of Defense (DOD), State Department, Central Intelligence Agency (CIA), and DHS all owned critical components of the overall effort to rescue Afghans who helped our soldiers during the war. DOD owned the transportation and, begrudgingly, the housing of Afghans until they were resettled in the United States. The State Department managed all diplomatic relationships with both the Afghan and Taliban governments, as well as other countries where Afghans fled, such as Pakistan and Uzbekistan, when they could not reach Kabul. The State Department also funds nine nongovernmental organizations (NGOs) that oversee resettlement of refugees in the United States. As we will see later, these nine refugee resettlement NGOs become central players in the story of our Afghan allies. DHS owned dual roles in the evacuation. One was as the lead immigration agency. We had to quickly process the immigration status of the Afghans. Additionally, we were the lead agency for vetting the Afghans to ensure they did not pose a threat to the United States and no possible security threats made their way to the homeland.

It was on this last point—the security and vetting aspect of DHS's role in the evacuation—that Secretary Mayorkas was most vocal. He repeatedly insisted on the most extensive vetting of the Afghans coming to the United States. He also insisted vetting was done before they could step foot on American soil. Several immigration novices involved in the discussions argued for initially flying the Afghans to places like Guam for vetting. Mayorkas and Tien fought back hard against that option. As Mayorkas said, "If you fly them to Guam, you might as well fly them to Kansas" because once on American soil they have all kinds of rights like a right not to be held against their will.[18] They could simply stroll off the plane in Guam, take a commercial flight to anywhere in the United States, and disappear.

If a terrorist hid among the throngs of Afghans coming to the United States, he had free rein to carry out an attack once he touched down on U.S. soil. Thus, security vetting of the Afghans was critical prior to arrival in the United States. Mayorkas held his ground on this point against fierce opposition.

He also held his ground on the type of vetting. He insisted that it be the most extensive vetting possible. Normal vetting procedures went out the window for the Afghans as their government, law enforcement, and military databases were either nonexistent or controlled by the Taliban. Normally if someone travels to the United States from a more developed country like Germany or Japan, DHS checks for convictions of any crimes in their home country or presence on any watchlist. After being ravaged by war for nearly two decades, diligent recordkeeping was not a priority for the Afghan government.

What the Afghan government lacked in recordkeeping, however, the U.S. military and several three-letter agencies made up for in biometric information on Afghans. In fact, the U.S. government may have collected more biometric information on the population of Afghanistan than any other country in the world—particularly on our enemies there. For nearly twenty years, if we captured or even questioned someone in Afghanistan suspected of supporting our enemies, we collected their biometrics. Fingerprints, facial images, and in some cases retina or voice were stored in our databases. In fact, the military sourced biometrics from everywhere. For example, if a bomb went off in a market in Kabul, some soldier was sent down to the site of the attack to gather up shrapnel and dust it for fingerprints and other biometrics.[19] So we possessed a lot of info on our enemies in Afghanistan. Mayorkas insisted on full biometric vetting before any Afghan was allowed to step foot on U.S. soil. Biometric scanning was also paramount as many of our Afghan allies fled their homes with nothing but the shirts on their backs. They often possessed no identification except for their biometrics.

Mayorkas won the fight. The highest levels of government concluded that when the Taliban routed the Afghan military, and we had no time to scan people there, Afghans would be flown to U.S. military bases in a third country for extensive vetting before they were taken to the United States. When Tien predicted Kabul would fall in a week or two, I immediately wondered what countries would accept these people and what biometric scanning equipment existed at military bases there.

Lily Pads

We wound up transporting the Afghans to U.S. military bases in Germany, Qatar, Bahrain, and a few other countries for vetting before they advanced to the United States.[20] Tien asked me to ascertain what vetting equipment and trained personnel were available at these bases. Of course, it turned out that no vetting equipment compatible with DHS's systems was available on any of the bases. Thus no people on base knew how to operate the equipment they didn't have.

Within hours of the NEO being initiated, I embarked on a mission to locate hundreds of biometric ID scanners compatible with our system and personnel skilled in operating them. Of course, after sourcing it, we had to transport all these people and equipment to the "Lily Pads," as the military bases where the Afghans were vetted came to be known. This initially appeared to be a straightforward task. Biometric ID scanners are present in every airport in the United States, and we have thousands of people across DHS trained to use them. Unfortunately for me, those biometric scanners are generally bolted down in the airports where they reside. Also, the countries that the machines (and their operators) were destined for required COVID-19 tests. That could delay travel for weeks as the tests available in the summer of 2021 were not as ubiquitous or fast as those we have today.

To remedy these challenges, I phoned anyone that may have a bead on biometric ID scanners. Eventually DHS's fixer-in-chief, Janene Corrado, sourced a guy who operates a nondescript warehouse in Chantilly, Virginia. He housed around five hundred of these scanners. He was likely the only person in the United States who was aware those scanners were stored in that warehouse. To this day, Janene and I remain puzzled about why all those devices were amassed at that random warehouse. To identify trained personnel, we recruited people at or near the military bases. Recruiting locals enabled us to forgo airplanes and their corresponding COVID-19 test delays.

These locals could immediately get on base and vet Afghans as the refugees were showing up by the planeload every day.

I located some USCG guys in Bahrain, and we surged a group of U.S. contractors living in Germany. Those folks were sufficient to train the military guys on the base to use the equipment. We quickly realized, however, the scanners deployed to the Lily Pads were not sufficient. The evacuation transported more than one hundred thousand people from Afghanistan.[21] A few hundred scanners that often broke and operated off spotty internet connections were not processing people fast enough. The Lily Pads were beginning to run out of room for new arrivals. The C-17s, however, kept showing up overflowing with people desperate to flee Kabul.

It turned out that DOD had thousands more scanners around the world, but they were not compatible with our system. By incompatible, I mean that the two systems operated on separate classified networks with separate end-to-end encryption. These were heavily secured and highly regulated military and law enforcement systems. Making the systems talk to one another was not as easy as flipping a switch. The interagency wrung its hands for a week or two as we watched the Lily Pads overflow with Afghans. We were getting dangerously close to a point where flights would have to be stopped. However, every second counted for our Afghan allies on the ground in Afghanistan. The Taliban was in firm control of the country and delivering retribution to those who helped NATO and its allies.[22] With so many lives at risk, we could not let the C-17s stop flying to unload Afghans on the Lily Pads.

Thankfully a DHS programmer came up with a hack to both the DOD and DHS systems that made them compatible. He was buried in an arcane office no one has ever heard of at DHS, the Office of Biometrics and Identity Management (OBIM). Once we confirmed his tech fix worked, we elevated him and assigned him a bunch of extra developers to duct-tape-and-bubble-gum the systems together. Our chief information officer at DHS, Eric Hysen, hailed from the likes of Google and was considered a civic tech wizard in the government. He estimated we achieved five years of DOD and DHS data integration in a matter of days.

Now DHS's immigration and law enforcement databases were able to talk to those in the military and thus allow DOD scanners to vet Afghans via both

DHS and DOD data. DOD flipped the switch of its global logistics juggernaut. It is remarkable to see what the Pentagon can do when it decides on a course of action. Within a day or two, thousands of machines appeared at the bases with trained military personnel. Reliable Wi-Fi miraculously appeared. In short order, we were vetting thousands of Afghans to decide if they were safe to migrate to the United States.

Stranded at the Airport

As the Afghans steadily processed through the Lily Pads, we found ourselves at another bottleneck. The Lily Pads were conceived to evaluate whether the person was a security risk to the homeland. The screening overlooked details like whether they had health problems, post-traumatic stress disorder (PTSD), or any number of other ailments. The limitations I mentioned around surging nonmilitary personnel to the Lily Pads deterred us from sending the type of medical and psychiatric personnel required there.

As a result of the limitations at the Lily Pads, we insisted on administering these health screenings before people departed the U.S. airport where they landed and could potentially join the U.S. population. So we conjured up another makeshift screening facility at Dulles International Airport[23] and later Philadelphia Airport to evaluate refugees for everything from COVID-19 to PTSD.[24] The new screening facility ballooned to resemble a refugee camp inside the airport. We quickly ran out of room for all the Afghans arriving at Dulles. At one point, DOD proposed erecting an entirely new hangar to house all the prescreened Afghans. This proposal contained a host of issues, however, not the least of which were potential risks to air travel security if the military just showed up with all its construction equipment and started building structures on the tarmac.

As a result, I began calling around to the airlines to see if they could address our space issue in a way that didn't entail the military commandeering half the airport. I figured the airlines had the most skin in the game to figure out a solution that did not disrupt their flights to and from Dulles. After careening down multiple dead ends, I reached an executive at Dulles who discovered an extra hangar United used for storage. He warned us to secure the industrial equipment and erect a barrier to keep people away from some of the more dangerous tools.

I informed him that we were holding at bay a cadre of military engineers replete with Bobcats, cranes, and jackhammers itching to throw together a convention center–sized facility at the airport. So, I figured they could handle moving some equipment around for us.

Overnight the United hangar was transformed into a refugee facility housing thousands of Afghans awaiting further screening. After this round of screening, Afghans could just meander out of the airport and join American society. Many migrants who had friends or family in the United States did just that. Once connected with those relatives, they would complete their naturalization process, get a job and a home, and put their kids in school like any other American.

Unfortunately, only a small minority had close friends and family in the United States. Everyone else required some level of initial support. For those of us raised in the United States, activities like finding a new home, enrolling our children in school, landing a job, or passing a driver's test are irritating but for most ultimately achievable. For new migrants with no support network, these present daunting obstacles that are all but insurmountable. Most refugees who arrive in the United States through a legal process are offered support from NGOs and financial resources funded by the federal government. Since the Afghans arriving in the United States were those who helped our soldiers, diplomats, and aid workers in a combat zone, all decision-makers insisted they be offered access to at least the same services other refugees received.

Unfortunately a glaring problem arose from the straightforward decision to offer the Afghans refugee services. The nine refugee NGOs the State Department funds to resettle refugees had little warning this deluge of refugees from Afghanistan was soon to be thrust upon them. Also, the evacuation from Afghanistan happened late in the fiscal year. So, most of the resettlement agencies already exceeded their capacity to resettle refugees for the year. Many of these NGOs were global enterprises with robust infrastructure and decades of experience, like Catholic Charities. However, they were still NGOs. This meant they operated on a shoestring budget and relied on volunteers for much of their productivity. These NGOs grasped the historic importance of quickly integrating Afghan refugees into American society. They regularly asserted they could supercharge resettlement output by 30 or 40 percent from a typical year. However, we were asking them to increase their production by around 500 percent in three months.

Safe Havens

The nine resettlement NGOs were so overwhelmed that the State Department could not determine how many Afghans to assign each one because all were over capacity. Scrambling yet again, we resolved to temporarily house the refugees on eight domestic military bases we referred to as the "Safe Havens."[25] Mayorkas was adamant the camps function as cities with health services, childhood education, English classes, job seeking services, naturalization services, and more. He urged us to ensure the Afghans were set up for success in the United States. The last thing the country wanted as a capstone to its longest war was scores of homeless Afghans wandering the streets after everything they had done for us.

To that end, Mayorkas tapped Robert "Bob" Fenton Jr., an old FEMA hand, to oversee the resettlement effort. Fenton was experienced in managing facilities for displaced local refugees in time of disaster. A hulking man of at least six feet four inches and 250 pounds, Fenton displayed the appearance of someone who must have played linebacker in college. He had recently risen to favor with the Biden inner circle for his part in overseeing FEMA's successful role in COVID-19 vaccine dissemination.

As Mayorkas suggested, seemingly overnight Fenton turned eight military bases into villages supporting every aspect of life. Despite Fenton's Herculean efforts, the Safe Havens were the third stop on the Afghans' journey to the Land of Opportunity. They were growing restless. They didn't seek handouts. They sought clarity on when this chaos would end and they could settle into a stable life. In fact, while at the Safe Haven in Quantico, I polled a group of men about leaving the ad hoc village there. An oil company in Mississippi had recently contacted us about providing good-paying jobs for the Afghans.

I gauged their interest in leaving the free room and board provided by the government in exchange for a physically demanding job in the heat of the Deep South. Through their interpreter, they admitted never hearing of a place called "Mississippi." Regardless, their only follow-up question was whether they could head to "Mississippi" right then and there and start these manual labor oil jobs and, consequently, the rest of their lives.

Companies were falling all over themselves to offer the Afghans jobs. Overall, the outpouring of support for the Afghans from the business community, volunteers, religious organizations, and civil society was inspiring and renewed faith that the United States can step up and do what's right when it desires.

Unfortunately, all that pent-up goodwill was butting up against one final confounding obstacle. Over the course of about six weeks, we encountered one new, unforeseen challenge after another. None of the challenges came with a playbook to address them. Fenton was even checking out forty-five-year-old reports from the Library of Congress on the Saigon evacuation to inform his planning for the Afghans.

Every few weeks after the NEO, we had a totally novel, largely unforeseen disaster gut punch us and demand an immediate solution. Usually this happened before we fully solved the last problem. Whether it was security vetting at the Lily Pads, the health screening at the airport refugee locations, and now the bureaucratic processing delays at the military base Safe Havens, we couldn't catch a break. Every step in the process found novel ways to torture us and, worse, the Afghans. This was all made more taxing by the life-or-death consequences testing our ability to solve these problems.

Thankfully, Fenton was working his magic as a bureaucracy buster to move Afghans off the bases and into homes in their new communities. The military built separate wooden housing facilities on the bases. The barracks were occupied by soldiers assisting with the relief effort. These makeshift barracks lacked basic heating and air-conditioning. Military bases were no place to house thousands of refugees indefinitely. Babies born on these bases required professional pediatric care. Victims of tragedy in Afghanistan required treatment for PTSD. Children needed to be in proper schools. However, there was one daunting problem that loomed larger than all others: winter.

The upside of all the evacuation delays meant the brutal summer of 2021 transitioned to fall. More humane fall temperatures eased stress on the refugees living in un-air-conditioned makeshift shantytowns. However, the milder fall transformed to . . . winter. Winter would bring plummeting temperatures and harsh weather conditions. The unheated makeshift barracks were ill-equipped to protect the Afghans from these conditions. As we watched October and November give way to the holidays, apprehension turned to dread.

Housing Crisis

We queried the resettlement agencies incessantly about what bottleneck prevented Afghan families from leaving the Safe Haven bases. We reminded the NGOs that we were the U.S. government and consequently swung a pretty big bat. If they encountered an obstacle, they should let us take a swing at removing it. One NGO after another across the country cited the same problem: no apartments. Nearly everyone in Washington engaged in solving the Afghan resettlement crisis was a national security or foreign policy expert. None of us knew anything about domestic housing policy.

Thus, we hadn't the foggiest idea that we were in the middle of the hottest rental market in U.S. history. There was a 98 percent apartment occupancy rate nationwide.[26] Also, most Afghans received limited assistance for only a few months of rent while they got on their feet. So they weren't sought-after tenants. Further, any job an Afghan initially secured would be in the Amazon warehouse or Uber driver category. So rents needed to be around $2,000 per month or less.

Worse still, the NGOs dealt with mom-and-pop landlords they could negotiate leases with on a case-by-case basis. NGOs were not connected to huge corporate apartment conglomerates with massive legal departments that could make blanket arrangements for thousands of apartments at once. These mom-and-pops spread across the country didn't collectively possess enough apartments to house all the Afghans. I knew absolutely nothing about U.S. housing policy or the apartment rental industry. It seemed no one else involved in the resettlement process did either. For days we sat there with absolutely no idea what to do. The feeling was akin to when you are waiting in line at the airport and for some reason the line just stops moving. You sit there watching the clock and mess with your phone waiting for the line to move, but it doesn't. You look around trying to figure out if there is another line to get in as you watch your departure time inch closer. However, you know there isn't another line. You are stuck in this line. Helpless.

Airbnb generously offered to put the Afghans up in thousands of apartments around the country for free or dramatically reduced rates.[27] Many of the NGOs took them up on the offer as we exerted enormous pressure on the NGOs to resettle Afghans off the Safe Haven bases. However, everyone recognized this was merely a stopgap measure. No matter how generous Airbnb intended to be, they couldn't put these folks up forever. Eventually the Afghan families needed long-term homes. Stashing them in yet another form of temporary housing just prolonged that. Temporary housing also had third- and fourth-order effects like not enrolling kids in a permanent school. Not securing primary care doctors or psychiatrists. It delayed applying for stable employment for adults. Most of all, these folks wanted to become productive members of society and get on with their lives. Further, the Afghans languished for so long in each step of the process, we spotted signs of trauma from the resettlement process itself.

Finally, at least when these folks lived on the Safe Haven bases we provided basic services. Those services were not long-term solutions, but they fulfilled basic needs nonetheless. Conversely, if Afghans were deposited in Airbnbs, they received little to no basic services. Worse still, if we didn't identify long-term housing by the time their federal funding ran out or Airbnb needed the unit back, tens of thousands of homeless Afghans could be wandering the streets of America. Not a great look for the Shining City on a Hill.

This was devastating for the refugees who risked their life for America when we needed it. We had to place people in long-term housing. Full stop.

Since I couldn't conceive of a better strategy, I started contacting everyone I knew who worked in residential real estate. Morgan Ryan, who worked with me in the Front Office of DHS, employed the six-degrees-of-separation strategy to connect with apartment renter trade associations. It turns out that by tapping into the network of the President of the United States, you can get to almost anyone. Within weeks, we had many of the major apartment rental groups on board to source apartments. Also, we found people like Mary Pat Bonner, a fundraiser for philanthropic causes who had nearly every rich person in the United States on speed dial. Many of them worked in real estate. Her hairdresser was Afghan. Mary Pat listened to heart-wrenching story after story as the Afghan woman styled her hair. The hairdresser and her stories lit a fire in Mary Pat's soul. I think she alone sourced around twenty-five thousand apartments pro bono. Morgan found thousands more.

We asked apartment building owners to dig deep and lift requirements for background checks, deposits, and more. We attempted to inspire the real estate moguls. I explained that they were not just supporting those who supported our brave men and women in battle. Rather, they were protecting the young Americans who enlist to fight our *next* war. The real estate executives' support for the Afghans was critical to convince the local population of our next war that if they side with the United States and not our opponent, we will take care of them. If they have our soldiers' backs, the United States will have theirs.

This may sound corny, but we really believed it. The vast majority of the apartment building owners we spoke to across the country did, too. There was still much hand-wringing over details around the apartments. However, with the units identified, Fenton was able to move people off the bases before ice started to form on the roofs of the makeshift barracks in the bases.

We breathed a sigh of relief and caught our breath from the crises of the summer of 2021 and the Afghanistan withdrawal.

It was around this time we were informed about fentanyl's grim new milestone. For the first time, deaths attributed to fentanyl surpassed more than one hundred thousand souls in 2021.[28] The fatality rate climbed nearly ten times higher than the combined annual death toll of the previously most deadly drugs like heroin and cocaine.[29]

We all had heard fentanyl was a problem. However, one hundred thousand fatalities was a macabre psychological marker that elevated it to a new echelon of crisis in the country. All the other calamities we encountered engendered their own state of emergency in the T-shaped corridors of DHS Front Office. However, none of them—not the Colonial Pipeline cyberattack, the Haiti assassination and subsequent humanitarian crisis, the Southwest

Border migrant surges, or even the Afghan evacuation and resettlement—were responsible for significant loss of American lives. At this rate, fentanyl now annually killed nearly double the number of Americans lost in the entire Vietnam War.

This catastrophe of human suffering required a response unparalleled to any other we executed before.

Notes

1　Hobbs, Allegra. "The Colonial Pipeline Hack: Exposing Vulnerabilities in U.S. Cybersecurity." Sage, July 6, 2021. https://doi.org/10.4135/9781529789768.

2　"Department of Justice Seizes $2.3 Million in Cryptocurrency Paid to the Ransomware Extortionists Darkside." U.S. Department of Justice, June 7, 2021. https://www.justice.gov/archives/opa/pr/department-justice-seizes-23-million -cryptocurrency-paid-ransomware-extortionists-darkside.

3　Hoffman, Abe. "Hospital Once Home for Ezra Pound." *New York Times*, June 23, 1982. https://www.nytimes.com/1982/06/23/us/hospital-once-home-for-ezra-pound.html.

4　Porter, Catherine, Michael Crowley, and Constant Méheut. "Haiti's President Assassinated in Nighttime Raid, Shaking a Fragile Nation." *New York Times*, July 7, 2021, sec. World. https://www.nytimes.com/2021/07/07/world/americas/haiti -president-assassinated-killed.html.

5　"Haitian First Lady Hospitalized after Attack." *New York Times*, July 8, 2021. https:// www.nytimes.com/video/world/americas/100000007856785/haiti-first-lady-injured -hospitalized.html.

6　"Four Florida Men Arrested in Plot to Kill Haitian President, Grand Jury Returns Indictment against 11." U.S. Department of Justice, February 14, 2023. https://www .justice.gov/opa/pr/four-florida-men-arrested-plot-kill-haitian-president-grand-jury -returns-indictment-against.

7　"FACT SHEET: U.S. Assistance to Haiti." White House, July 13, 2021. https://www .whitehouse.gov/briefing-room/statements-releases/2021/07/13/fact-sheet-u-s -assistance-to-haiti/.

8　"Haiti: Political Instability, Gang Violence and Disease." International Rescue Committee, July 14, 2023. https://www.rescue.org/article/haiti-political-instability -gang-violence-and-disease.

9　Roth, Samantha-Jo. "Coast Guard: Number of Haitians Trying to Reach the U.S. by Boat Triples in a Year." Spectrum News 13, October 5, 2021. https://mynews13.com /fl/orlando/news/2021/10/05/number-of-haitians-trying-to-reach-the-u-s--by-boat -surges.

10 Hernández, Arelis, and Nick Miroff. "Thousands of Haitian Migrants Wait under
    Bridge in South Texas after Mass Border Crossing." *Washington Post*, September 16,
    2021. https://www.washingtonpost.com/national/haitian-migrants-mexico-texas
    -border/2021/09/16/4da1e366-16fe-11ec-ae9a-9c36751cf799_story.html.

11 See "How to Seek Asylum in the U.S." USA.gov. https://www.usa.gov/asylum.

12 See "Transactional Records Access Clearinghouse (TRAC)," Syracuse University,
    December 2023. https://trac.syr.edu/phptools/immigration/asylumbl/, or Roy, Diana.
    "Seeking Protection: How the U.S. Asylum Process Works." Council on Foreign
    Relations, May 10, 2023. https://www.cfr.org/backgrounder/seeking-protection-how
    -us-asylum-process-works.

13 Jordan, Miriam. "Title 42 Is Gone, but Not the Conditions Driving Migrants to the
    U.S." *New York Times*, May 15, 2023, sec. U.S. https://www.nytimes.com/2023/05/14/
    us/migrants-condition-title-42-ends.html.

14 Gottesdiener, Laura. "Biden Tells Migrants to Stay Put: Central Americans Hear
    a Different Message." Reuters, March 31, 2021. https://www.reuters.com/article/
    world/biden-tells-migrants-to-stay-put-central-americans-hear-a-different-message
    -idUSKBN2BN1BA/.

15 "Hurricane Ida Recap: Devastation in Southeast Louisiana, Then Record Flooding in
    the Northeast." Weather Channel, September 2, 2021. https://weather.com/storms/
    hurricane/news/2021-09-02-hurricane-ida-recap-louisiana-south-northeast.

16 Rogers, Katie. "A Baby Passed over a Wall in Kabul Has Been Reunited with Family,
    the Military Says." *New York Times*, August 20, 2021, sec. World. https://www.nytimes
    .com/2021/08/20/world/asia/afghanistan-kabul-baby.html.

17 Barnes, Julian E. "Intelligence Agencies Did Not Predict Imminence of Afghan
    Collapse, Officials Say." *New York Times*, October 7, 2021. https://www.nytimes.com
    /2021/08/18/us/politics/afghanistan-intelligence-agencies.html.

18 "Zadvydas v. Davis, 533 U.S. 678 (2001)." Justia Law, n.d. https://supreme.justia.com/
    cases/federal/us/533/678/.

19 "Biometrics on the Ground and in the DOD." U.S. Army, July 22, 2011. https://www
    .army.mil/article/21940/biometrics_on_the_ground_and_in_the_dod.

20 Office of the Inspector General. *Evaluation of the Screening of Displaced Persons from
    Afghanistan*. Report No. DODIG-2022-065. U.S. Department of Defense, February 17,
    2022. https://media.defense.gov/2022/Feb/17/2002940841/-1/-1/1/DODIG-222-065
    .PDF.

21 Dawi, Akmal. "The Massive, Costly Afghan Evacuation in Numbers." Voice of
    America, February 18, 2022. https://www.voanews.com/a/the-massive-costly-afghan
    -evacuation-in-numbers/6449553.html.

22 Ormiston, Susan. "'I'm Scared': Afghan Who Worked with Foreign Partners Fearful of Taliban Visits." CBC, August 18, 2021. https://www.cbc.ca/news/world/taliban-door-visits-afghanistan-1.6144297.

23 Bowman, Tom. "What It's Like Inside the U.S. Processing Center Welcoming Thousands of Afghans." NPR, September 7, 2021. https://www.npr.org/2021/09/07/1034794347/what-its-like-inside-the-u-s-processing-center-welcoming-thousands-of-afghans.

24 Kean, Efrat R., Maura Sammon, Cheryl Bettigole, Sage Myers, Setareh Mohammadie, Naomi Rosenberg, and Patricia Henwood. "Operation Allies Welcome Medical Response Unit at Philadelphia International Airport: A Framework for Medical Triage of High Volume of Displaced Persons Arriving by Air." *Population Health Management* 27, no. 4 (2024): 257–66. https://doi.org/10.1089/pop.2024.0003.

25 "Operation Allies Welcome." U.S. Department of Homeland Security, n.d. https://www.dhs.gov/archive/operation-allies-welcome?utm_source=chatgpt.com#:~:text=Welcome%20Center%20Event%20Locations%20and%20Dates.

26 Parsons, Jay. "Demand for Apartments in 2021 Smashes Previous Record High by 66%." RealPage Blog (blog), January 7, 2022. https://www.realpage.com/analytics/demand-apartments-2021-smashes-previous-record-high/.

27 "20,000 Afghan Newcomers Housed." Airbnb Newsroom, January 28, 2023. https://news.airbnb.com/20000-afghan-newcomers-housed/.

28 Kornfield, Meryl. "U.S. Surpasses Record 100,000 Overdose Deaths in 2021." *Washington Post*, May 11, 2022. https://www.washingtonpost.com/health/2022/05/11/drug-overdose-deaths-cdc-numbers/.

29 "Drug Overdose Deaths: Facts and Figures." National Institute on Drug Abuse, September 30, 2024. https://nida.nih.gov/research-topics/trends-statistics/overdose-death-rates#Fig 5.

2

Hunting Coyotes

We searched for a strategy to combat fentanyl. As often happens, instead of constructing the strategy from scratch, we scoured for an existing program to tailor to the new challenges. The first operation that caught our attention was a program we had built in 2021 to combat human smugglers. These smugglers routinely exploited, abused, and even murdered migrants on their way to the United States.[1] The strategy was attractive to us for fentanyl because of a few key components. It targeted the network of criminals transporting and abusing the migrants—not solely the kingpin or figurehead of the criminal organization. Additionally, the program was already targeting cartels throughout Latin America, including the main cartels in Mexico responsible for trafficking the vast majority of fentanyl into the United States.[2] We had done the hard work of assembling an interagency group to gather intelligence and carry out operations against these cartels. So, there was already a platform across the national security, intelligence, and law enforcement agencies that could be repurposed for fentanyl. What follows is an explanation of how the counter-human smuggler operation was constructed. That program would later form the basis of our strategy to fight fentanyl.

We began the counter–human smuggler operation as an add-on, almost an afterthought, to the broader migration strategy of the Department of Homeland Security (DHS). Literally thousands of immigration and law enforcement experts worked around the clock—from the DHS secretary, to the department's top attorneys, to policy experts, to border patrol sentries—on a range of measures to manage the thousands of migrants showing up at the border every day. They also assembled a host of tactics to stop migrants from departing their home countries in the first place. DHS officials tried everything from running advertisements in Mexico and Central America to discourage migration to negotiating with regional governments to block migrants from reaching the United States. DHS even worked with news outlets in the region to report on planes returning migrants back home after failed attempts to enter the country.[3] DHS Deputy Secretary John Tien and I determined, however, that there was one rock yet unturned. Little was being done to disrupt and degrade operations of the migrant smugglers.

Countering Human Smugglers

A key complication to stem the relentless tide of migrants surging toward the Southwest Border was legal frameworks of Latin American nations. For them, remittances present a major source of income.[4] Also, unlike in the United States, migrants do not ignite political controversy in Latin America. In the United States, some parts of the electorate embrace immigrants. Other swaths of the electorate are wary of what effect an influx of migrants may have on their local school district or job market. Unfortunately, there also exists a large, dark underbelly of the American electorate harbors xenophobic or racist views of migrants.[5] Conversely, in much of Latin America, people personally knew members of their family who migrated to the United States. Many are the beneficiaries of remittances sent home. For example, in El Salvador, not only do remittances constitute nearly one-quarter of their gross domestic product (GDP),[6] a third of their population resides in the United States.[7] Imagine if one-third of your family and friends lived in Canada. It would likely engender sympathy toward migrants from any country in Canada.

Consequently, the migration laws in Latin America reflect this sympathy. Migration is considered a human right.[8] Like in any other part of the world, animosity runs deep throughout the region between neighboring countries in Latin America. That animosity, however, rarely extends to migrants from neighboring Latin American countries passing through the region. This is also due in part to the unlikelihood of migrants remaining in countries along the route to the United States. These migrants become a source of income to vendors along the route as they must eat, buy toiletries, and bathe. So, folks in Latin America harbor a large degree of empathy for the migrants.[9] Thus, traveling without a visa from Honduras through Guatemala or Ecuador to Mexico or from Colombia through Panama is not a crime as it is to enter the United States without official immigration documents.[10]

In fact, the Panamanian government transports the migrants for free from their southern border to their northern border and even feeds them along the way![11] DHS officials pleaded with regional governments to turn away migrants headed through their country on the way to the United States. DHS was repeatedly rebuked because the local government insisted the migrants broke no laws. Thus, the government had no grounds to deport them. In fact, most nations in the region lack an equivalent to the U.S. Border Patrol.[12] So even amenable governments could not halt the flow of migrants entering their southern border en route north to the United States. They lacked billions of dollars of border monitoring infrastructure and thousands of border patrol agents we maintain on our border.

The United States largely failed to convince these nations to change their laws. Nor would regional governments invest billions to erect a border patrol apparatus they deemed unnecessary. The global community seemed to align with the Latin American governments, too. Regional governments' policies were consistent with the United Nations (UN) Migrant Human Rights Declaration.[13] U.S. policies were not consistent with those of the UN.[14]

So, again and again, our operation was drawn back to degrading capacity of the smugglers, not the migrants.

Many of the human smugglers also engaged in human trafficking. Human smuggling involves one person willingly paying a guide to deliver him safely from one place to another.[15] Human trafficking occurs when one person is transported against her will, often for sex work or other forms of modern slavery.[16] Human trafficking is outlawed across Latin America. The UN Migrant Human Rights Declaration was in part crafted to combat it. Because migrants have such a high approval rating in Latin America, trafficking of migrants was considered a grave sin. Smugglers also committed other crimes like smuggling drugs or guns. By targeting the criminal organizations driving the migration trade, we gained far more cooperation from the local governments than otherwise possible. It became clearer with each rock we overturned that the smugglers were an ideal target at which to aim our fire.

Somehow, amid managing the crises mentioned in Chapter 1, we found time to hatch a plan aimed at degrading the criminal networks smuggling humans to the United States. This operation ultimately laid the groundwork for our national fentanyl strategy. At the time we were ignorant to the connection; however, we later uncovered that the human smugglers we targeted in Mexico were directly linked to the cartels smuggling fentanyl into the United States. For years conventional wisdom held that major cartels in Mexico, such as Sinaloa and Cartel de Jalisco Nueva Generación (CJNG), focused solely on darker crimes like narcotics and weapons trafficking. Human smuggling appeared almost beneath them. Experts long assumed this a task relegated to the aforementioned guides colloquially referred to as "coyotes."

Rocky Pummels Coyotes

A coyote is typically a guy from the local community who acquired the knowledge and relationships necessary to transport someone from point A in Latin America to point B in the United States. Before 9/11 we had a fraction of the security infrastructure on the border we do now. Back then, a typical migrant often didn't require a coyote. They just purchased a bus ticket to a border town in Mexico and then sprinted across the border when they got a chance. Years ago, migrants came and went with the seasons and little trouble. For a host of reasons, which we will address later, this practice has changed dramatically. So, too, has the coyote industry. Those changes have been overwhelmingly detrimental, especially for migrants.[17]

We had yet to uncover this new reality, however. It wasn't until Tien convinced the intelligence community to spy on human smugglers that we discovered the cartels had coopted the industry.[18] Our goal was to reduce the daily influx of migrants arriving at the border. We also knew the smuggler networks abused migrants.[19] We also knew they operated sophisticated direct marketing programs that spread misinformation to migrants. The misinformation convinced migrants that "today" was the perfect time to travel due to fabricated looming immigration policy changes in the United States, weather, the pandemic, or any number of other lies.[20]

In response, thousands of senior officials and border enforcement personnel were involved in mitigating the influx of migrants once they arrived. Officials deported those they could legally deport. They implemented programs to process and vet migrants, identify bad actors, and capture information on those claiming asylum. They also had thousands addressing the challenges associated with administering vaccinations, coordinating testing, and introducing quarantine measures in the middle of a global pandemic. Finally, hundreds of personnel were dealing with the nuances of families or small children traveling without an adult. All these activities to simply manage the massive daily influx of migrants were crucial to maintain order and prevent dangerous criminals from entering the country. Coyotes, however, avoided the spotlight in all these efforts.

Our coyote operation aimed to impose costs on the smuggler networks, not the migrants. Morgan Ryan and I discussed this shift in our focus from migrants to smugglers all the time. Morgan lived and breathed this project. Tien affectionately named it "Rocky" after the cartoon character Rocky from the eponymous *Rocky and Bullwinkle* show. Our initial shorthand for the project during its infancy was "secret squirrel." We kept the plan secret to avoid attracting too many cooks in the kitchen who would kill it in the cradle. Once we obtained approval from the DHS secretary, Alejandro Mayorkas, to move forward with the program, we assigned it a proper name inspired by a proper squirrel. The name also evoked a double entendre referring to Russian spies. Rocky and Bullwinkle's primary nemesis were the doltish Boris and Natasha. The number of Russians crossing the southern border illegally had risen since the Ukraine War. This in turn raised red flags about the motives of the Russians sneaking across the border. These disquieting facts made the name "Rocky" all the more appealing.

Morgan and I worked together in the private sector before joining the Joe Biden administration. We both uprooted our respective families from Chicago to Washington to accept our presidential appointments to the DHS Front Office. Our mantra was that we didn't transport our families across the country and leave a firm we built together to chase poor downtrodden economic migrants around the Western Hemisphere. The migrants' lives were desperate enough without us exacerbating their desperation. In contrast, we were excited to make life miserable for the human smugglers. The smugglers preyed on poor, downtrodden people and profited from their plight. The coyotes rape, exploit, abandon people to die, or house them in terrible circumstances and then extort more money from them to complete the trip. Once Morgan and I zeroed in on targeting these transnational criminal networks instead of migrants, we opened up a whole different paradigm for tackling root causes of migration.

Root Causes

We often rolled our eyes at arguments made by one flank of the immigration debate about addressing "root causes" of migration.[21] Their argument posits the only strategy to prevent mass migration to the United States is to solve all the problems in the countries people emigrate from so they stay home. While noble, the argument contains several fatal flaws. First, addressing root causes can take a generation or more. DHS would have ten thousand people appearing at the border tomorrow and the day after that and the day after that. We could not wait a generation for the economy in Honduras or El Salvador or rural Mexico to improve. For example, there was zero chance of us fixing the Honduran economy in the next decade. We could inject billions into any one of those countries' economies with no immediate expected return on investment. Corruption, climate change, and limited modern economic infrastructure would stifle any potential speedy economic development.

Second, the main driver of migration was a U.S. unemployment rate of 3.5 percent in 2022.[22] Most economists consider 3.5 percent to be full employment of the population.[23] Meaning anyone who wants a job can obtain one. The economy boomed as COVID-19 receded.[24] One economic survey after another reported on companies that couldn't fill orders or staff their kitchen or construction project for lack of workers. People in Honduras, El Salvador, and elsewhere in Latin America languished jobless. Conversely, their friends and family in the United States flooded WhatsApp, a free social media app, with tales of fortune. Unlike their countrymen back home, those who traveled to the United States comparatively made money hand over fist. They also conveyed urgent pleas from U.S. employers. Good-paying jobs awaited anyone brave enough to trek to the United States. So, the most impactful "root cause" we needed to "fix" was to increase the U.S. unemployment rate. A higher U.S. unemployment rate meant fewer jobs for migrants. There is one problem with this solution. By extension, it means more U.S. citizens would find themselves jobless as well. More unemployed Americans was obviously problematic. No one wants the unemployment rate in the United States to rise.

Finally, there was the pesky fact that the United States is notoriously bad at nation building.[25] We can brand it otherwise, but ultimately addressing "root causes" is nation building at its core. It is undoubtedly a moral, ethical, and noble cause to build schools, root out corruption, establish economic development programs, and stop deforestation in Latin America. Further, there are incredibly sound diplomatic arguments one can make as to why we should fund all of those initiatives and more. However, unfortunately, there is little data to support the claim that any of those initiatives will slow the pace of migration in the short term. Thus, addressing the root causes of migration in the region is unlikely to have any impact on the rate of migration for decades.

On the other hand, if we examine root causes from a different perspective, new opportunities present themselves. If one could disrupt the networks of smugglers, one could degrade the networks' ability to move migrants across Latin America to the border immediately. Disrupting the smugglers should also decrease the disinformation messages they deliver to migrants inducing them to travel for erroneous reasons like fake asylum deadlines. Moreover, disrupting the coyote network reduces their ability to prey on migrants.

Not Your Father's Coyotes

We zeroed in on the smuggler networks as our target. Intelligence reports we tasked out on the smuggling networks materialized from the field describing cartels as the central player. The lion's share of smugglers consisted of small groups of coyotes. The cartels, however, levied a tax on coyotes transporting migrants through their territory.[26] Over time, though, we noticed a shift. Whether by choice or by intimidation, increasingly coyotes answered directly to the cartel.

Further, we believed even Russian organized crime groups were conspiring with the cartels to smuggle thousands of Russians into the country.[27] The Russian invasion of Ukraine appeared more and more likely by the day. Consequently, demand to migrate from Russia to the United States rose. Moreover, it was the cartels who bought precursor chemicals from Chinese chemical companies.[28] Cooked it into fentanyl. Then smuggled it into the United States and poisoned Americans in prime years of life. The blurry criminal network trafficking migrants came into focus. A Venn diagram of evil eventually crystallized. Targeting the intersection of cartels with human smuggling, Russian organized crime, the Chinese chemical industry, and fentanyl distribution offered the most lucrative opportunity to bolster American security and inflict maximum damage on adversaries.

We hoped to convince other agencies, in particular the military, to work with us by presenting them with the Venn diagram of evil. The Defense Department is the big kid on the block. They had the big budget—roughly eight times that of DHS—and big guns to bring to the fight.[29] We posited that Rocky disrupted the cartels who were directly involved in Russian and Chinese activities in the region as well as fentanyl.

We spent weeks building our case and briefing senior White House officials like DHS advisor Liz Sherwood-Randall, Domestic Policy Council chair Susan Rice, and DHS secretary Alejandro Mayorkas on the concept. A key question each raised was how we could impact the criminal syndicates if those arrested would largely be apprehended in countries globally renowned for corruption. Judges and law enforcement in many countries where coyotes operate are routinely bribed as a normal course of business.

Our answer was that we aimed to disrupt and degrade the criminal networks—not simply the kingpins who oversaw the loosely affiliated networks. For centuries, kingpins evaded justice or were quickly replaced with even more diabolical gangsters. Despite El Chapo and Pablo Escobar being neutralized, organized crime still reigned in much of Latin America.[30] We were not opposed to taking down a kingpin; however, we wanted to degrade the overall function of the network. For example, we were more interested in pursuing the brokers who hid cartel money, cartel vehicles that transported migrants, and safe houses that stashed people than the single boss at the top. Think of it this way: if you wanted to degrade the capability for Amazon to serve its customers, it would be more effective to shutter its warehouses and ground its fleet of trucks than arrest Jeff Bezos. The White House and Mayorkas approved our smuggler network disruption plan.

Taking a Page from the War on Terror

Now that we had obtained sign-off on the disruption concept, Tien and I went to work contacting all relevant parties in the intelligence community (IC). Tien had worked with the Office of the Director of National Intelligence (ODNI) director Avril Haynes in the Barack Obama administration and asked her to help support our efforts throughout the IC. She immediately agreed to help. We then trekked to every three-letter agency you have heard of and many you haven't, including the National Security Agency (NSA), Central Intelligence Agency (CIA), the Defense Intelligence Agency (DIA), the National Geospatial Agency (NGA), the National Reconnaissance Office (NRO), State Bureau of Intelligence and Research (INR), the Treasury Office of Foreign Assets Control (OFAC), the National Counterterrorism Center (NCTC), DHS Intelligence and Analysis (I&A), and Coast Guard Intelligence. We also solicited support from the Joint Staff, Office of Secretary of Defense Policy, Northern Command and Southern Command. We scoured the national security establishment for existing models we could leverage for our disruption operation.

We identified a counterterrorism operation in Jordan run by the Department of Defense (DOD) that emphasized law enforcement powered by intelligence and diplomatic capabilities in countries where bombing terrorists was not an option.[31] The Jordan operation enabled allied countries to take out terrorists. Also, the Jordan operation sought to disrupt and dismantle terrorist networks instead of only decapitating a kingpin. We began to consider Rocky through the lens of a counterterrorism strategy like the one in Jordan that sought to disrupt the entire terrorist network.

In the process, NSA alerted us that it was already collecting on our cartel targets. Unfortunately, NSA had not zeroed in on intelligence about coyotes but, rather, other geostrategic issues like Russia and China. So, unless the intelligence was about activities it prioritized like Russia or China, it just tossed that intelligence away. It was akin to a movie editor cutting out scenes she isn't interested in and leaving them on the cutting room floor. So even though the IC collected much of the intelligence we sought, we weren't receiving the intelligence needed to take action. It sat on the cutting room floor of NSA. We trekked across the Potomac River from DHS to DIA headquarters at Joint Base Anacostia-Bolling to kiss the ring of the commander there and listen to a dog-and-pony show of all their superspy capabilities. We listened intently about their cloak-and-dagger skills. Despite their hands being full in Ukraine, they offered us intelligence support. Similarly, after we kissed the ring and sat through yet another dog-and-pony show at NGA, they offered us intelligence support and use of satellites to view Latin America with previously unavailable methods. NRO offered analytic support to assess the imagery gleaned from NGA. NORTHCOM was less than forthcoming. OSD Policy flat-out denied our request for support with this mission. In a truly bizarre bureaucratic deflection, senior officials there instructed us to ask the British or Canadians for help funding third-party entities like the Belize military to take up this mission instead of DOD.

We were incredibly frustrated by the recalcitrance of DOD. Since Franklin Delano Roosevelt's "Arsenal of Democracy" speech in 1940, the United States has funded our military at an astronomical level.[32] This funding was to ensure the United States maintained the capability to fight a two-front war simultaneously as it had in World War II. We just pulled out of Afghanistan. We had not declared war on Russia over Ukraine. So, we were not officially at war with anyone at that moment. If the Russian and Chinese connection to the cartels wasn't enough to convince DOD this was a national security threat, we didn't know what was. Fortunately, Tien had a long-standing relationship with Dr. Liz Sherwood-Randall and Ambassador Susan Rice, having worked together on the NSC during the Obama administration. He explained our strategy to pursue the coyotes in the national security language they understood. Neither of these hard-nosed women required much convincing.

Both received regular reports on Russian and Chinese activity in the region, the fentanyl crisis, and the number of migrants crossing the border. They made the case to relevant counterparts within the administration that the counter–human smuggler plan would save lives and reduce suffering.

Most important, it would improve our national security.

Consequently, we finally made progress with combatant commands. NORTHCOM and SOUTHCOM understood the threat. Migration did not rank on their top list of "Great Power" concerns like Russia and China. Despite that, they accepted we could not allow terrorists, Russians, Chinese operatives, or cartel members to carry out their nefarious activities in the region. Thus, NORTHCOM and SOUTHCOM gathered information on smuggler network activities. The intelligence community dramatically stepped up its efforts. As a result, the fruits of its labor produced insights central to our effort to take the fight to the smugglers.

Most important, Homeland Security Investigations (HSI) and Customs and Border Protection (CBP) ramped up efforts to disrupt smugglers across the region. DHS deployed more than thirteen hundred personnel to the Southwest Border as well as foreign countries within the path of smuggling routes.[33] The increased personnel in Latin America enabled them to target human smugglers. CBP also intensified efforts to arrest smugglers at the border. CBP passed intelligence collected on smugglers at the border to HSI so HSI could refine its smuggler targets. Now the intelligence community, the combatant commands, CBP, and HSI all collected intelligence on the smugglers. The intelligence was fed back to HSI or partner nations to take action. We began identifying opportunities to disrupt and degrade smuggler networks on a massive scale.

April Anvil

Mayorkas green-lit this effort in February 2022. By the end of March, HSI and CBP surged hundreds of agents across the region. We kicked the operation off in April and called it April Anvil. The name contained humor and bravado, both of which provided the troops something to rally around. By launch date in April, we had thousands of people developing intelligence and analyzing it for opportunities to disrupt the smugglers. Hundreds of U.S. and allied agents acted on the intelligence to dismantle smuggler networks through arrests, asset freezes, and straightforward interventions like impounding buses and tractor trailers used by the smugglers. April Anvil was a full-blown attack on the human smuggling networks, the scale of which had never been attempted before.

Until April Anvil commenced, we nervously sat on pins and needles waiting to find out if any of this would yield results. Months later our analysis bore out the results: where we had the most HSI agents and allied nation support, we witnessed smuggler activity drop most precipitously. It is impossible to prove a causal relationship between more agents in a country and decreased human smuggler activity, but there was a corollary relationship.[34]

It also logically followed that all the friction our agents caused for the smuggler networks degraded the networks' overall effectiveness. For example, even a small thing like impounding buses and tractor trailers was particularly maddening for the smugglers. Normally, sourcing a new bus or tractor trailer would prove simple for a smuggler. This was 2022, however, so post-pandemic automotive supply chain shortages depleted the availability of vehicles around the globe.[35] A smuggler could always steal a bus in a pinch. However, we just kept impounding their buses. The average smuggler in Guatemala, for example, can only steal so many buses before he angers someone who matters. Generating that type of friction, along with shutting down safe houses, arresting foot soldiers, and confiscating weapons, impacted smuggler capacity.

By June we were arresting hundreds of smugglers a week and confiscating thousands of vehicles, safe houses, weapons, and money. This level of success in less than two months of activity since Mayorkas approved our plan provided us some breathing room. It enabled us to take some time to assess Rocky and to think about new opportunities for disruption and ways to make ourselves even more effective.

Later in the spring of 2022, Russia, while preoccupied with its unexpectedly bogged-down military aggression in Ukraine, was known to maintain close ties with the regimes in Cuba, Nicaragua, and Venezuela. Coincidentally, Cuba and Venezuela had more people appearing at the border every day than anywhere else in the region next to the Central American countries and Mexico. We were alerted that Venezuela had the largest pent-up demand of migrants in the region. Venezuela remained one of the most populous nations in the region. Corruption, economic mismanagement, and sanctions had sent its economy spiraling. It quickly acquired the dubious distinction as one of the world's newest entrants on the list of failed states. Venezuela's decline was a significant potential problem for us. We learned hundreds of thousands or even millions of Venezuelans were poised to leave Venezuela at any moment.[36]

Just as disconcerting was that a significant number of Russian nationals arrived at the border in San Diego every day. Thousands of Russians crossed the border every month as it descended further into war.[37] We believed most of these people were fleeing the oppressive Russian authoritarian regime in search of a better life. Any proper Russian military or intelligence officer wouldn't stoop to this mode of entering the country. Russian agents had established routine methods to enter the country with aliases, fake documents, and disguises. However, we couldn't be too sure. Russia viewed the United States as ringleader of the global coalition emboldening the Ukrainian resistance with money, arms, and people. A real Russian agent would simply fly into JFK airport and enter with an alias. However, maybe Vladamir Putin wanted to send in, say, a group of Russian hackers to position themselves to gain access to our critical infrastructure, like electric grids or water systems. If so, funneling them across the Southwest Border may be a viable option. These conspiracy theories may sound paranoid. Nonetheless, at DHS it's our job to be paranoid.

One area on which presidents Obama, Trump, and Biden agreed was the threat posed by Chinese companies supplying Mexican cartels with chemicals to produce fentanyl. These companies shipped tons of precursor chemicals for fentanyl to the cartels. The cartels then manufactured the fentanyl in Mexico to be smuggled to the United States. We couldn't find any evidence the Chinese government was behind the companies trafficking the chemicals. As far as we could tell, the People's Republic of China (PRC) was either unaware or turning a blind eye to it. Further complicating the matter, most of the precursor chemicals were legal to sell on their own. Regardless, the same cartels controlling the coyotes smuggling humans across the border were the ones buying these precursor chemicals from the Chinese, cooking it into fentanyl, and then smuggling it into the United States.[38]

We argued that all these issues taken together justified mobilizing an interagency group to target the smugglers. Whether it was thousands of migrants showing up at the border each day, unknown Russian refugees, or Chinese precursor chemicals, all roads seemed to lead to the cartels that controlled the northern border of Mexico. The cartel dons had absorbed the coyotes into their criminal enterprise. Cartel smugglers were those facilitating Russian travel and illegal crossings. The cartels were concocting fentanyl pills and smuggling them into the United States at unprecedented rates. Armed with the intelligence we had uncovered about the coyotes, the Russians, and the Chinese fentanyl, we thought assembling an interagency group to target the smuggler networks was a no-brainer. The White House National Security Council agreed. Soon we brought together the group and were pounding on the cartel smuggler networks.

Guatemala and Tractor Trailer Murders

A key turning point in our effort to disrupt the smuggler networks occurred on June 27, 2022. Tragedy struck and laid bare how little regard the smugglers had for human life. A tractor trailer carrying sixty-four migrants stalled in San Antonio, Texas. The smugglers driving it fled. They left fifty-three to die in the refrigeration container.[39] Our CBP and HSI agents had been confiscating these tractor trailers left and right since we started the disruption campaign. However, we didn't impound this one in time. It was a massacre. This massive loss of life compelled the president to declare we would pursue the smugglers responsible for the murders to the ends of the earth. He cited our work as evidence we were taking the cartels seriously and punching back hard. But the president wanted more than tough talk against these sociopaths. The HSI agents spun into action. Within hours, they had leads on those involved. Two weeks later HSI arrested four people involved in the deaths.[40] More important, agents nabbed the perpetrators before they escaped to Mexico. As a result, the suspects were tried in a U.S. court and, if convicted, will serve time in a U.S. prison.[41]

At the same time, our efforts downrange in other Latin American countries yielded results. A Guatemalan woman was killed while being smuggled into the United States less than a year before we started April Anvil. An investigation ensued. We surged HSI agents to Guatemala specifically to support existing investigations against the most heinous smuggler crimes like this one. While we planned the disruption campaign, the criminal Guatemalan smuggling ring involved in her murder popped onto HSI's radar. They investigated the perpetrators with a Department of Justice (DOJ) task force and uncovered one of the largest smuggling rings in Guatemala. As usual, the smugglers were agnostic as to what they trafficked: people, narcotics, or weapons.

The mass arrests came down on Thursday, August 21, 2022, five months after we started the disruption effort.[42] More than five hundred Guatemalan law enforcement and military officials were involved along with dozens of DHS and DOJ officials. It was the largest arrest of extraditable individuals for murder related to human smuggling in one day in Guatemalan history. In all, fourteen people affiliated with the smuggling ring were arrested. As expected, they were not just smuggling people. Our agents seized cash, weapons, drugs, and other contraband.[43] The White House was ecstatic. Both Mayorkas and Tien took to social media to make sure our folks got credit where credit was due.[44]

Mom-and-pop coyotes of years past were more illicit travel agents than anything else. The takedown in Guatemala included dozens of weapon-wielding thugs managing a logistics operation that included de facto control of multiple hotels as safe houses, several vehicles to transport humans or contraband, and loads of narcotics. These were gangsters who reported into a cartel corporate infrastructure, not the mom-and-pop operations of a bygone age.

The arrests also claimed the distinction of the first extradition of its kind in Guatemalan history. Only a few weeks earlier our agents also arrested those responsible for murdering more than fifty migrants in a tractor trailer.[45] These were crowning achievements of the smuggler disruption effort. As usual, DOJ took most of the credit, and, as usual, DHS allowed itself to be sidelined and pushed out of the spotlight. However, Tien, Morgan, and I didn't care. It was exhilarating to witness the effort achieve such a massive impact. It was even more gratifying to witness deadly criminal rings that murdered innocent migrants brought to justice.

Around this time, I delivered the keynote speech at the largest naturalization ceremony ever held at Wrigley Field in Chicago. I sat sweating in a dark suit at Wrigley Field in sweltering Chicago summer heat. I waited my turn to welcome the nearly seven hundred new American citizens accompanied by thousands of friends and family. I was gratified to know that, at that same moment, hundreds of Guatemalan military and law enforcement personnel suited up for a massive raid on these murderers. The raid was replete with military helicopter air support and dozens of HSI agents. No one sweating in the Friendly Confines knew it that day, but just two days later those several hundred personnel in Guatemala would descend on the criminal network and bring the migrant woman's killers and their accomplices to justice.

Aside from bringing these murderers to justice, maybe the most important aspect of Rocky was that we were illuminating the cartel network. It was now clear these cartels controlled migration on the northern border of Mexico. Intelligence officials also had uncovered that fentanyl precursor chemicals were being shipped from China to the same cartels in Mexico who had recently usurped the migration business from the coyotes. However, among senior policymakers there was still a sense that the threat was diffuse. The coyotes, fentanyl, and Russian migrants all seemed mercurial and unconnected. The coyotes and fentanyl precursors pointed to a couple of the biggest cartels on the planet: the Sinaloa cartel and the Cartel de Jalisco Nueva Generación (CJNG) cartels that controlled the northern border of Mexico.

We weren't clear, however, if or how the Russian migrants fit into the scheme. We concluded they were a significant anomaly and came from a place of such keen interest that, at the very least, studying their path to the United States could reveal valuable insights into the criminal networks behind these nefarious activities. We were still unclear whether we were up against one cartel—or several. Were we fighting a series of criminal syndicates spanning the globe from the Russian mob to the triads in Asia to cartels in Latin America? Rather, could we be fighting one mega cartel that was capable of coopting mass migration from the coyotes, fentanyl from the Chinese chemical companies, and now smuggling tens of thousands of Russians halfway around the planet? We had acquired enough intelligence to begin painting a picture of our foe, but it had yet to come into focus.

Notes

1 "Smuggling of Migrants: The Harsh Search for a Better Life." United Nations Office on Drugs and Crime, n.d. https://www.unodc.org/toc/en/crimes/migrant-smuggling .html.

2 "DHS, DOJ Announce Significant Enforcement Operation, Disrupting, Dismantling Prolific Human Smuggling Operation." U.S. Immigration and Customs Enforcement, November 18, 2024. https://www.ice.gov/news/releases/dhs-doj-announce-significant -enforcement-operation-disrupting-dismantling-prolific.

3 "DVIDS—Search—Removal Flights." DVIDS, n.d. https://www.dvidshub.net/search/ ?filter[unit]=ICE&q=removal+flights&sort=date&view=grid.

4 Gammeltoft, Peter. "Remittances and Other Financial Flows to Developing Countries." *International Migration*, February 11, 2003. https://doi.org/10.1111/1468 -2435.00216.

5 Hout, Michael, and Christopher Maggio. "Immigration, Race and Political Polarization." *Daedalus* 150, no. 2 (January 2021). https://doi.org/10.1162/DAED_A _01845.

6 Valev, Neven. "El Salvador: Remittances, Percent of GDP." Global Economy, 2023. https://www.theglobaleconomy.com/El-Salvador/remittances_percent_GDP/.

7 Moslimani, Mohamad, Luis Noe-Bustamante, and Sono Shah. "Facts on Hispanics of Salvadoran Origin in the United States." Pew Research Center, August 16, 2023. https://www.pewresearch.org/fact-sheet/us-hispanics-facts-on-salvadoran-origin -latinos/.

8 See Article 14 of the Universal Declaration of Human Rights. "Universal Declaration of Human Rights." United Nations, n.d. https://www.un.org/en/about-us/universal -declaration-of-human-rights. See also the 1951 UN Refugee Convention: UNHCR— the UN Refugee Agency. "The 1951 Refugee Convention." United Nations High Commissioner for Refugees, n.d. https://www.unhcr.org/about-unhcr/overview/1951 -refugee-convention.

9 Marroquin, Andres, and Antonio Saravia. "Perception of Immigrants in Latin America." *Migration Letters* 19, no. 2 (March 2022). https://doi.org/10.33182/ml.v19i2 .1170.

10 Amarelle, Cesla, and Elisa Fornalé. "Challenges and Features of Migration and Trade Policies towards Latin America." In *The Palgrave Handbook of International Labour*

Migration, edited by Marion Panizzon, Gottfried Zürcher, and Elisa Fornalé. New York: Palgrave Macmillan, 2015. https://doi.org/10.1057/9781137352217_21.

11 Thornett, Robert C. "Panama's Border Crisis and U.S. Immigration Policy." *American Affairs*, August 16, 2022. https://americanaffairsjournal.org/2022/08/panamas-border-crisis-and-u-s-immigration-policy/.

12 Hiemstra, Nancy. "Pushing the US-Mexico Border South: United States' Immigration Policing throughout the Americas." *International Journal of Migration and Border Studies* 5, no. 1–2 (2019): 44. https://doi.org/10.1504/ijmbs.2019.099681.

13 International Convention on the Protection of the Rights of All Migrant Workers and Members of Their Families. United Nations, December 18, 1990. https://www.ohchr.org/en/instruments-mechanisms/instruments/international-convention-protection-rights-all-migrant-workers. See also Castillo, Carlos Maldonado. "The Cartagena Process: 30 Years of Innovation and Solidarity." *Forced Migration Review*, May 2015. https://www.fmreview.org/maldonadocastillo/.

14 Keaten, Jamey. "Aspects of US Restrictions on Asylum-Seekers May Violate International Protections, UNHCR Chief Says." AP News, June 13, 2024. https://apnews.com/article/unhcr-refugees-trends-sudan-united-states-gaza-6192947a3eba407cdbebac4e8c0a7197.

15 Kangaspunta, Kristina, and Andy Guth. "Trafficking in Persons." *Illicit Trade*, 2011. https://doi.org/10.1787/9789264251847-5-EN.

16 Smith, Katherine Taken, Hannah Michelle Martin, and L. Murphy Smith. "Human Trafficking: A Global Multi-billion Dollar Criminal Industry." *International Journal of Public Law and Policy* 4, no. 3 (2014): 293–308. https://doi.org/10.2139/SSRN.2316169.

17 Burnett, John. "The Security Crackdown after 9/11 Permanently Altered Life at the U.S.-Mexico Border." WUNC, September 9, 2021. https://www.wunc.org/2021-09-09/the-security-crackdown-after-9-11-permanently-altered-life-at-the-u-s-mexico-border.

18 Palacios, Simón Pedro Izcara. "Evolution and Operation of Human Smuggling Networks in Mexico." *Política y Cultura*, no. 59 (June 2023): 105–32. https://doi.org/10.24275/ohry4244.

19 Medina, Brenda. "Deadly Human Smuggling through Mexico Thrives in 'Perfect Cycle of Impunity.'" International Consortium of Investigative Journalists, April 30, 2024. https://www.icij.org/inside-icij/2024/04/deadly-human-smuggling-through-mexico-thrives-in-perfect-cycle-of-impunity/.

20 Hutchens, Landon. "El Paso Sector Warns Migrants Not to Be Led by Misinformation." U.S. Customs and Border Protection, December 15, 2023. https://www.cbp.gov/newsroom/local-media-release/el-paso-sector-warns-migrants-not-be-led-misinformation.

21 Call, Charles T. "The Imperative to Address the Root Causes of Migration from Central America." Brookings, January 29, 2021. https://www.brookings.edu/articles/the-imperative-to-address-the-root-causes-of-migration-from-central-america/.

22 Dizikes, Peter. "Economic Migrants." *MIT Technology Review*, February 23, 2022. https://www.technologyreview.com/2022/02/23/1044199/economic-migrants/.

23 Daly, Mary C., Bart Hobijn, and Robert G. Valletta. "The Recent Evolution of the Natural Rate of Unemployment." Discussion Paper 5832. Institute of Labor Economics, July 11, 2011. https://papers.ssrn.com/sol3/papers.cfm?abstract_id=1882851.

24 "Chart Book: Tracking the Recovery from the Pandemic Recession." Center on Budget and Policy Priorities, April 3, 2024. https://www.cbpp.org/research/economy/tracking-the-recovery-from-the-pandemic-recession.

25 Saikal, Amin. "Half a Century of Failed US Adventures." *Arena*, November 9, 2023. https://www.uwa.edu.au/news/article/2023/november/half-a-century-of-failed-us-adventures.

26 Perez, José Ignacio Castañeda. "'Boom of Opportunities': How Smugglers, Mexican Cartels Profit from US Border Restrictions." *AZ Central*, December 27, 2022. https://www.azcentral.com/in-depth/news/politics/border-issues/2022/12/16/how-cartels-profit-migrants-desperation-along-u-s-mexico-border/10704315002/.

27 Felbab-Brown, Vanda, and Diana Paz García. "Russia, Ukraine, and Organized Crime and Illicit Economies in 2024." Brookings, February 6, 2024. https://www.brookings.edu/articles/russia-ukraine-and-organized-crime-and-illicit-economies-in-2024/.

28 Felbab-Brown, Vanda. "China, Mexico, and America's Fight against the Fentanyl Epidemic." Brookings, March 21, 2024. https://www.brookings.edu/articles/china-mexico-and-americas-fight-against-the-fentanyl-epidemic/.

29 "House Approves H.R. 4365, the Department of Defense Appropriations Act." House Committee on Appropriations, September 28, 2023. https://appropriations.house.gov/news/press-releases/house-approves-hr-4365-department-defense-appropriations-act.

30 Villa, Santiago. "After Pablo and El Chapo: How Investigative Outlets Are Covering Organized Crime in Latin America." Global Investigative Journalism Network, July 10, 2024. https://gijn.org/stories/latamfocus-organized-crime/.

31 "US Heading Anti-jihadist Intelligence Sharing Operation—Report." *The Times of Israel* (blog), March 25, 2021. https://www.timesofisrael.com/liveblog_entry/us-heading-anti-jihadist-intelligence-sharing-operation-report/.

32 Roosevelt, Franklin Delano. "The Arsenal of Democracy." FDR Library, 1940. https://www.fdrlibrary.org/documents/356632/390886/lendlease_fireside.pdf/6a8052ab-f166-4137-bd62-879c3bd77b90.

33 "Fact Sheet: Counter Human Smuggler Campaign Update: DHS-Led Effort Makes 5,000th Smuggler Arrest in Fewer Than 6 Months." U.S. Department of Homeland

Security, 2022. https://www.dhs.gov/archive/news/2022/10/06/fact-sheet-counter
-human-smuggler-campaign-update-dhs-led-effort-makes-5000th.

34 Miller, Rebecca, and Sebastian Baumeister. "Managing Migration: Is Border Control
Fundamental to Anti-trafficking and Anti-smuggling Interventions?" *Anti-Trafficking
Review*, no. 2 (September 2013): 15–32. https://doi.org/10.14197/atr.20121321.

35 St John, Savannah. "A Look Back at the Automotive Industry in 2022." Resilinc, June
20, 2024. https://www.resilinc.com/blog/automotive-industry-2022/.

36 John, Mauricia. "Venezuelan Economic Crisis: Crossing Latin American and
Caribbean Borders." *Migration for Development* 8, no. 3 (September 2019): 437–47.
https://doi.org/10.1080/21632324.2018.1502003.

37 Masri, Michael, and Will Neal. "Escaping Russia for the United States, via Mexico."
New Lines Magazine, November 9, 2023. https://newlinesmag.com/first-person/
escaping-russia-for-the-united-states-via-mexico/.

38 "The Expansion and Diversification of Mexican Cartels: Dynamic New Actors
and Markets." International Institute for Strategic Studies, December 12, 2024.
https://www.iiss.org/publications/armed-conflict-survey/2024/the-expansion-and
-diversification-of-mexican-cartels-dynamic-new-actors-and-markets/.

39 Melhado, William. "First Defendant in San Antonio Tractor-Trailer Tragedy Pleads
Guilty to Smuggling Charges." *Texas Tribune*, September 27, 2023. https://www
.texastribune.org/2023/09/27/texas-migrant-tractor-trailer-truck-deaths-suspect/.

40 Dobbins, James, J. David Goodman, and Edgar Sandoval. "Migrants Found Dead in
Texas Trailer." *New York Times*, June 28, 2022. https://www.nytimes.com/live/2022/06
/28/us/migrants-san-antonio-tractor-killed.

41 Melhado. "First Defendant in San Antonio Tractor-Trailer Tragedy."

42 "Major Enforcement Operation in Guatemala City Secures Arrest of Human
Smuggler." Homeland Security Investigations, August 23, 2024. https://www.dhs.gov
/hsi/news/2024/08/23/major-enforcement-operation-guatemala-city-secures-arrest
-human-smuggler.

43 "Major Enforcement Operation in Guatemala City Secures Arrest of Human
Smuggler."

44 "Major Enforcement Operation in Guatemala City Secures Arrest of Human
Smuggler."

45 Gore, Hogan. "DOJ Arrests 7 Connected to 2022 Human Smuggling Operation That
Left 53 Dead in San Antonio." *Austin American-Statesman*, August 23, 2024. https://
www.statesman.com/story/news/crime/2024/08/23/texas-human-smuggling-arrests
-53-dead-san-antonio-2022-doj/74907080007/.

3

Putin's Long Arms

One of the biggest question marks hanging over our operation to thwart criminal networks operating on the border was the Russians. Putting aside concerns regarding U.S. and Russian relations over Ukraine, a more basic question plagued us. How? How were thousands of Russians appearing at the border every week? Also, why were they all arriving at the land port of entry in San Diego?[1] It seemed impossible that a lone industrious coyote or even a series of entrepreneurial coyotes facilitated transit from Russia and through Mexico to the exact same spot on the border for months on end coincidentally. We wanted to put a nail in the coffin of any theory still espousing lone coyotes as drivers of the massive flows of migrants or fentanyl to the border. Assessing the travel arrangements of the Russians could illuminate how the criminal networks operated. We surmised that the most expedient method to uncover how the Russians got here was to simply ask them face-to-face. As Russian migrants were in short supply at the Department of Homeland Security (DHS) Front Office, I decided to take a trip to San Diego to chew the fat with a few Russian detainees at the U.S. Immigration and Customs Enforcement (ICE) detention facility there.

On April 29, 2022, John Tien and I traveled to San Diego for an innocuous employee recognition ceremony where Tien keynoted and presented awards. He loved doing this type of thing. As a former army colonel, he relished pressing the flesh with the troops and thanking people for their service. He excelled at it, too. Tien had been in the private sector for the last decade making millions at Citibank. However, he was a soldier at heart. He had served in the DHS deputy cabinet secretary job for nearly a year. He knew all too well that more than any other agency, the men and women of DHS were expected to grind out every day in thankless frontline security roles like Transportation Security Administration (TSA) agents, border patrol agents, coastal patrol sailors, or Federal Emergency Management (FEMA) emergency responders. The troops could tell he internalized their plight, and they loved him, too. He was so incredibly earnest. They couldn't help but feed off his endearing gratitude. When most people say, "Thank you for your service," they sound patronizing. When he says it, he genuinely means it, and they all could feel that. Further, DHS's law enforcement folks were constantly under attack by the "Defund the Police" crowd. Rightly or wrongly, they felt particularly under siege by a Democratic administration that embraced many of the "Defund the Police" political activists—if not their policy positions. Ironically, the law enforcement guys at ICE and Customs and Border Protection (CBP) felt abandoned by probably the most pro-cop president in modern history. So to have a senior leader from a Democratic administration, like Tien, patting them on the back and saying we have theirs was a welcome endeavor.

Days before the employee recognition event, I back channeled a request to talk to Russian detainees to the deputy director of ICE, P. J. Lechleitner, who had been instrumental in executing Rocky and pursuing the human smugglers. As mentioned earlier, we gathered intelligence that the number of Russians claiming asylum at the San Diego port of entry had been growing for more than a year. This was disconcerting, but not surprising, as Putin cracked down on dissidents in Russia. He seemed to revert to his Soviet surveillance-state roots. Further, many young men and their wives or girlfriends sought to avoid conscription into the Ukraine War. These migrants were coming in record numbers every month. They presented themselves to border patrol agents and "claimed fear."[2] In this case, the migrants claimed they were in fear of being sent to battle or jailed as dissidents of the war. True or not, migrants are coached to make these types of assertions by the smugglers because it entitles them to have their case heard in court.[3]

The courts were still backed up with millions of cases. A Russian could wait five to seven years before their court date arrives.[4] The ICE detention facilities consistently overflowed with detainees. Russians with no criminal record who don't appear to pose a risk to the American public are released into the country. There they await trial. They can roll the dice in court to determine if their asylum claim is upheld or rejected; However, they can also blow off the court date and stay in the country indefinitely or leave.

It seemed logical enough that these Russians might simply be what they appeared. They appeared to be run-of-the-mill refugees fleeing a repressive regime. That being said, Russia had attacked Ukraine in an act of unprovoked aggression. We took nothing for granted. Putin was incensed at NATO, and in particular U.S. support for the Ukrainian resistance. One senior White House official captured the sentiment in an early meeting on the topic. We mentioned the record number of Russians presenting themselves at the border in San Diego. The official retorted, "Russians? What are fucking Russians doing at the Southwest Border? We shouldn't be letting *any* fucking Russians in the country! They just attacked a sovereign nation!"

Because of the potential threat, I wanted to eyeball some of these folks. I hoped to glean any useful information about who these people are and why they are here. How did they get here, and what did they intend to do while here? As a routine course of action, the Russians were questioned by CBP and ICE officers when initially detained. If any detainee was found to have derogatory information in our numerous databases, they were sent to secondary screening for questioning. Additionally, if any of them displayed suspicious behavior, they were further questioned. However, reading reports from agents who processed hundreds of migrants a day was not the same as sitting down and talking to the migrants face-to-face.

After our black SUVs rolled in to Coast Guard Base San Diego for the DHS employee award ceremony, Tien got out and strode into the base commander's office. It was customary to pay the commander a courtesy visit in advance of any event on his base. When Tien stepped out of the SUV with his security detail, I slipped out the back and entered yet another black SUV driven by two local ICE agents. We sped away to the ICE Otay Mesa Detention Center to rub shoulders with some Russians.

The two agents and I exited San Diego against traffic of commuters schlepping downtown. They explained that, once released from the detention facility, the Russians didn't stay long in San Diego. Instead, they quickly struck out for other destinations in the interior of the country. Generally, they went to major urban areas like Chicago, New York, and Los Angeles. We speculated as to why they all were coming to San Diego as opposed to another port of entry. My theory was that whichever Russian organized crime syndicate moved the migrants likely had a deal with the Sinaloa cartel, which controlled Tijuana.[5] I was eager to ascertain information as to exactly how this relationship between the Russian and Mexican criminal syndicates worked. As we arrived at the detention facility, I was struck by how much it resembled a sprawling penitentiary. Several layers of twenty-foot-high fences topped with barbed wire encircled the massive clay-colored complex. It stood behind the fencing and blended into the mountains behind it.

I was greeted there by multiple guards and, of course, the private prison contractor who managed the facility. They warned me not to expect to glean much from the conversations. The Russians were well coached by their smugglers to keep tight-lipped with the Feds. They had arranged for me to talk to two groups of about a dozen each. One consisted of men and the other, women. Traversing the cavernous halls, I was struck at how out of place these Russians were. Nearly everyone else in the facility was Hispanic—not only the asylees but also the guards, janitorial staff, and leadership. One notable exception, of course, was the private prison contractor. He was white. I entered the prison library and spotted about a dozen young Russian men, wearing COVID-19 masks, seated at a table; most sported poorly maintained prison beards. They were all in generally the same prison outfit of gray and orange shirts and pants and orange Crocs.

Googling to Freedom

As predicted, the men, all apparently in their twenties, recounted nearly identical stories. They received no support from smugglers or the Russian mob. They just googled how to get to America and, from there, bought plane tickets to Tijuana. Once in Tijuana, they purchased a car. The detainees insisted they were forced to buy a car because the Mexicans won't rent cars to Russians. I was later told that this practice is likely a result of Mexican car rental businesses being burned too often. Once emigrated, the theory goes, the Russian migrants don't return the car or pay the fee. The men insisted they were persecuted by the Russian government. They worried they would be picked up by the Russian Federal Security Service (FSB) at any moment back home and thrown in prison or forced to fight in Ukraine.

Why they were targeted in particular by the Russian government none of them could say. They alleged the Russian government persecuted people randomly. None of them claimed to be activists. Nor did they proclaim any interest in reforming Putin's government. I asked why they didn't emigrate to Europe instead. I argued it was much less complicated and expensive to travel to Europe than to the United States. They cited the assassination of Russian FSB agent Alexander Litvinenko in the United Kingdom and said the "long arms" of Putin reached across Europe.[6] Thus, they felt they would only be safe in the United States. This is certainly a line they were coached to say as multiple interviewees repeated the "long arms" line multiple times. In terms of engagement with Mexican smugglers, they claimed no connection to any Mexicans, smuggler or otherwise. The Russians just sequestered themselves in a hotel. Eventually they bought a car and drove here. They claimed to receive no assistance obtaining a hotel room or car. The Russians' sole support was Booking.com or Airbnb. They had no interaction with Mexican smugglers and avoided the police. They suspected the cops were corrupt and would demand bribes.

Aside from being Russian migrants who all just happened to appear specifically in the San Diego port of entry, and *only* the San Diego port of entry, aided by some adroit googling, they were otherwise unremarkable.

A couple of the guys worked in construction. One was a DJ. A few others claimed to be students. A couple of the guys said they were entrepreneurs and aspired to start a business. More disconcerting, there were a few who claimed to be in "IT" or "telecommunications."

These professions were eyebrow raising. Putin vaguely threatened a cyberattack in retaliation to Biden's support for Ukraine.[7] At that moment, DHS cyber officials at the Cybersecurity and Infrastructure Security Agency (CISA) were working around the clock to detect and prevent a possible Russian cyberattack. This definitely piqued my interest. One potential scheme could be for Russia to sneak a bunch of hackers in via the Southwest Border and disperse them around the country to hack our critical infrastructure in a coordinated attack.

"Huh. We gotta follow up on those guys," I noted. They all reported their trips were orchestrated via a particular encrypted texting app. That was critical intelligence as it provided a channel to identify future Russian mobsters communicating with migrants and analyze their conversations. Often these text group chats were not difficult to join and monitor.[8] This information would likely capture the interest of our intelligence community. They were now investing significant resources to map human smuggling networks. The nexus of human smuggling and Russians was a clear place to concentrate efforts.

I wrapped up my conversation and headed next door with the female guards to interview the Russian women. The interviews were largely more of the same. The women had clearly been coached on what to say. Their stories mirrored the men's. The only support they cited was provided by Google for flights to Tijuana, for a hotel and the annoyance of being required to buy a car.

They didn't talk to Mexicans. Especially not Mexican cops.

Deadly Long Arms

The women also claimed to be threatened by the Putin regime with imminent imprisonment. They didn't emigrate to Europe instead because, just as Putin poisoned Litvinenko, he could reach them with his "long arms." There was that "long arms" phrase again, just like in my conversations with the men. How is it possible that two dozen people being held in separate rooms repeat the same metaphor and are not coached to say it? In Russian, the phrase "*длинные руки*" (pronounced "dlinnyye ruki") literally means "long arms" and conveys the idea that a powerful or nefarious actor has an extended reach or influence, often beyond borders or through various agents.[9] Regardless it is quite odd they all employed the same turn of phrase to describe Putin's global assassin networks. This was yet another possible sign of coaching by smugglers.

The women insisted safety would only be assured in the United States. I pressed them, saying, "No offense, but you are all nurses, students, and teachers, not a former FSB whistleblower like Litvinenko.[10] I don't think Putin has any inclination to assassinate you." They dismissed my argument. Yes, they were average people. However, the Russian operatives were ubiquitous (except in the United States, apparently). Migrants in places like Europe would eventually be hunted down by these metaphoric long arms.

I dug deeper into travel patterns. Despite the women's insistence they had not employed smugglers, I wasn't convinced. I wanted to dig deeper to ascertain what assistance they likely received. Initially I fixated on a consistent detail vaguely referenced in every story. They all flew to Istanbul and then on to Mexico. Why Istanbul? What drew them there? It turned out they chose Istanbul because it was one of the few countries that didn't require Russians to obtain visas. Istanbul also offered direct flights to Mexico. When pressed, they insisted Istanbul was irrelevant. They just laid over for a day and then flew to Mexico.

I asked if they believed the Russian government monitored Russian civilian communication in cyberspace. "Of course," they retorted. The women treated the question as naive to say the least. Clearly, they believed Putin's "long arms" extended into cyberspace. Like the men, they claimed to be in constant danger of being corralled and thrown into prison at any moment back home. So how, then, were they comfortable googling these extensive travel plans in Russia? Weren't they exposing their plans to the risk of detection? Upon further reflection on this perceived inconsistency, they revised the sequencing. Now they collectively remembered that only the Turkey leg of the trip was sorted out in Russia. The rest of the googling was completed in Istanbul. The women uniformly asserted that searching for flights to Turkey was not suspicious activity. It would not raise alarm bells or activate Putin's long arms. I probed further. This was a lot of illicit migrant travel planning to cram into less than a twenty-four-hour layover. They again amended the collective memory. Actually, they stayed in Istanbul a "few days" while they finalized travel plans.

Russian and Turkish criminal organizations are known to collaborate.[11] Practically the flight plans made sense if the mob was involved. The uniformity of inconsistencies in their stories exposed that something was askew; however, I wasn't obtaining much actionable intelligence. My amateur sleuthing had only led me to a conclusion we knew before I endeavored on this junket. The Russian migrants garnered assistance from someone, probably organized crime. We still didn't know who or how. Then a detail I had glossed over leaped out at me. The Russians didn't fly direct to Tijuana. They usually flew to Mexico City or, mostly, Cancún. Bingo. Cancún is well known for being totally compromised by the Russian FSB and organized crime.[12] The Russian government doesn't clearly delineate where the FSB ends and Russian organized crime begins. The Russian intelligence apparatus and its mob blend together. In fact, Russian cyberespionage agents are tacitly allowed to moonlight as cybercriminals to make ends meet financially.

A few of the women said they actually stayed a few extra days in Cancún to hang out on the beach and "clear their minds." It was unclear how they could avoid talking to any Mexicans over the course of a "few days" in Cancún. It's even unlikely they could avoid Russian mob or Russian intelligence in a city wired by the Russians.[13] So now it seemed that, if we were to focus on Cancún, we could begin to generate more intelligence about the Russian and Mexican organized crime smuggling humans into the region.

Now, I had obtained the encrypted app and Cancún intelligence. Yet, I was still frustrated listening to these women all reading from the same script as the men. As I was warned, they and the men were obviously coached to recite all this to any questioner. I thought one of the Russians might divulge more one-on-one. Obviously, there was potential danger for any of them who spoke out of turn. Anyone in the group could be a Russian government informant or member of the mob. Surely in a group setting they would clam up. Reprisal for saying too much could be deadly. The guards and I thanked them, and they were all escorted back to their quarters. The female guards conspicuously kept one woman back in a way the others wouldn't notice. I sat with her and my facility handlers. I told her point-blank I had no interest in a few Russian refugees. Rather, I wanted to understand what involvement Russian and Mexican organized crime—and, moreover, the Russian government—had in their migration. We knew for a fact that Russian organized crime collaborated with Mexican cartels on a host of illicit activity.[14]

She swore Russian organized crime wasn't involved. She insisted, instead, that since Putin came to power, "criminality" had plummeted. (I think she meant the second time Putin came to power, after Dmitry Medvedev stepped down.) Now it was just "the cops" committing all the crime, she reported. This idea that maybe the cops were a stand-in for the mob on human smuggling was a new perspective I hadn't considered. We knew Russian intelligence services worked closely with Russian organized crime.[15] It followed that Russian local cops were part and parcel with the mafia on human smuggling there, too. Local cops were notoriously more corrupt than federal. There were just so many more of them. It was easy for the mob to find bad apples. This was true in many parts of the world.[16] If local cops in Russia masterminded human smuggling there, that idea was novel indeed.

It also begged the question: What criminal syndicate in Mexico was so powerful that it could cut an exclusive deal with the Russian cops to move thousands of Russian migrants around the globe to San Diego? Furthermore, did the Mexican gangsters edge out their rivals for the Russian cop deal by being the lowest bidder of other Mexican competitors? Did they win the business because they were able to outfight their rivals for the Russian business? Alternatively, was there a Mexican criminal syndicate so entrenched and established that it sustained long-standing relationships with the Russian syndicate, making it the natural choice for Russian gangsters—or cops—to conduct their business smuggling anything across the U.S. border?

A Sherpa

After this trip and the last few months of Rocky, I knew enough to be dangerous but not enough to be strategic. The White House and DHS leadership were excited about all the smuggler bashing. So much so, they demanded more. The question was, more of what? The top brass at Homeland Security Investigations (HSI) directed their folks to execute much of the smuggler disruption. These seasoned agents appreciated that we valued their efforts in this fight. At the same time, we were getting a little too close to their cases for comfort. So far all this attention from the Front Office was welcome. However, they were wary of leadership directing agents on particular cases or to pursue specific nodes of the criminal network. These concerns led to Tien's consistent refrain that if we waded too much into details we risked "Ollie North"-type errors. Aside from being ensnared by Colonel North's pitfalls, HSI was also wary of us wasting time and energy for their already overworked agents.

HSI leadership wanted to focus on activities that would significantly degrade smuggler capability. They didn't want to expend resources on what Tien referred to as "substrategic" targets. So HSI relocated a top agent from the Miami field office to the DHS Front Office. His role was to guide me in elevating our disruption operation. Agents despise when leadership, in particular political leadership, directs their activity. So, they sent us one of their top performers to make sure the DHS Front Office did not deploy HSI agents on a bunch of wild goose chases.

"Crockett" (not his real name—he is still an agent and prefers to remain anonymous) was straight out of central casting. Hair high and tight, he always had a badge and sidearm. As part of his deal to come Sherpa me through the special agent world of HSI and cartels, he negotiated that ICE issue him a black SUV that was itself a surveillance device and weapon. These guys are always ready. He immediately gravitated to the Russian issue. I explained that we strove to focus our anti-smuggler efforts on overlapping threats like fentanyl and Russia. He professed genuine appreciation for this focus.

He and his colleagues dedicated their lives to protecting our national security. Many HSI agents cut their teeth on counterterrorism operations over the last twenty years. As the war on terror waned, however, they had been assigned mundane duties at the border[17]—a far cry from hunting down members of al-Qaeda. These agents yearned for the type of sleuthing they signed up for during the war on terror. Attacking the cartel network that controlled much of the northwest Mexican border where Russians appeared was exactly the investigative work they craved.

HSI agents are the real deal, like FBI or CIA. Many disdain being associated with other parts of ICE. They especially begrudge getting tainted by the truly reprehensible actions of other divisions of ICE. In particular, they tend to deplore actions of the Trump administration that prioritized rounding up grandmas and toddlers instead of real threats to the homeland like terrorists and cartel members.

Crockett couldn't be further from the "round up the grandmas and toddlers" crew. He aspired to take down real bad guys. As he often said, he woke up every morning trying to stop "bad-guy stuff." To Crockett, "bad guy stuff" encompassed things like the Russian mob working with Mexican cartels to smuggle potential Russian operatives into the United States. Certainly bad-guy stuff included fentanyl produced with Chinese chemicals and trafficked into the country by Mexican cartels. Bad-guy stuff compelled him to kick the covers off in the morning. Crockett was deeply motivated to assemble operations that punched bad guys in the nose all day.

In his first week working in the DHS Front Office, he identified a firm HSI had on contract to find child pornographers. He planned to use the tool to investigate the Russians. I want to pause here and elaborate on HSI's role as the U.S. government's lead agency to combat online child exploitation.

HSI is the agency that investigates and takes down maybe the most heinous criminals in humanity: child predators and child pornographers.[18] HSI is not the part of ICE that runs deportations. That falls to a different office called Enforcement and Removal Operations (ERO).[19] It is instructive to note for a moment what the term *investigate* means in the context of child pornography. It means watching hundreds of hours of child pornography and other forms of child abuse. I would not last one day in this job before I slit my wrists.

The agents who stomach this day in and day out to take down the worst of humanity are true heroes. Sometimes they must watch a particular rape happen over and over because there is a sound in the background or a reflection on the TV of something—anything—that could be a clue as to where the child is being kept. These are heroes the press never covers. Child porn articles are too depressing for the general public to read, click, and post on social media. So, these agents toil away in darkness, with no recognition or appreciation for this soul-crushing work. They regularly require significant counseling for what they must watch to protect our children. These folks are the real Captain Americas. Certainly, what they endure and accomplish every day is more heroic than anything I have seen Captain America do in movies.

Our resident Captain America, Crockett, sourced this tool they use to find child predators. He figured out in a matter of days how we could find Russian human traffickers. It was just a matter of time before we found out who the main smugglers were. We later found their top stash houses in the Sinaloa cartel territory, which were a few hotels in Tijuana and other methods. Within weeks, HSI had a group of agents working the Russian issue full-time.

When we launched Rocky, I wondered whether the cartels had become involved in human smuggling or whether the old mom-and-pops were still at the helm. The last two months of Rocky and my interviews with the Russians eradicated any shadow of a doubt. It was clear the Sinaloa cartel and Cartel de Jalisco Nueva Generación (CJNG), who own the northern border of Mexico, had usurped the migration trade from the mom-and-pops.[20]

Thanks to Crockett and his colleagues, we were advancing on multiple fronts against the smugglers. Whether it was efforts to stymie the smugglers transporting Russians or the smugglers that killed fifty-three migrants in a tractor trailer or the smugglers who left a Guatemalan girl for dead, we now had multiple fronts open against the smuggler networks. Those efforts and others like them delivered significant blows to the smugglers.

The Summit

In the summer of 2022, the White House requested details on Rocky to showcase at the Summit of the Americas held in Los Angeles. We had only been prosecuting the Rocky campaign for two months. Yet the call came down from the NSC to me and to Tien's chief of staff, Mary Ellen Callahan: produce something tangible the president could highlight at the summit.

The administration was snubbed publicly by multiple nations. Chief among them was Mexico, who refused to attend the summit under the auspices of Cuba not being invited.[21] A more likely cause was that it made for good local politics. Mexican president Andrés Manuel López Obrador scored points with local constituents any time he poked a finger in the United States' eye.

The absence of several Western Hemisphere nations was particularly problematic for the White House. Joe Biden was rallying the global community against Russia's invasion of Ukraine. NATO sought to forge a global united front against Russia.[22] Particularly unsettling for the administration was the position adopted by its closest neighbor to the south. Mexico's relationship with the United States was at times strained. Still, it was considered a close ally. The Obrador administration, however, had yet to firmly condemn Russia and side definitively with NATO. Mexico's hedge between the United States and Russia over Ukraine strained relations. Lack of support curbing the ten thousand migrants a day who arrived at the United States' doorstep via Mexico added salt to the wound. Worse still, the unabated flow of fentanyl to the United States deepened the rift.

The summit was not shaping up to boost Biden's sagging poll numbers in advance of the midterms. Instead, it risked projecting shaky leadership rather than a steady-handed commander of the Free World. West Wing officials insisted on portraying strength in a time of global crisis. The summit also provided an opportunity to rebound from the chaos Americans witnessed unfold in Afghanistan. This was a moment to remind the world it needed U.S. leadership to stand up against belligerent regional hegemons.

The summit offered the United States—and, in particular, Biden—an opportunity to command the world stage and engender confidence from the rest of the world. Other nations may harbor petty grievances with the United States, but these gripes were indeed quite petty. Ultimately, standing with freedom and democracy far outweighed siding with aggression and authoritarianism. So far Biden *had* commanded the world stage. He successfully rallied NATO, the European Union, and other key allies to stand with the United States against Russia.[23] The lead-up to the Summit of the Americas, however, risked exposing a fissure within the global democracies' stand against Russia.

Detailing the cost inflicted on the smuggler networks presented an opportunity for the Biden administration. The president could highlight that the United States was not standing idly by while these smugglers had their way at the border. Instead, every day and across the hemisphere the United States took the fight to the smugglers. It didn't matter whether they were a plaza boss in Mexico or an illicit tractor trailer driver or a coyote smuggling Russians. The United States attacked these networks at every level, every day. Further, other governments in the region were active participants in this effort.

The White House agreed with the messaging. They issued a statement spotlighting the countersmuggler operation during the summit. The president even closed his keynote speech at the summit with details about it. Secretary Mayorkas was dispatched to elaborate on the effort in an exclusive CNN interview.[24] The following is an excerpt of the language we wrote for the POTUS speech and secretary interview:

Ruthless criminal organizations exploit migrants and America's commitment to human rights. Human smuggling organizations aren't the small mom-and-pop outfits that used to operate along the Southwest Border. They are sprawling, sophisticated international criminal organizations profiting from the multibillion-dollar human smuggling industry. They are affiliates or wholly owned subsidiaries of violent drug cartels and transnational gangs wreaking shocking violence across Latin America. For far too long, they have operated with impunity

As a result, I [Biden] have ordered law enforcement agencies to undertake a first of its kind effort, unprecedented in scale, to disrupt and dismantle these human smuggling networks. The Department of Homeland Security (DHS) has committed nearly $50 million and surged over 1,300 personnel in Latin America and along the Southwest Border to take the fight directly to these vicious criminals. The smugglers can't hide from our brave men and women at DHS and their partner law enforcement agents in the region. Our international partnerships are strong, and we collaborate to bring the swift hand of justice down on these violent gangs.

In the last two months alone marquee programs DHS recently launched like Operation Expanded Impact, led by Homeland Security Investigations (HSI), and Operation Sentinel, led by Customs and Border Protection (CBP), have deployed over 1,300 agents to execute over 20,000 law enforcement actions to disrupt and dismantle human smuggling organizations in Latin America. These agents have worked with international partners to attack these smuggling gangs at every point in their infrastructure. Our agents seize financial assets, raid stash houses that house migrants, impound buses and tractor trailers used to smuggle humans, and seize their illicit cargo. Moreover nearly 1,500 smugglers have been arrested through this program in the last eight weeks alone. These efforts exceed a 600 percent increase in law enforcement actions taken against human smuggling organizations compared to efforts in previous years. In short, this is the first time in American history a law enforcement campaign of this scale was launched to attack criminals' ability to smuggle humans everywhere in the Western Hemisphere.

These disruption actions are producing results. We are already seeing the criminals change their tactics. They changed the routes used to smuggle humans. They shifted stash house locations away from the border to avoid our raids. They increased prices for smuggling and no longer guarantee passage at the border.[25]

We were making progress.

Notes

1 Gómez, Marinee Zavala Ana. "Russian Migrants Set up Camp at San Ysidro Point of Entry." NBC 7 San Diego, March 18, 2022. https://www.nbcsandiego.com/news/local/russian-migrants-set-up-camp-at-san-ysidro-point-of-entry/2897927/.

2 Rivera, Salvador. "Russian Asylum-Seekers Secure Most CBP One Appointments in San Diego." BorderReport, April 6, 2023. https://www.borderreport.com/immigration/russian-asylum-seekers-secure-most-cbp-one-appointments-in-san-diego/.

3 "Smugglers Coaching Migrants to 'Defy' Authorities, Police Chief Says." KGET 17 News, n.d. https://www.kget.com/video/smugglers-coaching-migrants-to-defy-authorities-police-chief-says/10347360/.

4 Shah, Tejas. "Immigration Courts Backlogs Continue into 2024." *National Law Review*, January 12, 2024. https://natlawreview.com/article/immigration-court-backlogs-continue-2024.

5 Beittel, J. S. "Mexico: Organized Crime and Drug Trafficking Organizations." Congressional Research Service, updated June 7, 2022. https://sgp.fas.org/crs/row/R41576.pdf.

6 "President Putin 'Probably' Approved Litvinenko Murder." BBC, January 21, 2016. https://www.bbc.com/news/uk-35370819.

7 Sganga, Nicole. "President Biden Warns of 'Evolving' Russian Cyber Threat to U.S.: 'It's Coming.'" CBS News, March 21, 2022. https://www.cbsnews.com/news/russia-cyber-attack-threat-biden-warning/.

8 Roussi, Antoaneta. "Cops Infiltrate 'Ghost' Encryption App Used by Drug Lords, Mafia." *Politico*, September 18, 2024. https://www.politico.eu/article/police-ghost-encryption-app-drug-lords-mafia-europol/.

9 Lokshina, Tanya. "They Have Long Arms and They Can Find Me." Human Rights Watch, May 26, 2017. https://www.hrw.org/report/2017/05/26/they-have-long-arms -and-they-can-find-me/anti-gay-purge-local-authorities-russias.

10 "Russia behind Litvinenko Murder, Rules European Rights Court." BBC, September 21, 2021. https://www.bbc.com/news/world-58637572.

11 Ford, Alessandro. "Turkish Bananas: The Cocaine Road to Russia and the Persian Gulf." InSight Crime, October 13, 2023. https://insightcrime.org/news/turkish -bananas-the-cocaine-road-to-russia-and-the-persian-gulf/.

12 Baverstock, Alasdair. "Russian Mafia Is Stealing Millions from Cancun Tourists Using 'Most Advanced ATM Skimming Devices Ever.'" *Daily Mail*, September 16, 2015. https://www.dailymail.co.uk/news/article-3236513/Russian-mafia-stealing-millions -Cancun-tourists-using-advanced-ATM-skimming-devices-bought-online-550.html.

13 Monge, Yolanda, and Elías Camhaji. "US General: Russia Has More Spies Deployed in Mexico Than in Any Other Country." *El País*, March 26, 2022. https://english .elpais.com/international/2022-03-26/us-general-russia-has-more-spies-deployed-in -mexico-than-in-any-other-country.html.

14 "Mexicans, Russian Mob New Partners in Crime." *Washington Times*, May 28, 2001. https://www.washingtontimes.com/news/2001/may/28/20010528-023346-7901r/.

15 "Gangsters at War: Russia's Use of Organized Crime as an Instrument of Statecraft." Global Initiative, November 6, 2024. https://globalinitiative.net/analysis/gangsters-at -war-russias-use-of-organized-crime-as-an-instrument-of-statecraft/.

16 Holmes, Leslie. "The Police and Organised Crime." In *Rethinking Organized Crime*. Northampton, MA: Edward Elgar, 2024. https://www.elgaronline.com/monochap/ book/9781802206234/book-part-9781802206234-11.xml.

17 U.S. Department of Justice, U.S. Department of Homeland Security, Office of the Inspector General, Office of Inspector General, and Evaluation and Inspections Division. "A Joint Review of Law Enforcement Cooperation on the Southwest Border between the Federal Bureau of Investigation and Homeland Security Investigations." Evaluation and Inspections Division, July 2019, 23–26. https://oig.justice.gov/reports /2019/e1903.pdf.

18 "Child Exploitation." U.S. Department of Homeland Security, n.d. https://www.dhs .gov/hsi/investigate/child-exploitation.

19 "Enforcement and Removal Operations." U.S. Immigration and Customs Enforcement, February 4, 2025. https://www.ice.gov/about-ice/ero.

20 Verza, María. "How Mexican Cartels Manage the Flow of Migrants on Their Way to the US Border." AP News, October 30, 2024. https://apnews.com/article/mexico -migrants-cartels-smuggling-chiapas-us-border-67d4851eefa60981bceb772 bf26d7204.

21 Spetalnick, Matt, and Dave Graham. "U.S. Bars Cuba, Venezuela from Americas Summit; Mexican Leader Sits Out." Reuters, June 7, 2022. https://www.reuters.com/world/americas/us-excludes-cuba-venezuela-nicaragua-americas-summit-sources-2022-06-06/.

22 "Biden: U.S. Continues to Lead Global Partnership, Stands Firm with NATO." U.S. Department of Defense, July 10, 2024. https://www.defense.gov/News/News-Stories/Article/Article/3836362/biden-us-continues-to-lead-global-partnership-stands-firm-with-nato-allies/.

23 "Biden: U.S. Continues to Lead Global Partnership."

24 Alvarez, Priscilla. "First on CNN: Biden Administration Launches 'Unprecedented' Operation to Disrupt Human Smuggling as Caravan Moves North." CNN, June 10, 2022. https://www.cnn.com/2022/06/10/politics/alejandro-mayorkas-interview-cnntv/index.html.

25 Katz, Eric. "Biden Announces 'Unprecedented' Federal Deployments to Crack Down on Human Smuggling." Government Executive, June 13, 2022. https://www.govexec.com/management/2022/06/biden-federal-deployments-human-smuggling-international-agreement/368105/.

4

Fentanyl

Entering the Ring

Soon after we spiked the football at the Summit of the Americas, fentanyl surged to the front page.[1] News of the number of dead from drug overdoses, primarily caused from fentanyl-related poisoning was released. The year shaped up to be one of progress instead of setbacks. Earlier in the year, we had successfully resettled most of the Afghans. Rocky was rolling through one smuggler network after another. After the June 2022 summit, it appeared we had turned a corner from the chaos we inherited in 2021.

As mentioned in chapter 1, for the first time in modern history, the Centers for Disease Control (CDC) and National Institutes of Health (NIH) reported that more than one hundred thousand people died from drug overdoses in the United States in 2021.[2] This horrific news was chilling. We knew fentanyl was a problem before we took office. Thousands of agents and analysts pursued fentanyl cases daily. Still, this grim milestone dramatically ramped up pressure to stem the tide of corpses piling up across the country. To energize those unfamiliar with the fentanyl crisis, we cited macabre statistics. We penned lines like "This is like a 747 crashing every two days in America" or "Every year nearly double the number of people who died in Vietnam die from fentanyl"[3] or "This is the same number of Americans that died every year in World War II."[4]

Thanks to John Tien's prodding, the intelligence community regularly produced intelligence products on the situation at the northern border of

Mexico. Through various forms of intelligence collection—from satellite to signals intelligence to human intelligence—we acquired a far more clear view of the inner workings of the cartel and smuggling patterns. We were astounded to realize that the same cartels who wrested control of human smuggling operations from the mom-and-pop coyotes generated upward of $10 billion a year in revenue from migrants.[5] As mentioned previously, this was a huge departure for the cartels—particularly Sinaloa and the Cartel de Jalisco Nueva Generación (CJNG). They had grown their criminal empires through trafficking primarily two key commodities: marijuana and cocaine.

To be sure, Sinaloa and CJNG were equal opportunity mobsters. They were agnostic as to what contraband they trafficked. The criminal enterprises are generally pretty careful about not engaging in specific business lines that are too hot, where even a high profit margin isn't worth taking down the core enterprise. For example, there has always been an understanding that if terrorists were knowingly trafficked by cartels, this would be a red line for the United States, which would have unacceptable negative consequences for the core marijuana and cocaine trafficking business. Otherwise, whether prostitutes, rare animals, avocados, or migrants, the cartels trafficked anything they could make a buck off. Most of the gangsters' profits and nearly all of their time and attention for the last sixty years, however, was geared toward marijuana and cocaine with a smattering of other drugs like heroin and methamphetamine.[6] Diversifying their business to migration and synthetic drugs like methamphetamine—and, more recently, fentanyl—was a transformational departure from their business model. Something catastrophic must have disrupted the cartel business model. Any business executive is loath to change a business model that works. The cannabis and cocaine model transformed the narco-tycoons into some of the richest executives in the world. For example, El Chapo, the infamous leader of the Sinaloa cartel, was reputedly worth more than $1 billion, making him one of the richest people in the world.[7] If the model wasn't broken, there was little reason to fix it.

President Biden insisted the scourge of fentanyl be elevated to a top priority of his administration. He wanted it attacked at every level. Before Rocky, we didn't appreciate the level to which the two cartels that controlled the northern border of Mexico had assumed control of human smuggling. We honed our focus on those two cartels—Sinaloa and CJNG.[8] We connected these dots, and soon the other shoe dropped. Of the two cartels, Sinaloa was responsible for the vast majority of the fentanyl in the United States.[9] We also just demonstrated the lion's share of the Russians moved through Sinaloa territory. Sinaloa scored the trifecta of trafficking Latin American migrants, Russians, and fentanyl. We had a target to aim at: the Sinaloa cartel.

We also had gained experience through Rocky. We constructed a model operation to combat several cartels' human smuggling networks. We could leverage that model to disrupt Sinaloa's fentanyl networks. Rocky had gained its own momentum and was self-sustaining. Now we quickly shifted focus from maintaining Rocky to intensifying our counterfentanyl operation.

Our counterfentanyl operation needed to be distinct from Rocky. This was because the coyotes smuggling migrants maintained a completely separate line of business for Sinaloa than fentanyl trafficking. Our intelligence validated that cartels very rarely forced migrants to act as mules for fentanyl. To be clear, the cartels know best that the worst possible place to hide fentanyl was on a migrant. This is because the cartel trains the migrants not to run *from* the border patrol but rather run *toward* border patrol and claim asylum. The very next thing that happens to a migrant after claiming asylum is they are searched before being processed. So, the best way to lose a load of fentanyl to Customs and Border Protection (CBP) was to stash it on a migrant. Thus, the cartels were not employing the migrants to carry the fentanyl. So Rocky was not a useful vehicle to prosecute a campaign against Sinaloa's fentanyl operation.

Sinaloa, however, was employing the exact same infrastructure for fentanyl as it was for migrants. It was using similar routes, logistics contractors, drivers, money launderers, and stash houses. Further, there is a similar structure to receive and distribute contraband in the United States. So, we could establish a program with the same principles as Rocky and just target the fentanyl line of business at Sinaloa while Rocky continued to target Sinaloa's coyote line of business. Furthermore, replicating the law enforcement logistics that were in place for Rocky can easily be transitioned to counter fentanyl.

However, one key problem surfaced: U.S. law enforcement is drastically outnumbered in Mexico. After more than a decade of bloody conflict with the cartels, Mexican president Andrés Manuel López Obrador implemented a "hugs not bullets" policy. "Hugs" coupled with rampant corruption throughout law enforcement and the military meant that Mexican government actions to combat the cartels were at a nadir.[10] Moreover, my back-of-the-envelope math showed that, with the Department of Homeland Security (DHS), the Drug Enforcement Administration (DEA), and the Federal Bureau of Investigation (FBI), among others, we had roughly one thousand agents and officers in Mexico. A quick Google search divined that approximately 175,000 people are on the drug lords' dole in Mexico.[11] These narco-empires operated with impunity in their territory. They could even outfight the national government on their home turf.[12]

More disconcerting was Chinese entanglement with Sinaloa. Aside from discovering that Chinese brokers supplied all the precursor chemicals for fentanyl, our agents uncovered fentanyl production operations recruiting Chinese nationals as chemists.[13] Finally, the illicit tycoons' money laundering operations were largely funneled through elaborate Chinese money laundering schemes.

Taking It to Sinaloa

We mirrored the foundation established with Rocky to dramatically increase operations against fentanyl coming across the border. For example, Homeland Security Investigations (HSI) initiated an investigation months earlier after a routine traffic stop. They pinched a load of drugs hidden in the perp's vehicle. That case eventually led us to a fentanyl lab in Mexico controlled by the Sinaloa cartel. HSI confiscated more fentanyl in that operation than we did in the entirety of 2021.[14] Time and again Sinaloa turned out to be ground zero in the fight against fentanyl. As mentioned previously, the narco-enterprise produced the vast majority of the fentanyl in the United States. CJNG had entered the fentanyl market, but it was a bit player in fentanyl trafficking compared to Sinaloa.[15]

The U.S. government knew very little about Sinaloa as a network. We knew a lot about its leadership. The "Chapitos," or children of infamous cartel boss El Chapo, ran much of the cartel.[16] El Chapo famously tunneled out of incarceration and oversaw the sprawling multibillion-dollar criminal enterprise. The Sinaloa empire is so gargantuan it would likely rank as a Fortune 50 company if it were measured as a legitimate business.[17] We were shocked at how little the U.S. government had pieced together about an enterprise that massive and global. The intelligence and law enforcement communities did not know Sinaloa like it knew al-Qaeda. It didn't even know Sinaloa as well as IBM knows Microsoft or Ford knows Toyota. There was no single part of the government that had something like a business intelligence assessment of the Sinaloa enterprise and global supply chain.

Multiple parts of the government understood a lot about certain people or aspects of the cartel. The DEA, for example, was expert in compiling encyclopedic details on Sinaloa kingpins. CBP understood Sinaloa's border smuggling routes in intricate detail. However, each part of the government, whether DEA, CBP, HSI, or FBI, generally only grasped its piece of the elephant. None possessed an understanding of the entire network. For example, we possessed little insight into Sinaloa executives' U.S. holdings. We had no idea how its logistics directors managed their fleet of tractor trailers, drones, planes, submarines, ships, and other modes of transportation.

DEA amassed painstakingly detailed information about Sinaloa's narcotics line of business. Conversely, it knew little about Sinaloa's booming migration business vertical. The FBI might acquire in-depth analysis on key corrupt government officials in bed with Sinaloa dons. Yet the FBI understood little about Sinaloa's illegal fishing corporate vertical. HSI closely tracked the Sinaloa capos migration line of business. But it remained in the dark regarding the gangsters who administered their local extortion racket. Very few individuals had a grasp on ties between the web of licit businesses, money laundering operations, and real estate holdings. No one had a grip on how Sinaloa recruiters sourced and managed chemists for laboratories. HSI and DEA mapped the online narco-marketplace; however, the network of precursor chemical brokers we observed was only the tip of the iceberg. It was discouraging to realize how each agency had parts of the puzzle, yet there was hesitancy to collaborate and share intelligence.

We had little conception of the sprawling network of Chinese brokers that provided precursors to the narcos. There were hundreds of front companies online on both the open and dark web.[18] Every time we pursued one front company, it shuttered; however, a new one popped up immediately. The new LLC tweaked its name but provided the same service. It connected yet more Sinaloa brokers to the precursor chemical company in China.

Fortunately the agents at HSI had been investigating Chinese chemical front companies for about a year when we asked about it. They tracked front companies and identified package destinations. Agents interdicted chemicals before cartel henchmen snatched shipments from the ports. Yet there existed another reason we knew so little about Sinaloa's fentanyl operation. Until a few years earlier, finished fentanyl was delivered straight from China via the U.S. Postal Service, FedEx, or UPS.[19] Once China outlawed the production of fentanyl for all but approved medical uses, the Sinaloa cartel chemists scaled up their fentanyl production.[20] This inflection point was when fatalities surged.

Unfortunately it turns out that Sinaloa has a better distribution network for drugs in the United States than the U.S. Postal Service, UPS, and FedEx combined. The agents at HSI evolved along with the fentanyl trade. Within a few months of criminalization in China, agents tracked front companies, infiltrated Sinaloa communications, monitored shipments, and seized hundreds of tons of chemicals.[21] Tons of chemical shipments represented a significant shift in production. Seizing fentanyl chemicals is not the same as seizing marijuana or cocaine. Just a few pounds of precursors in a container the size of a large suitcase provides enough chemicals to fashion millions of pills. Those pills can murder millions of Americans.[22] So, tons of precursors was emblematic of just how many possible deaths loomed on the horizon in the United States. Despite our success seizing fentanyl, we had not achieved much progress locating the precursor chemical plants in China.

On the opposite end of the fentanyl supply chain, we understood aspects of the drug lords' money laundering operations; however, significant gaps remained. The laundering programs ranged from high-tech methods involving multiple cryptocurrency platforms on the dark web down to low-tech methods like concealing pallets of cash in cars back down to Mexico.[23] Alejandro Mayorkas and John Tien clamored for HSI to up its game and seize more mafiosi money. One industrious HSI agent from Los Angeles, Ponch (not his real name as he is still an agent and prefers to remain anonymous), scaled up an operation targeting washed physical cash. He arranged for a group of agents in Los Angeles to hit bag after bag of cash. Each bag only stored $50,000–$100,000 a pop. Over time, however, he picked millions of dollars from the pockets of the Chapitos.

We gleaned more nuanced information every day about the fentanyl supply chain and Sinaloa cartel. Nonetheless, we remained blind in many respects. We had yet to discover the vast majority of the fentanyl labs in Mexico. We lacked new methods to detect fentanyl pills coming across the border except for routine vehicle searches. We possessed almost no capability to track the overall business management of the fentanyl trade. To better understand the narco-enterprise, we traveled to Mexico City. There we broke bread with HSI and CBP agents in the field. These brave men and women were closest to the trafficking operations.

Just before Thanksgiving in 2022, there was a rare lull in the otherwise hectic pace of the DHS Front Office. Ponch, Morgan Ryan, and I slipped down to Mexico to meet with both our HSI agents and our vetted Mexican Transnational Criminal Investigative Units (TCIUs). Our vetted units were routinely polygraphed as prophylactic against the mobsters' uncanny ability to infiltrate Mexican law enforcement. These local Mexican agents kicked down the doors of bad guys for us. We also met with fascinating journalists and authors who had been covering the gangster warlords for decades.

Our first meeting was set with the longest-serving DHS attaché to Mexico in DHS history, named Edgar Ramirez. We were immediately reminded how little we knew about Sinaloa's intricate business operations. He explained that the gangster supply chain managers could sneak fentanyl precursors from China through the Mexican Pacific sea ports unabated. President Obrador's leadership team was well versed in this problem. So the Secretaría de la Marina (SEMAR), the well-respected and generally less corrupt Mexican marines, were assigned authority over the ports.[24] SEMAR's new role at the ports was a positive step. At least we had a far less corrupt portion of the Mexican military to plot with against Sinaloa. The flip side was that SEMAR lacked experience managing or inspecting ports. So we essentially started from zero with SEMAR. DHS headquarters sent teams down with experts from CBP, the Coast Guard, and HSI to jumpstart their capability for discovering contraband at the port.[25]

Nerve Center

The following morning, we received a classified briefing from the Mexican Embassy Fusion Center. The Mexican Embassy Fusion Center was the global hub of intelligence on Sinaloa. They also served as the tip of the spear in Mexico. The DEA, HSI, Central Intelligence Agency (CIA), Department of Defense (DOD), and other three-letter agencies worked hand in glove there. Their level of cooperation was a tacit admonition of our petty bickering in Washington. While the brief was classified, one message was no secret. The team was frustrated and beat down. They were some of the best agents and analysts the United States had to offer. Still, they knew they were no match for the narco-tycoons. For example, HSI employed thirty-five staff, and another fifty or so TCIUs, in Mexico. As mentioned previously, some estimates suggest the cartels had nearly 175,000 people laboring in some capacity for them.[26] Sinaloa paid everyone from corrupt politicians, to freelance truck drivers, to maids, accountants, and highly trained assassins.

DEA had a footprint in Mexico similar to HSI. Unfortunately, the DEA was on the Mexican government's shit list. DEA officials arrested the Mexican minister of defense on corruption charges a few years earlier.[27] The Mexican government was incensed. Arresting members of a head of state's cabinet breached diplomatic protocols. DEA argued that, regardless of protocol, the minister was as corrupt as the day is long. As a result, for the moment, DEA was in the penalty box with the Mexican government. So, they had one arm tied behind their back for the foreseeable future. The embassy team went on for more than two hours describing the capabilities of Sinaloa. Then they explained that our efforts, while world class, amounted to a mere drop in the bucket compared to what the gangsters brought to the fight.

This was also the first time I heard a reasonable person claim with sincerity that, if we were serious about this effort, we needed to declare war on the Sinaloa cartel. It was not a war like Richard Nixon's "war on drugs," which was as much a slogan as anything else. Rather, this was an actual war—like the war declared on al-Qaeda and the Islamic State of Iraq and Syria (ISIS). Everyone in the room acknowledged the dire ramifications for all levels of the U.S.-Mexico relationship. The political impacts would be severe at home, too. Despite that, these hard-nosed operatives felt it was the only way we could have a chance defeating Sinaloa narco-warlords.

Short of that, they argued, there was only one way to stop Sinaloa from flooding the United States with deadly fentanyl. We had to persuade the Mexican government to step in and do it. Unfortunately, they reported that the Mexican government was too corrupt to be persuaded. Some parts of the military and Justice Department, Fiscalía General de la República (FGR), were largely aboveboard.[28] But those were small forces. They are not a formidable opponent against Sinaloa. After the briefing someone explained the disparity:

A firefight between the gangbanger militia and Mexican military occurred in Sinaloa's stronghold. The militia outfought and chased off the military. A bust went bad in Sonora. A battered and bleeding group of military personnel were fighting their way out. The military deployed reinforcements. The cartel retaliated by lighting garbage trucks on fire at the local airport. Military planes loaded with reinforcements could not land. Fortunately, the remaining Mexican troops escaped on the only helicopter still operational. It was not lost on anyone that the military had come to take out Sinaloa C-Suite and the C-Suite's militia stood its ground.[29]

As I walked out of the morning briefing, I only half-jokingly asked our DHS handlers in the meeting if it was too early to have a drink. Later, we received a briefing from our HSI team and stumbled upon some potentially positive news. The team in Mexico believed Sinaloa chemists sourced their precursor chemicals from only around three hundred chemical companies in China and a few other countries. While three hundred was a big number, it wasn't unmanageable for the seven thousand agents at HSI and hundreds of staff at the Treasury Department.[30] HSI assessed most of these companies operated in the "formal economy," meaning the companies did not live solely in the illicit black market. If the companies conducted business in the formal economy, they may be publicly traded. They may have individual investors or appoint board members from Democratic allied nations. Further, most of the firm's licit chemical customers may reside in the United States or allied nations. Their finances may be held in a legitimate bank.

These three hundred or so companies operated in the formal economy yet conducted illicit business in the black market. That characteristic provided multiple attack vectors for our agents. Investigators could freeze bank accounts or seize assets. They could simply alert Western shareholders of illegal activity in their portfolio. The Feds could threaten the shareholders or customers with personal investigations. Ratcheting up pressure on investors or customers often compels those threatened to demand compliance with U.S. laws. We learned many of these Chinese chemical companies are behemoths.[31] Fentanyl precursor sales likely account for an infinitesimally small portion of total revenue. Nervous shareholders and customers would demand rigorous know-your-customer due diligence. Shareholder and customer outcry could be enough to induce a chemical company broker to lose the phone number of their Sinaloa client.

Merchant of Death

Later, insights from a new connection revealed still more pathways to take the fight to Sinaloa. Morgan and I broke bread in an fascinating conversation with celebrated Mexican author Jorge Fernández Menéndez[32] and famous journalist Bibiana Belsasso.[33] Menéndez is a world-renowned expert on cartels. Unprompted, they reiterated points delivered from the Mexican government months earlier. The Mexican government was deadly serious about the number of guns flowing south into Mexico from the United States. Sinaloa wears the crown for being the world's top drug dealer,[34] but the United States wears it for being the top arms dealer. U.S. weapons manufacturers' deadly assembly lines appeared to deposit full arsenals into the trunks of Sinaloa vehicles—vehicles bound for Mexico. These weapons supplied all the munitions necessary to fuel a never-ending war among the cartels and government.[35] Everything from pistols to rocket launchers racked up a death toll that ranked nearly seven Mexican cities in the top ten deadliest cities in the world. For a time, Juárez held the title for the deadliest city in the world. This meant someone living in Juárez was more likely to violently meet their maker than would a counterpart in Baghdad or Kabul at the height of each conflict.[36]

U.S. officials routinely threw up their hands and reversed roles with their Mexican counterparts. Instead of Mexican officials insisting they could do nothing to impede the cartel drug trafficking, it was the Americans insisting they could do nothing about U.S. weapons manufacturers arms trafficking. U.S. officials parroted back the same lines the Mexicans squawked at them. We proffered excuses about the Second Amendment and guns bought legally. The right to bear arms was not a fungible law but protected by the Constitution itself. Further, U.S. Customs was funded and required primarily to inspect cargo entering the United States, not leaving it. Moreover, even the multibillion-dollar inspection regime we architected to inspect cargo shipped to the U.S. only inspected about 5 percent of it.[37] Inspection rate targets for cargo coming into the United States were 99 percent, so spending any more resources searching cargo going south was infeasible.

This bleak assessment provided little incentive for the Mexican officials to work with us. We later learned the United States had only seized several hundred guns traveling to Mexico the previous year.[38] Those seizures were accompanied by little fanfare. Ironically, the upside of seizures that low is they could easily be doubled or tripled. The number would remain low, but if the numbers were moving in the right direction, it could provide us a political asset. We could be smart about letting the Mexican government take credit for the increases. Weapons made for great props at press conferences. The Mexican government could take credit for demanding the gringos triple weapons seizures backed by a glimmering weapons cache at press conferences in Mexico. Enabling Mexican politicians to take credit publicly for minuscule enforcement increases on our part could create the political space necessary for them to muster more assets to pursue Sinaloa.

Menéndez and Belsasso agreed. They posited we could gain far greater cooperation from the Mexican government if we demonstrated we were seizing more weapons. Enabling Mexican officials to take credit for the seizures at press events in Mexico would go a long way to engender goodwill. It was striking how passionate the two were about the gun issue. By contrast, in the United States officials relegate this to a bottom-tier issue primarily because of the aforementioned complications with interdicting the guns. Moreover, officials hold an unspoken belief the cartels will get weapons from somewhere else if not the United States. They argue limiting the flow of guns to Mexico from the United States is irrelevant. The overall problem of eradicating the criminal enterprise starts and ends with their main source of income, narcotics.[39]

This is decidedly *not* the view in Mexico. They admit the gangsters would source arms one way or another. However, the sheer magnitude of the arsenal the criminal militias maintain is only possible with a limitless supply of weapons from the U.S. gun industry. Not only is the supply endless but the carnage these weapons wreak is military grade. Sure, they would argue, gangsters will always find some number of pistols and rifles from another country. But the grenade launchers, missile launchers, RPGs, automatic machine guns with "cop killer" bullets, and armed helicopters, could only come from a couple potential suppliers on the planet. None is so close as the United States.[40]

The journalists' passion on this issue stuck with us. We revisited it time and again while reflecting on the looming battle with the gangster warlords. The weapons issue proved especially relevant for soliciting the support of the Mexican government in attacking Sinaloa. Morgan and I resolved that whatever plan we proposed must have a component to prevent the flow of weapons to Mexico.

The military-grade weaponry Sinaloa militias wield against the government was hammered home further when I met with our Transnational Criminal Investigative Units (TCIUs) the following day. The TCIUs are the aforementioned vetted units of elite Mexican agents who are routinely polygraphed and on the U.S. payroll. They work our cases. They arrest our criminal targets. They kick down the doors we can't in another sovereign nation.[41]

In a briefing at the U.S. embassy, we learned how poorly resourced they are. They struggle to fund a full team. They barely manage to finance offices and housing.[42] Despite resource challenges, they are viewed as the most elite law enforcement group in Mexico. After the briefing, I took them out for drinks at the rooftop bar of the Sofitel Hotel next to the U.S. embassy. The Sofitel rooftop bar functions as an unofficial watering hole for U.S. officials visiting the Mexico City embassy.

Morgan and I knocked back tequila and beers with these agents. For their safety, we do not use their names here. These guys regaled us with harrowing stories and showed us pictures on their phones of kicking down doors and rounding up serious thugs. The cartels' fierce arsenal came up again. The head of the TCIU unit dialed up a picture of a machine gun on his phone. The monster is designed to turn an armored jeep into Swiss cheese. He chose this picture because of his personal relationship with the beast. During one operation, he peered over top a hill to raid a mob safe house. The weapon was aimed right between his eyes. It certainly would have made short work of the body armor he wore. Instinctually he rolled back down the hill to regroup. Fortunately, the mobster lookouts didn't spot him. His team regrouped. Despite being seriously outgunned, they still staged the planned assault.

Fortunately, he survived. His unit cuffed the mafia cell and shuttered the safe house. He proudly displayed the victory with further pictures of him and his agents. They were covered from head to toe in military-grade battle armor. They posed next to helicopters brandishing weapons of their own. They presided over a cadre of grimacing blindfolded gangsters, heads slouching down.

Despite winning the day, he made clear he would rather not face these guys down while they sported weapons on par with his. In most other parts of the world, the government's competitive edge against criminals is its vastly superior capacity for lethal force. There will always be more criminals than cops. However, cops traditionally have access to better technology, infrastructure, and weapons. In Mexico, this is not always the case. Our TCIUs routinely find themselves outgunned by the cartels.

Field Agents Follow the Money

I pressed him on ideas to thwart the narco-empire's fentanyl business. He repeatedly encouraged me to go after their money and their "middle bosses" who manage their money. He contended there existed a vast but not unlimited Sinaloa "back office" of accountants, lawyers, and financial advisors to target.

If neutralized, these hidden assets could cripple Sinaloa's ability to manage its money. I complained that Mexican financial institutions were notoriously recalcitrant to seize cartel assets.[43] He acknowledged that. But he also pointed out that a huge amount of cartel money is kept in the United States in the form of real estate, cars, and licit and illicit companies.[44] He pointed out that we didn't need the Mexican government or banks to target those assets.

The next evening, we met with our American HSI agents and their leadership in Mexico City. We convened in a dark corner at a steakhouse. The agents all sat with their backs to the wall. Their comfort was dependent on monitoring who came and went from the restaurant. Servers brought an endless stream of tequila and mezcal. There I implored our agents for their most innovative ideas on degrading Sinaloa. They were on the front lines. Presumably, no one knew the issues better than they did. They were led by Mary (not her real name) and supported by both young and hungry guys like Victor (not his real name) and grizzled veterans like Tino. This was Tino's second tour of duty against Sinaloa. He had been fighting Sinaloa in Chicago for more than a decade before coming to Mexico.

Mary and team were adamant about targeting precursor chemicals from China. They also were in agreement with the TCIUs. We must put more effort toward targeting the finances of the narco-tycoons. They were more sanguine about the gun issue as they knew the political obstacles in the United States. To a person, they argued that once the precursors entered Mexico, it was game over. Fentanyl could be made in a home kitchen. Thus, the Sinaloa cooks weren't required to construct massive underground labs like they did for methamphetamine. Further, Sinaloa had peerless smuggling networks.[45] As had been true with cocaine and heroin since they first showed up on the streets of America, the United States can seize some of the drugs some of the time, but we have never been able to seize all of the drugs all of the time.

The experts we interviewed in Mexico provided a grim assessment. Sinaloa's gangster warlords operate with impunity on their turf. They boasted arms of a military-grade militia. Their major financial assets in the United States and Mexico went undisturbed. The main commodity required to concoct fentanyl slipped through their ports from Chinese ocean liners undetected. The labs required to cook fentanyl could fit in an average-sized residential kitchen.

Once produced, the poison was smuggled in a dizzying array of contraptions and routes to the border. Our official visit to Mexico was enlightening but not encouraging. Our only glimmer of hope was the dedication and resilience of the team on the ground. The TCIUs, the HSI agents, and their counterparts at the DEA and intelligence agencies were inspiring agents taking it to the bad guys every day. We just needed about ten times more of them.

Notes

1 "Approximately 1 Million Fentanyl-Laced Pills Seized in Drug Bust near Los Angeles." CBS News, July 15, 2022. https://www.cbsnews.com/news/fentanyl-pills-seized-in-dea -bust-near-los-angeles/.

2 McPhillips, Deidre. "Drug Overdose Deaths Top 100,000 Annually for the First Time, Driven by Fentanyl, CDC Data Show." CNN, November 17, 2021. https://www.cnn .com/2021/11/17/health/drug-overdose-deaths-record-high/index.html.

3 Richter, Felix. "Infographic: Fentanyl Fuels Surge in U.S. Drug Overdose Deaths." Statista, August 30, 2024. https://www.statista.com/chart/18744/the-number-of-drug -overdose-deaths-in-the-us/.

4 Leland, Anne. "American War and Military Operations Casualties: Lists and Statistics." Congressional Research Service, November 15, 2012. https://sgp.fas.org/crs /natsec/RL32492.pdf.

5 "Migrant Smuggling: Background and Selected Issues." Congressional Research Service, December 20, 2021. https://crsreports.congress.gov/product/pdf/IF/IF12003.

6 "Mexico's Long War: Drugs, Crime, and the Cartels." Council on Foreign Relations, August 5, 2024. https://www.cfr.org/backgrounder/mexicos-long-war-drugs-crime -and-cartels.

7 "#937 Joaquin Guzman Loera." *Forbes*, 2010. https://web.archive.org/web /20110810055603/http://www.forbes.com/lists/2010/10/billionaires-2010_Joaquin -Guzman-Loera_FS0Y.html.

8 "Mexico's Long War: Drugs, Crime, and the Cartels"; "National Drug Threat Assessment." Drug Enforcement Administration, May 2024. https://www.dea.gov/sites /default/files/2024-05/NDTA_2024.pdf.

9 "National Drug Threat Assessment."

10 O'Neil, Shannon K. "AMLO's 'Hugs Not Bullets' Is Failing Mexico." Council on Foreign Relations, October 23, 2019. https://www.cfr.org/blog/amlos-hugs-not-bullets -failing-mexico; "US Envoy Says Mexico Not Safe, Blames Ex-President for Failed

Security." Reuters, November 13, 2024. https://www.reuters.com/world/americas/us
-envoy-says-mexico-not-safe-blames-ex-president-failed-security-2024-11-13/.

11 Prieto-Curiel, Rafael, Gian Maria Campedelli, and Alejandro Hope. "Reducing Cartel
Recruitment Is the Only Way to Lower Violence in Mexico." *Science* 381, no. 6664
(September 2023): 1312–16. https://www.science.org/doi/10.1126/science.adh2888.

12 Dalby, Chris. "How Mexico's Cartels Have Learned Military Tactics." InSight Crime,
September 2, 2021. https://insightcrime.org/news/interview/how-mexicos-cartel-have
-learned-military-tactics/.

13 "Three Chinese Chemical Manufacturing Companies and Five Employees Charged
with Conspiring to Manufacture Fentanyl." U.S. Department of Justice | U.S.
Attorney's Office, Eastern District of New York, June 23, 2023. https://www.justice
.gov/usao-edny/pr/three-chinese-chemical-manufacturing-companies-and-five
-employees-charged-conspiring.

14 Chaparro, Luis. "A $200 Million Load of Fentanyl Was Just Seized in El Chapo's
Hometown." VICE, July 27, 2024. https://www.vice.com/en/article/mexico-sinaloa
-fentanylmexico-sinaloa-fentanyl/.

15 "National Drug Threat Assessment."

16 Chavez, Nicole. "What We Know about the Sinaloa Cartel and Its Leaders." CNN, July
28, 2024. https://www.cnn.com/2024/07/27/us/sinaloa-cartel-history-leaders/index
.html.

17 At its highest estimate, revenue of $39 billion would rank Sinaloa 110th on the
Fortune 500. See: Tikkanen, Amy. "Sinaloa Cartel | Leader Caught, Arrest, History,
Members, & Facts." *Encyclopedia Britannica*, May 12, 2025. https://www.britannica
.com/topic/Sinaloa-cartel; Sarath. "Fortune 500 Companies List (2024)." Eqvista,
March 17, 2025. https://eqvista.com/fortune-500-companies-in-the-us/.

18 "We Bought What's Needed to Make Millions of Fentanyl Pills—for $3,600." Reuters,
July 25, 2024. https://www.reuters.com/investigates/special-report/drugs-fentanyl
-supplychain/.

19 Serletis, George. "Deadly High-Purity Fentanyl from China Is Entering the U.S.
through E-commerce Channels." U.S. International Trade Commission, September
2019. https://www.usitc.gov/publications/332/executive_briefings/ebot_george
_serletis_fentanyl_from_china_pdf.pdf.

20 Greenwood, Lauren, and Kevin Fashola. "Illicit Fentanyl from China: An Evolving
Global Operation." U.S.-China Economic and Security Review Commission, August
2021. https://www.uscc.gov/sites/default/files/2021-08/Illicit_Fentanyl_from_China
-An_Evolving_Global_Operation.pdf.

21 "ICE HSI Announces Record-High Number of Criminal Arrests in FY 2019." U.S.
Immigration and Customs Enforcement, November 18, 2024. https://www.ice.gov/
news/releases/ice-hsi-announces-record-high-number-criminal-arrests-fy19.

22 Yang, Maya. "Police Seize Enough Fentanyl to 'Kill a Quarter of the Population of California.'" *Guardian*, November 4, 2024. https://www.theguardian.com/us-news /2024/nov/03/california-fentanyl-drug-bust.

23 "China Primer: Illicit Fentanyl and China's Role." Congressional Research Service, February 20, 2024. https://www.congress.gov/crs-product/IF10890.

24 Larson, Caleb. "Mexico's Marines Have a Plan to Break the Cartels Once and for All." *National Interest*, March 24, 2021. https://nationalinterest.org/blog/reboot/mexico %E2%80%99s-marines-have-plan-break-cartels-once-and-all-180927.

25 "Strengthening of Port Inspections in Mexico." Club de Carga, June 2, 2022. https:// clubdecarga.com/en/2022/06/02/fortalecimiento-de-inspecciones-portuarias-en -mexico/.

26 Prieto-Curiel, Campedelli, and Hope. "Reducing Cartel Recruitment."

27 Barr, William P., and Alejandro Gertz Manero. "Joint Statement by Attorney General of the United States William P. Barr and Fiscalía General of Mexico Alejandro Gertz Manero." Office of Public Affairs | U.S. Department of Justice, November 17, 2020. https://www.justice.gov/opa/pr/joint-statement-attorney-general-united-states -william-p-barr-and-fiscal-general-mexico.

28 Suárez-Enríquez, Ximena, and Úrsula Indacochea. "WOLA Report: A Fiscalía That Works in Mexico." Washington Office on Latin America, April 19, 2018. https://www .wola.org/analysis/wola-report-fiscalia-works-mexico/.

29 Dalby, Chris. "How Mexico's Cartels Have Learned Military Tactics." InSight Crime, September 2, 2021. https://insightcrime.org/news/interview/how-mexicos-cartel-have -learned-military-tactics/.

30 Feathers, Todd. "The Most Powerful Agency You've Never Heard of: Homeland Security Investigations." Muckrock, April 22, 2014. https://www.muckrock.com/news/ archives/2014/apr/22/operation-cornerstone-training-slides/.

31 "China-Based Chemical Manufacturing Companies and Employees Indicted for Alleged Fentanyl Manufacturing and Distribution." Drug Enforcement Administration, October 24, 2024. https://www.dea.gov/press-releases/2024/10/24/ china-based-chemical-manufacturing-companies-and-employees-indicted.

32 "Jorge Fernández Menéndez." Muck Rack, n.d. https://muckrack.com/jorge-fernandez -menendezanalista/articles.

33 "Bibiana Belsasso." Muck Rack, n.d. https://muckrack.com/bibiana-belsasso/articles.

34 "Sinaloa Cartel." InSight Crime, November 7, 2024. https://insightcrime.org/mexico -organized-crime-news/sinaloa-cartel-profile/.

35 Elinson, Zusha, and Cameron McWhirter. "As America Battles Fentanyl, Mexico Fights Flow of American Guns." *Wall Street Journal*, February 6, 2025. https://www .wsj.com/us-news/us-mexico-gun-weapon-smuggling-ecddf964.

36 "7 Mexican Cities among the 10 Most Dangerous in the World Based on Homicide Rate." *Yucatan Times*, November 6, 2024. https://www.theyucatantimes.com/2024/11/7-mexican-cities-among-the-10-most-dangerous-in-the-world-based-on-homicide-rate/.

37 Rosenblum, Todd. "Border Regulation Begins with Stronger Capacity at Official Points of Entry." Third Way, May 12, 2021. https://www.thirdway.org/memo/border-regulation-begins-with-stronger-capacity-at-official-points-of-entry.

38 "Firearms Trafficking: U.S. Efforts to Disrupt Gun Smuggling into Mexico Would Benefit from Additional Data and Analysis." U.S. Government Accountability Office, November 20, 2024. https://www.gao.gov/products/gao-21-322.

39 "Drug Trafficking Violence in Mexico: Implications for the United States." Federal Bureau of Investigation, n.d. https://archives.fbi.gov/archives/news/testimony/drug-trafficking-violence-in-mexico-implications-for-the-united-states.

40 "'Weapon of War': The U.S. Rifle Feared by Mexican Police—and Loved by Drug Cartels." NBC News, August 6, 2021. https://www.nbcnews.com/news/latino/weapon-war-us-rifle-feared-mexican-police-loved-drug-cartels-rcna1624.

41 "Transnational Criminal Investigative Units (TCIUs)." U.S. Department of Homeland Security, n.d. https://www.dhs.gov/hsi/task-forces/tciu.

42 "House Committee Hearing: Failure by Design: Examining Secretary Mayorkas' Border Crisis." U.S. Department of Homeland Security, March 15, 2023. https://docs.house.gov/meetings/HM/HM00/20230315/115476/HHRG-118-HM00-Wstate-CaganS-20230315.pdf.

43 Correa-Cabrera, Guadalupe, Charles Lewis, and William Yaworsky. "Mexican Money Laundering in the United States: Analysis and Proposals for Reform." *Journal of Illicit Economies and Development* 6, no. 1 (2024): 64–78. https://doi.org/10.31389/jied.224.

44 Correa-Cabrera, Lewis, and Yaworsky. "Mexican Money Laundering."

45 "Justice Department Announces Charges against Sinaloa Cartel's Global." U.S. Department of Justice, February 6, 2025. https://www.justice.gov/archives/opa/pr/justice-department-announces-charges-against-sinaloa-cartel-s-global-operation?utm_source=chatgpt.com#:~:text=cargo%20aircraft%2C%20private%20aircraft%2C%20submarines.

5

A Mass Poisoning

Zach

To fully grasp the difference between the fentanyl epidemic and a narcotics epidemic, it may be instructive to contrast my high school and college experience with that of Zach Didier. In high school, I had several friends who experimented extensively with all kinds of drugs. I will discuss one in particular here and use the pseudonym, Ken, to protect his privacy. Ken enrolled in high school in 1990. By the end of freshman year, Ken and nearly everyone in his friend group was drinking alcohol. Ken, like many people drawn to smoke weed, began inhaling by the end of sophomore year. LSD and magic mushrooms were quite popular in the 1990s.[1] Ken and most of his group who dosed LSD or mushrooms experimented with them sometime in junior year. After checking with a few friends, neither Ken nor I can remember people snorting cocaine in high school. However, it became a drug of choice for Ken and many of his friend group in freshman or sophomore year of college. By junior year, MDMA or "ecstasy" was rampant on campus and in the clubs Ken frequented. Ken and a small number of the remaining folks in his friend group proceeded to experiment with methamphetamine.

Ken recounts one guy in college who stumbled around parties dabbing a little meth on top of the weed in pipes people were smoking. He doesn't recall anyone ever asking the guy what the powder was before he layered it as a topping on their weed. Oxycodone and other prescription drugs were not yet as widely abused as they were in the 2000s. However, if someone got their hands on illicit prescription uppers or downers, Ken and his buddies blindly washed the pills down with booze. He says he never tried heroin but several of his friends did by their junior year in college. Today he says he would cringe to know how much time he spent high in our adolescent years. He spent months if not a whole year of his life stoned. Aside from the time Ken spent high, he spent so much time and energy seeking out drugs he chuckles that he is shocked he had time to work to pay for the drugs.

Ken and most of the rest of his friends grew out of this incredibly risky behavior in their late twenties and early thirties. Like many who engage in this activity, most grow up. Get real jobs. Marry and have kids. That trifecta of life responsibility (real jobs, marriage, and kids) sent them all by and large on the straight and narrow. A few of Ken's friends unfortunately fell into addiction and, even in their late forties, are still struggling with one or more monkeys on their backs. As far as Ken and I can remember, however, no one has died from any of these drugs. Friends have died from cancer, auto accidents, heart attacks, and the like. Some of those could be tied back to substance abuse indirectly. However, our unscientific poll has yet to turn up anyone from our adolescence who overdosed and died.

Not one.

Zach Didier entered high school in 2017. He earned straight As. He scored 1550 on his SAT. He was accepted into nearly all AP classes and secured near-perfect grades there. But his success didn't end there. He also achieved star-athlete status. He excelled on the varsity soccer and track teams. He even went on to star in the school play, *High School Musical*, in his junior year. He volunteered to deliver aid to those affected by fires that ravaged a nearby town in California. He was not a normal kid. He was an exceptional kid. Teachers, parents, peers, and basically everyone knew he would be successful in life. Moreover, he was one of those rare types of overtly successful people in life. People *wanted* him to succeed. In a world where nice guys often finish last, people were encouraged to believe that this nice guy was destined to make it. He was even accepted into five University of California schools, including his top choice, UCLA, one of the most competitive schools in the country to gain admission.[2]

Adults since Aristotle often wax nostalgic and talk derisively about "kids today."[3] Yet all agreed Zach provided evidence as to why there is hope for the upcoming generation. The day after Christmas, Zach went to dinner with his girlfriend and came home thirty minutes before curfew. He watched a Christmas movie with the family. He told his father he loved him and went to bed.

Zach's friends report he didn't drink or smoke weed. However, nowadays both are regulated. So short of getting in a drunk driving accident or alcohol poisoning, neither poses a significant immediate risk. None of his friends report that he did any illicit drugs. As we all know, high school kids are loath to rat out their friends. So, it's possible he tried other drugs. But after an in-depth investigation by his parents, school officials, and law enforcement, no one has found evidence he did drugs.

Except once.

Via Snapchat, Zach was approached by a dealer at the end of his first semester of his senior year of high school. The dealer found new users like Zach by geo targeting advertisements on Snapchat to kids who hung out at a particular mall that Zach unfortunately shopped at. He and some friends met the dealer at the mall. He purchased what was advertised as a Percocet. Actually it was a fake blue M30 pill that looked like an oxycodone. However, it doesn't seem Zach and his novice friends knew the difference between oxycodone and Percocet. His friends suggested he chose a "Percocet" because he had some pain from his intense workouts and thought the Percocet, as it was described to him, would alleviate some pain associated with lifting weights and enable him to work out harder. Unfortunately, the pill described as Percocet only contained fentanyl and some binder chemicals. So it took the shape of a prescription drug but was not. Whether Zach wanted it for workouts or just wanted to try the drug to see if it was fun is irrelevant. The outcome was the same; his father found him dead in his room after lunch on December 27, 2020.[4]

Contrast Zach's story with that of Ken. A few of Ken's friends were on the honor roll and were varsity athletes, too. Ken also performed in the school theater and volunteered in the community. That being said, even a cursory investigation by his parents much less the police routinely produced mountains of evidence that he and his friends were all consuming alcohol and drugs regularly. Zach may have just consumed this one pill. He may have consumed ten pills. But there is no evidence he consumed more than the one.

Ken and his friend group, to a person, consumed drugs thousands of times. Also, they spent hours upon hours sourcing drugs. Zach was micro targeted and recruited by a dealer on Snapchat.

Ken agrees that if he and his friends attended high school or college today and engaged in the behavior they did in the 1990s, they would likely all be dead. Yet none are. Most even went on to good colleges, and some got into elite universities like UCLA.

Unfortunately, Zach never found out he got into UCLA. His parents opened his acceptance letter three months after he died.

Something New

Before we delve too much further into how we planned to combat fentanyl, we should assess why fentanyl is categorically different than previous narcotics epidemics. Why is Zach dead and none of my friends are? If fentanyl was simply a new type of magic mushroom, we would not have the highest echelons of the U.S. government mobilizing massive resources to counter this horrific drug. Magic mushrooms generally don't kill people.[5] In fact, no other drug kills people at the rate fentanyl does.[6] The fatality rate of other drugs like cocaine and heroin hardly approaches the number of people killed by fentanyl.[7] This is largely because fentanyl more resembles a mass poisoning than a traditional drug epidemic. As a result, the shocking number of needless deaths from this nightmare drug has prompted serious concern in the West Wing and National Security Council (NSC).

Most Americans are unaware that the seniormost people in the U.S. federal government, from the president on down, have spent countless hours devising and executing plans to combat the unprecedented influx of fentanyl. Within the first year of the Biden administration, the fentanyl crisis was routinely afforded top priority alongside major national security issues like the war in Ukraine, China's global ambitions, climate change, and the Iranian nuclear program for high-level attention. Consequently, the national security elite spends more waking hours than any of them imagined they would to solve the ever-growing fentanyl crisis.

Sprawling federal enterprises previously dedicated to the war on terror have been repurposed to counter the scourge of fentanyl. Most law enforcement agents receive bonuses and raises based on successful arrests and convictions.[8] Now, in response to the fentanyl crisis, many of them only receive pay bumps if they disrupt the fentanyl supply chain and stymie cartel efforts to produce or transport the drug. New data analytic programs costing hundreds of millions of dollars have been established solely to disrupt the fentanyl trade. Legions of agents, soldiers, and diplomats have been toiling away in stale conference rooms and on classified videoconferences for thousands of hours over fentanyl.

These experts are plotting to thwart Mexico's largest cartel: Sinaloa. As discussed in chapter 4, the Sinaloa cartel generates the revenue of a Fortune 50 company and maintains quasi-governmental status in vast swaths of Mexico. It sources raw materials from China. It manufactures fentanyl. It traffics the drugs to the United States and delivers the proceeds—often through Chinese money laundering organizations[9]—back to Sinaloa cartel strongholds in Mexico. To combat a transnational criminal organization this sprawling and sophisticated, the U.S. government must pull every lever of power at its disposal. Even the global banking system and global supply chains are repeatedly altered so law enforcement can confiscate proceeds or interdict just a few kilograms of fentanyl.

Between restructuring agents' incentive systems, designing new data analytics programs, engaging senior government leaders, and mobilizing global banks and the international supply chain, the U.S. government has dramatically redirected its focus from other issues to address fentanyl.

Why has the leviathan U.S. government apparatus altered its normal routine so dramatically to address the fentanyl threat? Most people don't realize that fentanyl is not, at its core, a narcotics problem. The reason it receives so much senior-level attention is because it is

- ten times more lethal than any narcotics problem in American history;[10]
- a categorically different problem than a narcotics epidemic; and
- far more akin to a mass public poisoning.

Fatality Rate

For comparison, let's take a look at another synthetic drug: MDMA. Commonly known as ecstasy, MDMA came roaring onto the club scene in the late 1990s.[11] While law enforcement adapted to address the new substance, we didn't see George H. W. Bush or Bill Clinton spending much if any of their presidential capital on the issue. Nor did George W. Bush or Barack Obama. That's because ecstasy kills very few people.[12] However, Joe Biden and Donald Trump have spent countless hours discussing fentanyl with their advisors. Biden contacted the president of Mexico about it repeatedly. He even mentioned it in his State of the Union speech.[13] Trump rails against fentanyl in speech after speech and threatened a trade war with Mexico over it.[14] Fentanyl has drawn this level of presidential attention because the catastrophic number of fentanyl fatalities is the central problem—not the emergence of a new narcotic.

In fact, use of the deadliest and most addictive drugs has fallen precipitously since the late 1970s and early 1980s.[15] At the height of the hard drug craze in 1985, nearly 3.14 percent of the population reported using cocaine in the previous month.[16] Today those numbers have plummeted to 0.6 percent.[17] This decline is consistent with all drugs except marijuana as we have essentially legalized it in the United States.[18] There may be many reasons behind such a decline. These likely include better enforcement measures, better public awareness of the health risks, and less glorification of these drugs in popular culture. The claims that we are losing the war on drugs fly in the face of reality and all current data on the matter.

We are undeniably winning the war on drugs. Unfortunately, we are winning the war as it was intended to be waged fifty years ago. We are winning against combatants we sparred with for decades: like cocaine and heroin. We also "won" the war against marijuana by calling a truce and decriminalizing it in most states. Even the few so-called designer drugs that popped up, like LSD and MDMA, were niche enough to be easily curbed by authorities. Also, LSD and MDMA generally do not kill people. So, they did not warrant much of a fight anyway.

Of course, none of this is to say there are not still scores of individuals and their families devastated by the horrors of addiction and overdose from old-school narcotics like cocaine and heroin. However, the number of people in the United States taking the drugs our society set out to eradicate in the 1970s is irrefutably a fraction of what it was fifty years ago.

Despite this steep decline, more people succumb to overdoses than ever. So how is it possible the fatalities from drug overdoses rack up nearly ten times the deaths than even during the apex of drug culture in modern America? This arises as the central disturbing fact about fentanyl: it is far deadlier than any narcotic we have encountered previously. By comparison, before fentanyl hit the scene, the next most deadly drugs—cocaine and heroin—felled about five thousand people a year each.[19] Fentanyl and drugs cut with fentanyl are murdering nearly one hundred thousand people a year. To be sure, heroin and cocaine are far deadlier now than when Richard Nixon launched the war on drugs. Yet again, fentanyl is to blame. Heroin and cocaine are deadlier now because they are often cut with fentanyl. Quite simply, the overdose fatality rate exploded to ten times what it was a generation ago because fentanyl infiltrated our drugs and society, not because people are consuming more drugs.

Mass Poisoning

The second key aspect of the fentanyl epidemic that defines it as categorically different from any in human history is lack of choice. Unlike previous narcotics epidemics, most people ingesting fentanyl don't intend to take fentanyl. It is cut into their cocaine or heroin or even illicit Oxycodone, Xanax, or Adderall pills. This makes the problem categorically different from previous drug epidemics. People who die from cocaine or heroin overdoses (before they were both widely cut with fentanyl) were *intending to use* cocaine or heroin—not fentanyl. Intent on the part of the user to consume a specific drug doesn't mean the victim deserved to die. However, users of cocaine and heroin made a choice to consume those drugs, albeit often a poorly informed choice. At least an element of choice existed early on before addiction may have limited the degree of choice involved in consumption of the drug.

There exists no other narcotics epidemic in American history where the vast majority of victims were unaware they were taking a particular drug. Other potentially comparable epidemics like the oxycodone prescription opioid epidemic or morphine epidemic after the Civil War could claim victims were unaware the drugs were harmful or addictive. Doctors assured victims the drugs were safe when, in fact, they were not.[20] Even in those tragic cases, however, the user was fairly well informed about which drug they ingested. Obviously, individual awareness of narcotic consumption is central to preventing consumption of that narcotic. Simply put, if people are aware they are ingesting a drug, we can educate them to not take that drug. In fact, we have seen the abuse of prescription opioids like oxycodone decline over the past several years as the public and medical professionals became aware of oxycodone's risks.[21]

Unfortunately, public awareness campaigns are useless to stymie fentanyl trafficking because most users are unaware they are taking fentanyl. Instead, victims believe they are consuming less-deadly narcotics like cocaine or methamphetamine or even worse: a licit prescription medicine.

Fentanyl's insidious nature is compounded by the fact that it packs fifty times more potent punch than heroin.[22] It is also far more addictive than any other drug.[23] The deadly cascading effect of fentanyl is that unwitting users believe they are consuming another drug. Many perish after the first dose. Survivors of the first dose experience a more elevated high than expected and, after just a few doses, become hopelessly addicted. Once hopelessly addicted, the victims then desperately seek out fentanyl or other drugs laced with it. It is only a matter of time until they overdose and perish. In this way, the fentanyl crisis is more akin to a mass poisoning than an opioid epidemic.

Chinese Chemicals

Fentanyl claims more than one hundred thousand lives a year in the United States and is now the number one killer of people between the ages of eighteen and forty-five.[24] All our military-aged potential soldiers belong to this prime age-group. China likely did not devise this epidemic to decimate our pool of soldiers in anticipation of war, but they cannot claim ignorance of this fact either. China's decision to conveniently turn a blind eye to the mountains of fentanyl precursor chemicals flowing from its chemical industry to Sinaloa's narco-corporate empire is self-serving at best. Also, our agents uncovered fentanyl production operations that employed Chinese chemists. Finally, the cartels' money laundering operations are largely funneled through intricate Chinese money laundering schemes.

To be sure, the Chinese aspect of this ongoing tragedy further establishes it as a unique crisis unlike anything the United States has faced in its history. Before fentanyl, drugs in the United States were either homegrown or had originated in Latin America, like Colombia, or Europe—à la *The French Connection* As a general rule, China had not exported drugs to the United States since the days of the Opium Wars more than one hundred years ago. Even then, China consumed more opium than it exported, hence the wars.[25] Now, however, the gargantuan chemical industry in China churns out mountains of precursor chemicals for the cartels to make fentanyl and methamphetamine. For its part, the People's Republic of China (PRC) has been more aggressive at scheduling narcotics than the United States or its partners.[26] Scheduling a drug makes it illegal, and with drug trafficking punishable by death in China, once a drug is scheduled, it largely vanishes from the market there. In fact, when criticized for its role in the fentanyl epidemic, the PRC correctly cites its decision to crack down on finished fentanyl coming from China to the United States as evidence that it is not complicit in this epidemic.

To President Xi and Trump's credit, in 2018 we witnessed the disappearance of a massive illicit fentanyl industry from China seemingly overnight. Trump put the screws to the PRC, and they capitulated. The hundreds of thousands of fentanyl pills traveling via the U.S. Postal Service to users around the country dried up immediately after the deal was cut between Xi and Trump.[27] For all its authoritarian human rights abuses, the PRC does otherwise value its brand. It eschews any activity that would brand the country as a narcostate. Once Trump used his bully pulpit to taint their image, the PRC cut the fentanyl industry off at the knees.

Unfortunately for the American public, after the PRC shut down shipments of finished illicit fentanyl to the United States, its use exploded. Once Sinaloa was able to source precursor chemicals from China and make fentanyl itself, they put it in everything they could get their hands on.

The PRC rightly claims that most of the chemicals synthesized to produce fentanyl have legitimate uses for a host of necessary products like paint, swimming pool cleaner, and household cleaning products. Far be it from the PRC, they argue, to monitor what happens to the chemicals once sold to paint producers in Mexico, even if it is obvious that the amount of precursor chemicals was enough to make several hundred times more paint than the company could produce in a lifetime. What makes the shipments of precursors to Mexican cartels more bedeviling is that the PRC now refuses to talk to the United States on essentially any law enforcement matters.[28] In years past, we could both agree to pursue certain types of criminals both countries deemed a threat to their respective societies. Child predators, drug dealers, and terrorists were the types of bad guys law enforcement in both countries could collaborate to take down.

Relations are at such a nadir between the two countries that the PRC has essentially stopped picking up the phone even when our cops call about criminals we both want to eradicate. Further, the Biden administration, like Trump, consistently publicly admonished the PRC for the distribution of precursor chemicals to criminal syndicates. The Chinese, however, display few signs of concern about tarnishing their image or being branded as a narcostate related to the sale of precursors.

The PRC is likely unconcerned about their image related to precursors because the narrative is convoluted. To lay out the narrative around precursors, the United States could assert China is a narcostate because of its involvement in a dizzying array of points in an underground web of fentanyl trafficking. First, Chinese chemical companies peddle precursor chemicals to front company brokers. Those brokers then resell the chemicals to Sinaloa. The cartel then compiles chemicals from multiple local distributors for cartel labs. The cartel labs then synthesize the precursors into fentanyl. The fentanyl is then distributed to resellers in the United States. Those resellers then market the drug to mostly unwitting users. The proceeds from sales to end users are washed, often through Chinese money laundering networks. Laundered funds snake back to cartel bosses, who then use the washed proceeds to buy more precursors from the Chinese chemical industry. All that doesn't fit very well into a newspaper headline. Despite this convoluted narrative, it is exactly how the fentanyl trade unfolds.[29] The PRC could cripple the gangster chemists by turning off the spigot of ingredients used to make fentanyl.

Unfortunately, they do not. The PRC is recalcitrant likely both because relations are so fraught today *and* that this particular problem is killing hundreds of thousands of war-fighting-age Americans in the prime of their lives. So, the PRC has little incentive to help U.S. law enforcement curb the fentanyl epidemic and even has some incentives to look the other way.

In fact, we often wondered if this was China's attempt to exact revenge for the opium epidemic more than a hundred years earlier. We also wondered if the fentanyl epidemic was China's way of weakening our ability to successfully prevail in a war against them. The demographics being killed off in droves were the exact same demographic that made up most of our soldiers in the military. Both are low-income men lacking a college degree.[30] Few senior government officials are conspiratorial enough to believe the Chinese planned the fentanyl epidemic. Serious senior government officials know it is nearly impossible to pull off a real conspiracy without getting caught. People leak, make mistakes, and betray each other. Conspiracies involving even a small number of people routinely get sniffed out. Also, we have intelligence assets who monitor PRC activities obsessively. So, the Chinese are likely more lucky than good. Regardless, the result ends up the same. Tens of thousands of potential American soldiers are mowed down by fentanyl every year without the PRC ever firing a shot. The Chinese are directly involved in both supplying the chemicals to make the poison and the laundering service to wash money on its way back to the Chinese chemical industry.

Pentagon Pushback

Another significant difference between a typical narcotics epidemic and fentanyl is the internal debate over the role of the military. Take, for example, three of the last major drug epidemics in the United States: the prescription painkiller epidemic in the 2000s, the crack-cocaine epidemic in the 1980s, and the morphine epidemic after the Civil War. The military was not recruited to mitigate the prescription or morphine[31] epidemics. That was largely because our own medical industry was responsible for the epidemic.[32] The Department of Defense (DOD) supported the Drug Enforcement Administration (DEA) and others to combat Colombian cartels supplying coke to the United States during the crack-cocaine epidemic. However, as with fentanyl today, DOD played a supporting role. It provided intelligence, training, and operational support to law enforcement agencies combating the epidemic.[33] The military largely did not directly strike narcotics suppliers in any of these three major drug epidemics.

Here again nomenclature matters in government. The three epidemics just mentioned were narcotics epidemics. Fentanyl is a mass poisoning. As noted, few people not already horribly addicted to hardcore narcotics seek out fentanyl. This mass poisoning is disguised as a narcotics epidemic in part because we have no frame of reference to debate the appropriate response to a mass poisoning. In fact, it's so incendiary to announce a mass poisoning is being perpetrated on U.S. citizens that responsible policymakers demur when talk of poisoning arises. The question to DOD should be reframed this way: "Would the military's mandate include preventing a foreign actor from knowingly poisoning to death hundreds of thousands of Americans?" If that question was posed, we may arrive at a very different policy position from DOD.

So, nearly one hundred thousand Americans were poisoned from fentanyl proffered by the Sinaloa cartel in 2022. Our chief nation-state competitor, China, bookended Sinaloa's operation via chemical inputs and money laundering outputs. These two facts unequivocally argue that Sinaloa's gangster warlords are a top national security threat to the United States. Despite these facts, the Pentagon rejected attempts to enlist them. Only intelligence was provided in the fight against the Sinaloa warlords and their Chinese coconspirators. The top brass at the Pentagon argued that the intelligence support we received from NORTHCOM, SOUTHCOM, and the rest of the intelligence community (IC) exceeded their capacity to help us. Senior leaders in the national security establishment are sympathetic to DOD's view.

We can't wield the military as a Swiss army knife unsheathed to solve every crisis du jour. The military's responsibility is to fight and win the nation's wars. Period. DOD agrees fentanyl is a scourge that plagues the country. They argued, however, it would be much worse for DOD to take its eye off the ball. Its top goals were to defeat Russia in Ukraine and prepare for and deter China from starting a war. DOD officials acknowledge the crisis but immediately cite myriad obstacles related to lack of authorities and appropriated funds. In side conversations, though, DOD experts argue failure to deter China or Russia from starting a war with the United States, and subsequently losing a resulting war that could kill millions, would be a worse outcome than delayed progress on fentanyl.

DOD experts also logically ask what, specifically, the Pentagon should do to stymie the Sinaloa cartel from selling fentanyl in the United States that isn't already being pursued by law enforcement. The military argues it maintains a specific suite of capabilities not relevant for this problem. They can't start dropping bombs on Mexico as we are not at war with Mexico. Per the U.S. Constitution, only Congress can declare war. Until that happens, their hands are tied.

At the president's direction, generals could deploy Seal Team Six ninjas à la bin Laden. However, decapitating Sinaloa via one kingpin atop the cartel food chain would be insufficient to dismantle it. Our Special Forces would be required to capture or kill hundreds of gangsters. What if one of the operations didn't go as smoothly as the bin Laden operation? What if it devolved into chaos as depicted in the film *Black Hawk Down* when Special Forces executed a raid in Somalia?[34] Picture dozens of American soldiers killed and dragged through the streets of Coyocan. The tragedy would unfold live on YouTube. Outrage in the United States would then certainly lead to war with Mexico or at least war in Mexico against the Sinaloa cartel. Going to war in Mexico is in no one's interest, especially in advance of a looming war with China. So again, DOD experts ask, "What, specifically, should DOD do against the cartels that isn't already being done by law enforcement?"

Moreover, DOD experts also point out that Sinaloa is not shooting missiles at Kansas but, rather, distributing drugs. They largely have not embraced the idea that the fentanyl epidemic is a mass poisoning. They adhere to the conventional idea that fentanyl is a narcotic. Narcotics are the realm of law enforcement. The number of annual deaths in the United States due to fentanyl exceeds the yearly death rates from the Civil War, World War I, World War II, or Vietnam.[35] Yet DOD doesn't seem to believe fentanyl is their problem and fought the Biden administration tooth and nail any time it tried to solicit help. As a country we must decide what the military's role should be in the fight against fentanyl and the Sinaloa cartel.

Dropping bombs on a sovereign nation we have not declared war on or sending in Seal Team Six on a regular basis are likely nonstarters. So, what activities could the military realistically execute that would stem the flow of fentanyl? First, Cyber Command could take a series of actions to degrade cartel operations. In particular, it could tunnel deep into Sinaloa's extensive financial networks and slow, stop, or reverse payments and all manner of financial holdings. Also, information operations could pit cartel members, government officials, and rival cartels against each other to degrade their operations.

Further, DOD could use its considerable resources to erect an international coordination program like the one used to combat the Islamic State of Iraq and Syria (ISIS). The counter-ISIS program connected multiple nations' intelligence assets, law enforcement, and financial institutions against ISIS.[36] Finally, DOD has the resources to push Mexico in the same way it pushed Pakistan during the war on terror. It paid the Pakistani government to side with us against al-Qaeda.[37] We knew Pakistani officials skimmed billions off what we paid them. We counted on it. And we were the highest bidder. Al-Qaeda could never match what we paid the Pakistani government. DOD could offer the same deal to Mexico and finance them to prosecute war against Sinaloa with assistance from our law enforcement and intelligence capabilities. There are a lot of obvious problems with this approach, and Mexican leadership would chafe at it. However, a lot of the lessons we learned when dealing with Pakistan apply here—especially as al-Qaeda was no less ruthless than Sinaloa.

Both DOD and federal law enforcement agencies construct valid arguments for and against dragging DOD into the fentanyl fight. The military, rightly, constantly waves off demands to solve problems outside its mandate. Fentanyl, though, kills one hundred thousand Americans a year; is supplied by our chief strategic competitor, China; and is facilitated by the largest transnational criminal organization on our border. All those facts argue for an open debate among political leadership in the executive and legislative branches to arrive at a deliberate decision as to what the military's role should be in the fight against fentanyl.

No matter what the final result of these debates among elected and political leaders, as a country we must decide what the military's involvement in dealing with fentanyl and the Sinaloa cartel should be. As Zach's story describes, unlike morphine, crack-cocaine, or the prescription opioid epidemics in past eras, it is doubtful U.S. law enforcement and public health professionals can solve the fentanyl epidemic alone. Given the aforementioned reasons, the fentanyl crisis is something else altogether. It is something we have never dealt with before.

The mass poisoning of America.

Notes

1 Hunt, Dana. "Rise of Hallucinogen Use." U.S. Department of Justice | National Institute of Justice, October 1997. https://www.ojp.gov/pdffiles/166607.pdf.

2 "First-Year Profile—Fall 2023." Undergraduate Admission, n.d. https://admission.ucla.edu/apply/first-year/first-year-profile/2023.

3 Freese, J. H., ed. *Aristotle in 23 Volumes*. Vol. 22. Cambridge, MA, and London: Harvard University Press, 1926. https://www.perseus.tufts.edu/hopper/text?doc=Perseus%3Atext%3A1999.01.0060%3Abook%3D2%3Achapter%3D12.

4 Walike, Lauren. "Sacramento Man Sentenced to 17 Years in Prison in Zach Didier's Fentanyl Death." ABC10, September 2, 2022. https://www.abc10.com/article/news/local/rocklin/zach-didier-rocklin-fentnayl-placer-sentenced/103-5a988571-d6d0-4695-8685-92a9384612d8.

5 Van Amsterdam, Jan, Antoon Opperhuizen, and Wim Van Den Brink. "Harm Potential of Magic Mushroom Use: A Review." *Regulatory Toxicology and Pharmacology* 59, no. 3 (2011): 423–29. https://doi.org/10.1016/j.yrtph.2011.01.006.

6 "Facts about Fentanyl." Drug Enforcement Administration, n.d. https://www.dea.gov/resources/facts-about-fentanyl.

7 "Drug Overdose Deaths: Facts and Figures." National Institute on Drug Abuse, September 30, 2024. https://nida.nih.gov/research-topics/trends-statistics/overdose-death-rates#Fig 2.

8 Adamson, J. and Rentschler, L. "How Policing Incentives Affect Crime, Measurement, and Justice." *Economic Inquiry*, January 2025. https://doi.org/10.1111/ecin.13270.

9   "Collaboration between Chinese Money Laundering Organizations & Drug Cartels." Institute for Financial Integrity, February 4, 2025. https://finintegrity.org/collaboration-between-chinese-money-laundering-organizations-drug-cartels/.

10   Spencer, Merianne, Matthew Garnett, and Arialdi Miniño. "Drug Overdose Deaths in the United States, 2002–2022." NCHS Data Brief 491. National Center for Health Statistics, March 2024. https://doi.org/10.15620/cdc:135849.

11   Shah, Haleema. "MDMA's 40-Year Fight for Medical Approval Continues." *Vox*, August 1, 2024. https://www.vox.com/today-explained-podcast/363903/mdma-medicine-ptsd-fda.

12   Gill, James R., Jonathan A. Hayes, Ian S. deSouza, Elizabeth Marker, and Marina Stajic. "Ecstasy (MDMA) Deaths in New York City: A Case Series and Review of the Literature." *Journal of Forensic Sciences* 47, no. 1 (2002): 121–22. https://soar.suny.edu/bitstream/handle/20.500.12648/8154/Ecstasy%20%28MDMA%29%20Deaths%20in%20New%20York%20City-%20A%20Case%20Series%20and%20Review%20of%20the%20Literature.pdf?sequence =1 &.

13   "Fact Sheet: President's State of the Union Highlights DHS Efforts on the Front Lines Combating Illicit Opioids, Including Fentanyl." U.S. Department of Homeland Security, March 8, 2024. https://www.dhs.gov/archive/news/2024/03/08/fact-sheet-presidents-state-union-highlights-dhs-efforts-front-lines-combating.

14   Horsley, Scott, and Joe Hernandez. "Trump Imposes New Tariffs on Imports from Mexico, Canada and China in New Phase of Trade War." NPR, February 2, 2025. https://www.npr.org/2025/02/01/g-s1-46010/trump-tariffs-mexico-canada-and-china-imports.

15   Caulkins, Jonathan P., and Peter Reuter. "Reorienting U.S. Drug Policy." *Issues in Science and Technology* 23, no. 1 (Fall 2006). https://issues.org/caulkins/#:~:text=true%20for%20marijuana.-,CHANGING%20TIMES,-%2C%20CHANGING%20POLICIES.

16   "Drug Enforcement Administration History 1985–1990." Drug Enforcement Administration, n.d. https://www.dea.gov/sites/default/files/2021-04/1985-1990_p_58-67.pdf.

17   "Key Substance Use and Mental Health Indicators in the United States: Results From the 2022 National Survey on Drug Use and Health." Substance Abuse and Mental Health Services Administration, Center for Behavioral Health Statistics and Quality, 2023. https://www.samhsa.gov/data/sites/default/files/reports/rpt42731/2022-nsduh-annual-national-web-110923/2022-nsduh-nnr.htm?utm_source=chatgpt.com#sub3:~:text=The%20number%20of%20people%20aged%2012%20or%20older%20in%202022%20who%20used%20cocaine%20in%20the%20past%20month%20was%202.0%C2%A0million.

18 Kramer, Bill. "Has Marijuana Legalization Lost Momentum? Probably Not—Look to Legislatures." MultiState, April 7, 2023. https://www.multistate.us/insider/2023/3/17/has-marijuana-legalization-lost-momentum-probably-not-look-to-legislatures.

19 "Heroin Deaths Prior to 2013: Centers for Disease Control and Prevention, Table: Drug Overdose Deaths Involving Selected Drug Categories, Number and Age-Adjusted Rates: United States, 2000–2016." NCHS Data Brief 190. National Center for Health Statistics, n.d. https://www.cdc.gov/nchs/data/databriefs/db190_table.pdf#1; "Cocaine Deaths Prior to 2013: Centers for Disease Control and Prevention, Table: Drug Overdose Deaths Involving Selected Drug Categories, Number and Age-Adjusted Rates: United States, 2019–2020." NCHS Data Brief 428. National Center for Health Statistics, n.d. https://www.cdc.gov/nchs/data/databriefs/db428-tables.pdf#5.

20 "Opiate Addiction in the Civil War's Aftermath." Virginia Museum of History & Culture, n.d. https://virginiahistory.org/learn/opiate-addiction-civil-wars-aftermath.

21 Ahmad, F. B., J. A. Cisewski, L. M. Rossen, and P. Sutton. "Provisional Drug Overdose Death Counts." National Center for Health Statistics, 2024. https://www.cdc.gov/nchs/nvss/vsrr/drug-overdose-data.htm.

22 "DOJ/DEA Drug Fact Sheet: Fentanyl." U.S. Department of Justice | Drug Enforcement Administration, 2020. https://www.dea.gov/sites/default/files/2020-06/Fentanyl-2020_0.pdf.

23 Suzuki, Joji, and Sarah Wakeman. "Opioid Addiction: Why Is Fentanyl So Dangerous?" Mass General Brigham, May 5, 2023. https://www.massgeneralbrigham.org/en/about/newsroom/articles/opioid-addiction-fentanyl.

24 "DEA Administrator on Record Fentanyl Overdose Deaths." Get Smart about Drugs, n.d. https://www.getsmartaboutdrugs.gov/media/dea-administrator-record-fentanyl-overdose-deaths.

25 Zhang, Sheldon X., and Ko-lin Chin. "A People's War: China's Struggle to Contain Its Illicit Drug Problem." Foreign Policy at Brookings, 2016. https://www.brookings.edu/wp-content/uploads/2016/07/A-Peoples-War-final.pdf.

26 "News: April 2019—China: Announcement to Place All Fentanyl-Related Substances under National Control." United Nations Office on Drugs and Crime, n.d. https://www.unodc.org/LSS/announcement/Details/f2adea68-fbed-4292-a4cc-63771c943318.

27 Jiang, Steven, and Ben Westcott. "China Announces New Crackdown on Fentanyl in Win for US President Trump." CNN, April 1, 2019. https://www.cnn.com/2019/04/01/asia/china-us-fentanyl-trump-intl/index.html.

28 Martina, Michael. "U.S. Slams China's 'Unacceptable' Disruption in Countering Fentanyl." Reuters, August 8, 2022. https://www.reuters.com/world/asia-pacific/us-slams-chinas-unacceptable-disruption-countering-fentanyl-2022-08-08/.

29 "Supplemental Advisory on the Procurement of Precursor Chemicals and Manufacturing Equipment Used for the Synthesis of Illicit Fentanyl and Other

Synthetic Opioids." Press Release. U.S. Department of the Treasury and Financial Crimes Enforcement Network, June 20, 2024. https://www.fincen.gov/sites/default/ files/advisory/2024-06-20/FinCEN-Supplemental-Advisory-on-Fentanyl-508C.pdf.

30 Powell, D. "Educational Attainment and US Drug Overdose Deaths." *JAMA Health Forum* 4, no. 10 (2023). https://doi.org/10.1001/jamahealthforum.2023.3274.

31 Grafe, Melissa. "The 'Great Risk' of 'Opium Eating': How Civil War–Era Doctors Reacted to Prescription Opioid Addiction." Harvey Cushing | John Hay Whitney Medical Library, November 15, 2024. https://library.medicine.yale.edu/blog/great-risk -opium-eating-how-civil-war-era-doctors-reacted-prescription-opioid-addiction.

32 "What Led to the Opioid Crisis—and How to Fix It." Harvard T. H. Chan School of Public Health, November 22, 2024. https://hsph.harvard.edu/news/what-led-to-the -opioid-crisis-and-how-to-fix-it/.

33 "Colombia: U.S. Counternarcotics Assistance Achieved Some Positive Results, but State Needs to Review the Overall U.S. Approach." Report GAO-19-106. Report to the Caucus on International Narcotics Control, U.S. Senate. U.S. Government Accountability Office, December 2018. https://www.gao.gov/assets/700/697386.pdf.

34 Bowden, Mark. "The Legacy of *Black Hawk Down.*" *Smithsonian Magazine*, January 2019. https://www.smithsonianmag.com/history/legacy-black-hawk-down -180971000/.

35 Richter, Felix. "Infographic: Fentanyl Fuels Surge in U.S. Drug Overdose Deaths." Statista, August 30, 2024. https://www.statista.com/chart/18744/the-number-of-drug -overdose-deaths-in-the-us/.

36 "Counter ISIS Finance Group Leaders Issue Joint Statement." U.S. Department of the Treasury, February 8, 2025. https://home.treasury.gov/news/press-releases/jy2531.

37 "Combating Terrorism: U.S. Efforts to Address the Terrorist Threat in Pakistan's Federally Administered Tribal Areas Require a Comprehensive Plan and Continued Oversight." GAO-08-820T. U.S. Government Accountability Office, May 20, 2008. https://www.gao.gov/assets/a120110.html.

6

Sinaloa

If the first question to answer is, "Why is fentanyl different than a typical drug epidemic?"—the next logical question is this: "Who is the Sinaloa cartel and why is it, as opposed to any other criminal organization in the world, marshaling this mass poisoning across our country?"

The population of Sinaloa has roots that date back to Cortez and even the Aztecs. For our purposes, we will travel back as far as when a loosely knit band of merchants began shipping drugs north to the United States. Initially many of these products were legal in Mexico. Ironically, one exception is marijuana. The Mexican government outlawed marijuana seventeen years before the United States.[1] That being said, marijuana is not where the drug trade between the United States and Mexico originated.

Old-Time Chinese Precursors

The U.S.-Mexico drug trade kicked off much as we find it today. Precursor substances flowed from China to Mexico where they were cultivated and processed. Once the drug was ready for consumption, industrious Mexican merchants smuggled the drug to the United States. The precursor contraband was poppy seeds smuggled over by Chinese migrants.[2] These migrants came to Mexico to help build railroads, much like they did in the United States. Many Chinese, however, were forced south to Mexico by the Chinese Exclusion Act of 1882.[3] Unfortunately for the Chinese, they were not treated much better in Mexico. Mexican anti-Chinese riots killed many Chinese immigrants.[4]

Yet even more relevant for the development of organized crime in Mexico was that many of the Chinese poppy farmers emigrated to Western Mexico. As it turned out, the mountainous region of Sinaloa, Durango, and Chihuahua was perfect for growing poppy seeds to produce opium.[5] Colloquially known today as the Golden Triangle, it serves as the bastion of the Sinaloa cartel stronghold. In an odd twist of fate, had opium first landed on Mexico's east coast through Turkey and France, as it did in the United States, or had the Sinaloa region not housed an ecosystem welcoming to poppy seeds, the Sinaloa cartel may have never existed.[6]

Opium provided the enterprising criminals with valuable experience moving contraband north to the United States. The smugglers had to locate reliable smuggling routes. They had to ascertain which officials could be bribed. From that intelligence, they establish a protection racket from government leaders and law enforcement to ensure safe passage to their contraband. They developed expertise in maintaining a supply chain. They cultivated farmers to grow the poppies. They identified chemists who could cook the flowers into opium. They found teamsters with means and expertise to haul the drug to the United States. They established an intelligence network of informants in border towns to evade the suspicion of U.S. law enforcement. This experience was invaluable for the many small, unorganized criminal enterprises cutting their smuggling teeth on opium. This head start on other would-be mafiosi in Mexico proved decisive when the real smuggling bonanza ignited.

Prohibition, Prohibition

Illegal opium, like heroin today, was never in very high demand in the United States. In fact, much of the distribution was to the very Chinese and South Asian immigrants whose countrymen brought it over in the first place.[7] Legal opium was prescribed by doctors for a host of ills for which there was no cure. However, Joe Six-Pack had little interest in kicking back with an opium pipe.

By contrast, Joe Six-Pack had keen interest in kicking back with a six-pack of beer. Prohibition in the United States in the 1920s and early 1930s transformed the ragtag group of farmers with limited experience smuggling opium. They morphed into a hierarchical international criminal enterprise. In just a few decades, the Mexican mafia rivaled the largest criminal organizations in the world. Over time, organized crime groups in northwest Mexico rivaled the likes of the Cosa Nostra, Yakuza, or Russian mob.[8] As profits piled up, the banditos upgraded from ragtag to business class. They were soon in league with government officials who witnessed the massive sums tumbling back to Mexico. Somewhat unwittingly, an insidious corruption racket was constructed that protected the enterprise's efforts to move products north, minimize friction, and keep costs down. Prohibition in the United States professionalized the gangsters.

Prohibition did more than induce the smugglers to trade their ponchos in for pinstripes. It transformed a steady but sleepy tequila industry into a global behemoth. After Prohibition, tequila brands from Mexico competed on the global stage with Kentucky bourbon, Japanese sake, and Russian vodka at a level foreign to them just a few years earlier.[9]

Jose Cuervo Corporation and their brethren lauded the end of Prohibition. They now had distribution networks throughout the United States. Many Americans had acquired a taste for tequila over the decade and a half of Prohibition. Cuervo and others developed brand recognition and, for a time, remained a step ahead, with U.S. distillers playing catch-up. These competitive advantages, along with an American population newly allowed to drink their troubles away, ensured tequila sales would explode for the coming century.[10]

While the end of Prohibition in 1933 was a boon for Cuervo, it proved catastrophic for the smugglers. Mexican alcohol distribution to the United States went legit. Instead of bribing a host of local officials, they paid above-board duties to Mexican and U.S. customs officials. They paid sales taxes. They shipped products on legitimate transportation arteries across North America.

After Prohibition, there was little use for the smugglers in the alcohol industry; however, the criminal enterprise had expanded too vast to sustain itself on opium alone. Whether booze was legal in the United States or not, the smugglers' children still needed to eat. Corrupt government officials still extended their hands for a bribe. After wandering in the proverbial desert for a few years, the American temperance movement once again delivered for the gangsters of the Golden Triangle. In 1937, the Marijuana Tax Act effectively made marijuana illegal except for medicinal uses and research.[11] In just a few decades, this new prohibition catapulted the cartels into a criminal stratosphere completely alien to them just a few years earlier.[12]

The business acumen they acquired from alcohol prohibition provided an MBA in narco-capitalism for the would-be criminal plutocrats. These predecessors of the Sinaloa cartel in the Golden Triangle applied lessons learned from their illicit MBA to rapidly capitalize on the newfound marijuana market in the United States.

Corporate Consolidation

Miguel Ángel Félix Gallardo ("Félix") was born in the commercial and cultural heart of the Golden Triangle—Culiacan, Sinaloa—nine years after the United States enacted prohibition of ganja. He toiled up the ladder of law enforcement for the first several years of his career and even worked for the governor of the state of Sinaloa.[13] The experience was critical to his later success as the first true Mexican drug lord.[14] Instead of immersing himself in details of weed production or transportation, he received an insider's education on the intricacies of a corruption racket's architecture. Félix learned who had a ready hand out waiting for a bribe and who required coercion via pistol to accept a bribe. He learned who mattered in government and law enforcement. He developed a sense for who could be ignored or superseded with a bribe up the chain. The don also pieced together which low-level officials were in critical nodes of the network. For example, bank tellers, border checkpoint sentries and transit hub dispatchers provided lucrative targets to corrupt. He studied each person's weak spots. Everyone harbored a weak spot, whether it be money, women, drugs, or blackmail.[15]

These essential insights gleaned from constructing a corruption architecture fortified the Guadalajara cartel, as it later came to be known, as a cut above any other criminal enterprise in Mexico. Félix assumed the helm of the cartel in his late twenties / early thirties. The malaise of the 1970s gave way to the Wall Street–driven economic warfare of the 1980s. Not to be left out of the hostile corporate takeovers now in vogue, Félix embarked on a buying spree.[16]

The disparate local mafiosi now producing marijuana had professionalized their smuggling operations during the 1920s and 1930s. Yet their aspirations were parochial. These mobsters aspired to preside as big shots in a small town. They yearned for fancy cars, racehorses, designer clothes, and other gaudy accoutrements. Local gangsters wanted the women they grew up with to swoon over them and the men in power to cower before them. Few thought about their industry from a regional perspective. None attempted to seriously consider the path toward a global criminal empire. None but Félix.

Unlike his kindred spirits on Wall Street, Félix wielded a few more tools in his toolbox than the tycoons in corporate boardrooms across Ronald Reagan's America. Similar to his compatriots in the U.S. C-Suite, Félix, and allies like Rafael Caro Quintero (RCQ), made massive investments to acquire real estate. He also invested heavily in research and development.[17] Félix invested in a more diverse supply chain by adding a small fleet of planes to his transportation network. He also worked diligently to ensure a favorable government regulatory framework. However, unlike titans of industry in the United States, Félix didn't beat around the bush disguising his bribes as campaign contributions. They were just bribes.

Like in the U.S. agriculture sector, family farms were bought up and shuttered. Large-scale industrial weed plantations replaced the family farms, and the families in question became tenant farmers. Also, RCQ fashioned himself as a Mafiosi Monsanto. He experimented with new strains that produced higher yields and more potent pot.[18] His botany produced more durable defenses against pests and disguises from detection via the air from U.S. and Mexican spy planes. At one point, Félix and RCQ lorded over the largest corporate marijuana farm in the world at more than one thousand acres. Despite its size, they camouflaged the massive plantation, so it was not detectable from air surveillance.[19]

Unlike his brothers at the Chamber of Commerce, however, Félix raised a sprawling militia. That militia waged war for Félix in ways even the Wolf of Wall Street could not muster.

Félix tirelessly evangelized the virtues of consolidating all the gangsters under one roof with shared profits. However, as the Catholic Church learned a millennium ago, evangelism will only get you so far. Félix's militia included a division of assassins who smote down those nonbelievers who did not convert to vertically integrated narco-capitalism. In some of Félix's most egregious escapades, he ordered the assassination of a rival cartel holdout at the Guadalajara airport. Multiple bystanders were killed in the process. Aside from missing the target, Félix's assassination attempt struck fear in the hearts of all would-be rivals. His implicit message was clear: he could launch brazen attacks in public places with no reprisal from law enforcement. Félix was untouchable.[20]

Gruesome acts like these earned him the nickname, "El Padrino" (the Godfather). Like Vito Corleone in the eponymous movie, Felix was particularly ruthless when it came to the old guard attempting to stymie his rise to power. In one illustrative case, a mentor of Felix and key boss in the region, Pedro Avilés Pérez, was shot and killed during a police ambush. Pedro Avilés Pérez was considered a pioneer in drug trafficking and top don who stood in El Padrino's way. Felix knew he must topple Avilés Pérez if he were ever to assume command of the cartel. Authorities and cartel historians alike allege Felix orchestrated the hit via local cops to ensure he didn't miss his target while maintaining a veil of plausible deniability. Mentors and rivals alike were excised viciously and disinterestedly like tumors blocking the proper functioning of the cartel he was cultivating.[21]

Like Francis Ford Coppola's Godfather, El Padrino was a canny operator who also worked with U.S. authorities when it suited him. Unconfirmed reports by scores of journalists claim El Padrino cooperated with the Central Intelligence Agency (CIA) during the 1980s communist scare across Latin America. Félix is reported to have sought out CIA spies to cut a deal to secure government cover for his operations. In exchange, Félix allegedly facilitated drug money and guns flowing to the Contras in Nicaragua fighting the socialist Sandinistas.[22]

Forecast Includes Snow in Mexico

Through evangelism, absorption, coercion, torture, extortion, and murder, Félix's primary contribution to drug trafficking in Mexico was the consolidation of myriad small gangs of drug slingers into one cartel. The Guadalajara cartel established a monopoly on drug trafficking in vast swaths of Mexico. That narco-corporate empire provided a platform for Félix to realize his ultimate dream and crowning achievement of his career.

He wrested control of the cocaine trade from the Colombians to be the primary distributor of cocaine in the United States.[23]

Here again, Félix had help, albeit unwittingly, from U.S. authorities. For years federal agents targeted coke cartels in Colombia and successfully extradited some of their leadership. As a result, the narco-tycoons of Colombia scanned the underworld for relief. They scrambled for new distribution routes and middlemen to minimize the exposure of Colombian cartel bosses. El Padrino went hat in hand to the most well-known drug lord in the world at the time, Pablo Escobar. Félix offered Pablo the deal of the century.

Or so it seemed. Félix assured Pablo he would take on all the risk of smuggling and distribution in the United States. All Escobar had to do was grow and process the white lady. The Guadalajara cartel would take the baton from there. Félix spent painstaking years orchestrating an iron-clad corruption racket that bought off everyone from the lowly customs official up to governors, generals, and cabinet ministers. This canopy of protection afforded Félix a competitive advantage with Escobar over the few competitors left in Mexico. Félix's impeccably timed proposition intrigued and ultimately persuaded Pablo.[24]

Félix's timing was impeccable because Escobar desperately needed to turn down the heat. Like the Guadalajara cartel, Escobar's Medellín cartel purged the country of all but one major competitor, the Cali cartel.[25] Unlike Escobar, the Cali cartel was buttoned up and discreet. Escobar's brazen and ruthless theatrics, not to mention his political ambitions, had captured the world's attention. Consequently, all that attention prevented authorities in Colombia from looking the other way.

For years, Escobar followed the same strategy as Félix (in fairness to Escobar, Félix followed Pablo's strategy). He bribed, blackmailed, tortured, and massacred his way to a protection racket of corrupt officials up and down the chain of command in Colombia. Escobar's sprawling corruption and intelligence network enshrouded the government. To placate international outcries and demonstrate they had a grip on the situation, Colombian authorities cut a deal with Pablo to do time. Pablo conceded under the condition he build the prison that housed him and his henchmen. Dubbed La Catedral, the prison became his own global command center. From that command center, he directed his narco-empire. Needless to say, Pablo and his "incarcerated" henchmen continued to access any women, drugs, gourmet chefs, and entertainment they desired.[26]

However, unlike Félix, Escobar ran for political office *and won*.[27] His political ambitions and support garnered from poor farmers deeply disturbed the ruling class in Colombia. Colombia's elite were content taking Pablo's bribes and providing cover for him to sling drugs to gringos. However, a narco-kingpin gaining legitimate power ensconced in the Colombian Constitution was a bridge too far. He was ostracized from parliament and forced to step down just three months after taking office in 1982.[28]

Pablo did not take this well. He blamed the minister of justice, Rodrigo Lara Bonilla, for initiating the series of events that led to the end of his political career. Bonilla was assassinated. Escobar's hit men allegedly pulled the trigger shortly after he was publicly humiliated and removed from Congress. Always with a flair for the theatrical, Escobar did not have the justice minister killed at home in his sleep. The minister and his driver were gunned down on an open highway by assailants on motorcycles wielding machine guns.[29]

Escobar continued his political terrorism for years. In a subsequent presidential campaign, a top candidate, Luis Galán, suggested Escobar would be extradited if Galán was elected. After managing to survive an assassination attempt via an RPG hailing bullets down on him, Galán finally succumbed to a second assassination attempt at closer range. Escobar always sought to inflict terror on the psyche of future opponents. So, the assassination occurred as Galán stepped up to a microphone with thousands of adoring supporters as witnesses to the attack and TV cameras rolling.[30]

Escobar's terror campaign did not end with the assassination of presidential hopeful Galán. Escobar also ordered a hit on the leading presidential candidate, César Gaviria. The hit, however, was more than a simple assassination attempt. It was an over-the-top act of terror designed to strike fear in the minds of any government upstart who considered opposing him. On November 27, 1989, Escobar directed his henchmen to incinerate Avianca Flight 203, a Boeing 727 en route from Bogotá to Cali. The explosion and resulting crash massacred the 107 people on board, and several bystanders on the ground were killed by falling debris. Luckily, Gaviria changed his travel plans at the last second and escaped.[31]

This was one of the most stunning acts of terror in the post–World War II era. Escobar's latest grotesque massacre was yet another attempt to intimidate political leaders. The bombing's aftermath was carried live around the globe. It displayed jarring footage of rescue workers and morticians sifting through smoldering wreckage for those dead or alive.

The assassination attempts and bombings that formed the dystopian backdrop of his reign of terror marked the beginning of the end for Escobar. Four years later he was dead.

For its part, the Reagan administration made a concerted effort to shut down the flow of powder through the Caribbean to Miami and other ports in the United States. With pressure coming down on him both at home and abroad, Escobar desperately needed a release valve. He could not simultaneously fight a three-front war among his terrorist political campaign, the coke distribution cat-and-mouse with Reagan, and the conflict with upstart cartels. Some upstart cartels were already taking advantage of the myriad distractions diverting Escobar's attention away from his narco-empire.

Partially through luck, partially through impeccable timing, and partially through sheer drive, Félix surreptitiously established contact with Escobar in the midst of his three-front war. Escobar, and later his more discreet rival, the Cali cartel, gave the Guadalajara cartel a chance. Félix aimed to leave no doubt in Escobar's mind that he was the solution to all the Medellín cartel's problems with cocaine distribution to the United States. To this end, he turned to Amado Carrillo Fuentes or "the Lord of the Skies" as he was known.

Fuentes specialized in flying clandestine multiton drug shipments across Latin America and the United States.[32]

Navigating a small prop plane or schooner through the web of law enforcement traps set throughout the Caribbean was increasingly a recipe for imprisonment and confiscated coke. Conversely, the Lord of the Skies flew multiton loads of the white lady in Boeing 727s.[33] He glided from Colombia over airspace in Central America and Mexico monitored by local aviation officials. These poorly paid and easily threatened officials were bought off in each country and looked the other way.

Once in a border town like Juárez, Félix ensured the local crime boss, who was now in the Guadalajara cartel C-Suite, would distribute the powder. The cocaine arrived at cities in the United States via a dizzying array of distribution methods like yet smaller planes, people, cars, trains, tractor trailers and Pacific-based boats. The barrage of smaller shipments across the border overwhelmed customs officials. Félix distributed risk across the two-thousand-mile border. No single pinched shipment could impact the bottom line significantly.

Eventually, Félix shipped more nose candy to the United States than any Colombian cartel.[34] The Guadalajara cartel leveraged its decade of corporate consolidation to scale cocaine smuggling and distribution in the United States. The Colombians could not imagine the volume of cocaine flowing to the United States even a few months before meeting the Mexican Godfather. Later Escobar and his competitors happily agreed to reap smaller but more reliable profits. In exchange, the Colombian cartels traded some upside for less risk. Soon the Colombians evolved into coke wholesalers for the Mexican drug lords.

Individual foot soldiers who smuggled and distributed powder into the United States for the Guadalajara cartel took on significant individual risk. However, logistics managers spread that risk thinly across the network. One— or even one hundred—henchmen getting nabbed did not imperil corporate profits or stability.

Thus, in one fell swoop, Félix wrested control of the more profitable distribution and retail end of the cocaine market from Pablo and his competitors. The Guadalajara cartel Félix helmed now maintained a near monopoly on the three most popular drugs (marijuana, heroin, and cocaine) in the largest drug market on the planet: the United States of America.

Inheritance for Shorty

Félix had no illusions he would live to a ripe old age in a tranquil environment. Despite his smart suits and comfort strolling the halls of power in Mexico, he was, at his core, a bandito. Banditos don't live to old age. They definitely don't live to old age outside a jail cell. Félix met his demise in part due to a disastrous decision by a Guadalajara don to torture and murder a Drug Enforcement Administration (DEA) agent named Kiki Camarena. Félix had also amassed too much power for the comfort of military and political leadership in the country. He was arrested and jailed in 1989.[35]

The Godfather attempted to manage the cartel from prison as Escobar had done years earlier. However, over time, his power waned. Soon a vacuum appeared in Mexico's narco-capitalist market. Félix's cult of personality, ruthlessness, and cunning only barely held together the dons in the first place. Soon, fissures turned to fractures until open war ensued. The main fault lines manifested between the Juárez, Tijuana, and Sinaloa cartels.[36] Each inherited its own militia to protect its interests and smuggle drugs to the United States. Each inherited product lines for the two staples of American drug consumption: cocaine and marijuana. As a result, each inherited massive flows of cash. That revenue could afford an unlimited and increasingly deadly arsenal of weapons to wage a protracted battle for dominance.

Joaquín Archivaldo Guzmán Loera was born on April 4, 1957, in La Tuna, Sinaloa.[37] His family eked out an existence in squalor via subsistence farming. Guzmán grew up an uneducated peasant farmer. He dropped out of school at the age of seven. He toiled in the Golden Triangle's marijuana and poppy fields with his family. Joaquín quickly climbed the ladder of Félix's Guadalajara cartel. Guzmán's ruthless penchant for violence earned him a reputation as one not to cross. When Félix was convicted, Guzmán seized control of the Sinaloa faction of the cartel. He had witnessed multiple generations of his family toil under narco-jefes with nothing to show for it but repression and poverty.

He expanded his militia and began a life-and-death struggle for turf. Most important, the cartel business model required control of land on the border.[38] Without owning real estate on the border, he would always be subservient to a border boss who would levy taxes, cut into his margins, and relegate his loads to an afterthought.

He assumed the moniker "El Chapo," which is Mexican slang for "shorty," because of his slight stature. Shorty initially set his sights on the Tijuana corridor. This maneuver put him in direct conflict with the Tijuana cartel helmed by Benjamin Arellano Félix. Guzmán instigated the bloody conflict in an ambush at a nightclub frequented by the Arellano Félix family and lieutenants. The war waged for years, but eventually Guzmán won out and captured the Tijuana corridor. He had reassembled the Sinaloa and Tijuana components of the Guadalajara cartel.[39]

El Chapo bided time to fulfill his dystopian manifest destiny. All that was left to rebuild the Godfather's empire was the capture of Juárez. Juárez was ruled by the iron fist of Fuentes, the Lord of the Skies. He was the aforementioned fleet manager in the early Guadalajara-Colombian cocaine arrangement. In 1997, Fuentes died. The bizarre circumstances surrounding his death have spawned a litany of conspiracy theories.

Fuentes went under the knife for facial reconstruction surgery intended to permanently disguise him and allow him to flee the country. Complications with the reconstructive surgery purportedly led to his death. Those complications also led to the murder of physicians performing the surgery. The surgeons' deaths lead many to speculate that the Lord of the Skies continues to inhabit our airspace.[40]

Whatever the truth about Fuentes's disappearance, Guzmán seized the opportunity to reclaim Juárez. The prime real estate bordered El Paso, Texas, and was critical for the narco-empire's distribution hubs. It was the crowning jewel to reconstitute the Guadalajara cartel. The war lasted more than a decade and, at its height in the late 2000s, cost nearly three thousand lives in one year alone in Juárez,[41] securing it the macabre distinction as the deadliest city in the world, edging out places like Baghdad and Kabul.[42]

El Chapo bested his rivals to assume the crown once worn by Félix Gallardo. Once ensconced as undisputed kingpin, Shorty renamed the narco-empire the Sinaloa cartel. Atop the ashes of the Guadalajara cartel, he erected a sprawling criminal enterprise estimated as the largest criminal organization on the planet.[43] Shorty catapulted to the top of most-wanted lists. Ruthless consolidation was only one aspect of Guzmán's growth strategy.

Digging for Treasure

Lost or damaged products cut into the profits of any company with goods to transport. The Sinaloa cartel was no exception. Loads of drugs were invariably lost to customs agents on the border, local cops, or simply incompetent traffickers. Guzmán's relentless focus on corporate efficiency drove the organization to experiment with all manner of transportation methods across the border. Sinaloa experimented with small planes, partially submerged submarines, and a host of secret compartments in cars, semis, and trains. Sinaloa even created an R&D division just to devise new methods to sneak drugs across the border.[44]

Like so many corporate innovations, El Chapo's seems blatantly obvious. Yet at the time, it had not occurred to anyone despite nearly a century of dreaming up clever methods to move contraband into the United States. The main obstacle to secure passage of contraband across the border is customs agents. El Chapo surmised that moving the contraband through a place where there are no agents would increase the likelihood of safe passage. Concealing weed or coke in fake bananas or secret compartments in cars may slip more drugs through. However, the agents always get wise to new concealment methods. Even the narco-submarines had to contend with Coast Guard surveillance.

At some point, it dawned on Guzmán that there was one place no border agents were stationed: underground. He started small with tunnels just a few hundred feet long that originated at a small building in Mexico and terminated in another small building on the American side. Sometimes the buildings were so close, you could throw a baseball from one and hit the other. Later these tunnels extended miles. They were ventilated, lit, and even housed small train systems to more efficiently ferry contraband to the United States and profits and weapons back south. These tunnels were devilishly difficult to find. U.S.

authorities and Sonora police have even been forced to fly drones over the border to find the tunnels.[45]

This gangster, with only a third-grade education, for a time had outwitted the most powerful country on earth. The peasant farmer from el Tuna forced the United States to deploy its most high-tech devices like earth-penetrating drone surveillance to peer underground in an attempt to thwart him.

Initially the tunnels provided Sinaloa a boon in profits through reduction in lost loads. However, later the tunnels proved a dual-use technology.

Houdini

Like Félix and Pablo before him, Shorty wound up in prison multiple times. Similar to both kingpins, he also commanded his cartel from prison. Unlike the other narco-tycoons, El Chapo escaped from prison not once but twice. While in a high-security prison during his second incarceration, he tunneled out of prison on a motorcycle fitted to ride on the rail lines built underground. Aside from escaping from prison via tunnel, El Chapo repeatedly employed his intricate network of tunnels to evade authorities. Time and again, authorities were convinced they had him surrounded in a building only to find he had vanished via a trapdoor into a tunnel below.[46]

After a series of high-speed chases and outright firefights between the Sinaloa militia and Mexican military, however, El Chapo succumbed to the inevitable. As of this writing, he languishes in a maximum-security prison in Florence, Colorado.[47] The Sinaloa cartel was seized by his sons, derisively referred to as El Chapitos (Little Chapos), and allies like gangster El Mayo. Authorities hunted down and arrested several Chapitos and El Mayo nearly a decade after El Chapo's capture.[48] Sinaloa, however, still reigns supreme in Mexico.

The history of the Sinaloa cartel spans unorganized bands of opium and alcohol smugglers in the 1920s and 1930s that eventually led to the multibillion-dollar Sinaloa cartel we know today. Toppling the kingpin has barely impacted the scale and success of the cartel. In fact, Félix, El Chapo, Fuentes, El Mayo, RCQ, and dozens of other kingpins not mentioned here were captured or killed. Yet the narco-corporate enterprise centered on the Golden Triangle has only grown in power, profitability, and scale over the last one hundred years.[49]

In fact, Sinaloa's exponential growth would make any Wall Street corporate boardroom envious. Its durability under constant attack from competitors and occasionally from the government is nothing short of remarkable. Its ability to innovate on critical issues like pest-resistant marijuana strains and underground distribution channels would make even Google's R&D team feel inadequate. Further, its ability to orchestrate a pliant government protection racket would also be the envy of any corporate government relations shop in Washington, DC. This all raises one key question: If Sinaloa has such a well-established recipe for success, why upset the apple cart? Why add fentanyl to their product offerings if the current suite of products is enjoying overwhelming success? In particular, why add a product that kills so many more Americans than any other product they offer? Why add fentanyl when it will undoubtedly bring unwanted heat from the gringos and their own government?

We asked ourselves these questions every day.

Notes

1 Thompson, Matt. "The Mysterious History of 'Marijuana.'" NPR, July 22, 2013. https://www.npr.org/sections/codeswitch/2013/07/14/201981025/the-mysterious-history-of -marijuana.

2 Velázquez, Juan Fernández, and Benjamin Smith. "A History of Opium Commodity Chains in Mexico, 1900–1950." *Journal of Illicit Economies and Development* 4, no. 2 (2022): 113–27. https://doi.org/10.31389/jied.113.

3 Romero, Robert Chao. *The Chinese in Mexico, 1882–1940.* Tucson: University of Arizona Press, 2012. https://uapress.arizona.edu/book/the-chinese-in-mexico-1882 -1940.

4 "Mexico Apologizes for 1911 Massacre of Chinese in Torreón, Coahuila." *Mexico News Daily*, May 18, 2021. https://mexiconewsdaily.com/news/mx-apologizes-for -1911-killings/.

5 "Mexico Apologizes for 1911 Massacre of Chinese in Torreón, Coahuila."

6   Ghosh, Amitav. "The Blue-Blood Families That Made Fortunes in the Opium Trade." *Nation*, January 23, 2024. https://www.thenation.com/article/society/american-old-money-opium-trade-fortunes/.

7   Ekpechtl. "How Stigma Hurts Series: Opium and Chinese Repression." *UAB Institute for Human Rights Blog*, April 10, 2024. https://sites.uab.edu/humanrights/2024/04/10/how-stigma-hurts-series-opium-and-chinese-repression/.

8   "The Relationship between Italian Mafias and Mexican Drug Cartels—Part 1." Council on Hemispheric Affairs, December 2, 2013. https://coha.org/the-relationship-between-italian-mafias-and-mexican-drug-cartels-part-1-a-comparison/.

9   Valenzuela-Zapata, Ana Guadalupe, and Gary Paul Nabhan. *Tequila: A Natural and Cultural History*. Tucson: University of Arizona Press, 2003.

10 Valenzuela-Zapata, Guadalupe, and Nabhan. *Tequila*.

11 McKenna, Gerald J. "The Current Status of Medical Marijuana in the United States." *Hawai'i Journal of Medicine and Public Health* 73, no. 4 (April 2014): 105–8. https://pmc.ncbi.nlm.nih.gov/articles/PMC3998227/.

12 Puyana, Juan Carlos, Andres Mariano Rubiano, Jorge Hernan Montenegro, Glyn O. Estebanez, Alvaro Ignacio Sanchez, and Felipe Vega-Rivera. "Drugs, Violence, and Trauma in Mexico and the USA." *Medical Principles and Practice* 26, no. 4 (2017): 309–15. https://doi.org/10.1159/000471853.

13 Jubera, Drew. 2022. "Drug Lord." *Texas Monthly*, October 11, 2022. https://www.texasmonthly.com/true-crime/drug-lord-miguel-felix-gallardo/.

14 "The Felix Gallardo Organization (Guadalajara OCG)." Wilson Center, February 12, 2001. https://www.wilsoncenter.org/the-felix-gallardo-organization-guadalajara-ocg.

15 "The Felix Gallardo Organization (Guadalajara OCG)."

16 "The Felix Gallardo Organization (Guadalajara OCG)."

17 García, Jacobo. "Caro Quintero, the Old Drug Lord Who Revolutionized the World of Marijuana." *El País*, July 18, 2022. https://english.elpais.com/international/2022-07-17/caro-quintero-the-old-drug-lord-who-revolutionized-the-world-of-marijuana.html.

18 García. "Caro Quintero."

19 García. "Caro Quintero."

20 Miller, Marjorie. "Mexico Cardinal Slain; Caught in Gun Battle: Violence: 6 Others Are Killed at Guadalajara Airport. Rival Narcotics Traffickers Are Believed Responsible." *Los Angeles Times*, March 8, 2019. https://www.latimes.com/archives/la-xpm-1993-05-25-mn-39567-story.html.

21 Brook, John Lee. *Blood + Death: The Secret History of Santa Muerte and the Mexican Drug Cartels*. London: Headpress. 2016. Part I, Introduction: The Beginning

of the Cartels. https://books.google.com/books/about/Blood+Death.html?id
=JI5XDwAAQBAJ.

22   "CIA Allegedly Aided Guadalajara Cartel to Traffic Drugs and Torture DEA Agent."
Tequila Files, November 19, 2013. https://thetequilafiles.com/2013/11/19/cia-accused
-of-aiding-guadalajara-cartel-to-traffic-drugs-and-torture-dea-agent/.

23   Miller, Marjorie. "The Mexico Connection: Cocaine Cuts New Routes to the North."
Los Angeles Times, March 13, 2019. https://www.latimes.com/archives/la-xpm-1989
-04-13-mn-1718-story.html.

24   Grillo, Ioan. *El Narco: Inside Mexico's Criminal Insurgency*. New York: Bloomsbury,
2011. https://www.amazon.com/El-Narco-Mexicos-Criminal-Insurgency/dp
/1608194019.

25   Thomas A. Constantine, and Strategic Intelligence Section. "The Cali Cartel:
The New Kings of Cocaine." Drug Intelligence Report. Drug Enforcement
Administration, November 1994. https://www.ojp.gov/pdffiles1/Digitization
/152436NCJRS.pdf.

26   Grillo. *El Narco*.

27   "Pablo Escobar." InSight Crime, August 2021. https://insightcrime.org/colombia
-organized-crime-news/pablo-escobar/.

28   Bowden, Mark. *Killing Pablo: The Hunt for the World's Greatest Outlaw*. New York:
Atlantic Monthly, 2001. https://en.wikipedia.org/wiki/Killing_Pablo.

29   Bowden. *Killing Pablo*.

30   Bowden. *Killing Pablo*.

31   Ahmad, Hadi. "Cartel Bombing: The Story of Avianca Flight 203." AeroXplorer,
January 25, 2025. https://aeroxplorer.com/articles/cartel-bombing-the-story-of
-avianca-flight-203.php.

32   "Family Tree—Juarez Cartel | Murder Money & Mexico." PBS, November 18,
2015. https://www.pbs.org/wgbh/pages/frontline/shows/mexico/family/juarezcartel
.html.

33   "Private Jets to Airliners: The Use of Private Aircraft in Narco-Trafficking." AML
RightSource, n.d. https://www.amlrightsource.com/news/private-jets-to-airliners-the
-use-of-private-aircraft-in-narco-trafficking.

34   "Drug Trafficking Violence in Mexico: Implications for the United States." Federal
Bureau of Investigation, 2010. https://archives.fbi.gov/archives/news/testimony/
drug-trafficking-violence-in-mexico-implications-for-the-united-states?utm_source
=chatgpt.com#:~:text=Current%20estimates%20suggest%20that%20approximately
%2093%20percent%20of%20the%20cocaine%20leaving%20South%20America%20for
%20the%20United%20States%20moves%20through%20Mexico.

35 "Notorious Mexican Drug Lord—Known as the 'Boss of Bosses'—Leaves Prison after 33 Years." CBS News, September 16, 2022. https://www.cbsnews.com/news/miguel -angel-felix-gallardo-mexican-drug-lord-leaves-prison-after-33-years/.

36 Corcoran, Patrick. "How Mexico's Underworld Became Violent." InSight Crime, April 24, 2023. https://insightcrime.org/news/analysis/how-mexicos-traffickers-became -violent/.

37 Some outlets report a birth date of December 25, 1954. "Joaquín 'El Chapo' Guzmán Loera," Biography, January 3, 2020. https://www.biography.com/crime/el-chapo -joaquin-guzman-loera.

38 Miller, Marjorie. "The Mexico Connection: Cocaine Cuts New Routes to the North." *Los Angeles Times*, April 13, 1989. https://www.latimes.com/archives/la-xpm-1989-04 -13-mn-1718-story.html.

39 "Sinaloa Cartel." InSight Crime, November 7, 2024. https://insightcrime.org/mexico -organized-crime-news/sinaloa-cartel-profile/.

40 "Murdered Mexican Doctors May Have Killed after Operating on Drug Lord." BBC News, November 5, 1997. http://news.bbc.co.uk/2/hi/despatches/americas/23487 .stm.

41 "Mexico Drug War Fast Facts." CNN, March 20, 2022. https://www.cnn.com/2013/09 /02/world/americas/mexico-drug-war-fast-facts/index.html.

42 O'Connor, Emma. "Mexico's Ciudad Juárez Is No Longer the Most Violent City in the World." *Time*, October 15, 2012. https://newsfeed.time.com/2012/10/15/mexicos -ciudad-juarez-is-no-longer-the-most-violent-city-in-the-world/.

43 Oliveira, Astrid Prange de. "What Is the Sinaloa Drug Cartel?" *Deutsche Welle*, July 27, 2024. https://www.dw.com/en/what-is-the-sinaloa-drug-cartel/a-69788336.

44 Sullivan, John P. "Mexican Cartel Adaptation and Innovation." OODAloop, October 31, 2024. https://oodaloop.com/analysis/ooda-original/mexican-cartel-adaptation -and-innovation/.

45 Guzman, Alyssa. "Secret Tunnel Discovered by Drones Indicator of Stealth Super Gangs." *Daily Mail*, January 4, 2025. https://www.dailymail.co.uk/news/article -14244985/secret-border-tunnel-drones-steal-super-gangs-sneaking-arizona.html.

46 "Inside Mexican Drug Lord 'El Chapo's' 2nd Prison Escape." ABC News, n.d. https:// abcnews.go.com/International/inside-mexican-drug-lord-el-chapos-2nd-prison/story ?id=32414208.

47 "Supermax Prison: 5 Things to Know about the 'Escape Proof' ADX-Florence." Corrections1, September 6, 2024. https://www.corrections1.com/escapes/articles /5-things-to-know-about-the-escape-proof-supermax-prison-Nw3H6vQbd0EN 0mSd/.

48 Jorgic, Drazen. "US Arrests Mexican Drug Lord 'El Mayo' and Son of 'El Chapo' in Texas." Reuters, July 26, 2024. https://www.reuters.com/world/americas/mexican-drug-lord-el-mayo-is-us-custody-sources-say-2024-07-25/.

49 "Mexico's Long War: Drugs, Crime, and the Cartels." Council on Foreign Relations, August 5, 2024. https://www.cfr.org/backgrounder/mexicos-long-war-drugs-crime-and-cartels#chapter-title-0-4.

7

Narco-Capitalism

The seniormost policymakers in the national security establishment continually revisit one essential question: "Why is the fentanyl epidemic happening at all?" People always ask, "Don't the cartels want their customers alive to buy more of their drugs?" Why would they sell something that kills off their customer base? Obviously, the drug lords don't care if their customers are leading healthy, happy lives. They don't care how miserable their clients are, as long as they keep buying drugs. Around ten thousand annual overdose fatalities was a standard statistic before dealers cut fentanyl into street drugs and distributed them across the country.[1] The dealers likely chalk up the lost customers as inevitable collateral damage. It's the cost of doing business—the same way a pharmaceutical company knows in any given year there will be some unfortunate number of customers who experience fatal side effects.

In less than a decade, however, overdose fatalities in the United States have shot up tenfold to more than one hundred thousand a year.[2] A spike that severe could presumably decimate the entire illicit drug market in a few years. Moreover, millions of those open to smoking and snorting their way through young adulthood would surely forgo all drugs once word got out about the astronomical fatality rate. One would think this level of carnage would hit a tipping point, where people would forgo illicit drugs altogether and stick with regulated alcohol and marijuana. Narco-executives can intuitively integrate this logic into their business planning. Yet the drug endures.

As we will see, the main Mexican cartel responsible for the fentanyl industry in the United States is backed into a corner. Sales of its top commodities have plummeted. To recover lost revenue, it has dipped into illicit underground markets like human migration and extortion rackets with varied success. Eventually Chinese chemical companies who dominated the fentanyl market were forced to shutter operations on the order of their government. The Mexican cartel filled the void and expanded the fentanyl market in ways catastrophic to the United States.

Bad for Business?

As mentioned in chapter 4, the cartel that produces and distributes the vast majority of fentanyl in the United States is the Sinaloa cartel. The Sinaloa cartel is an unbridled capitalist corporate organization driven solely by profit through any means necessary. It ranks as one of the largest criminal organizations on earth and thrives or perishes according to unrelenting Darwinian market forces. There are no government bailouts for cartels that make poor business decisions. Thus, the fentanyl line of business seems wrongheaded at best, even suicidal, for the narcotics division of the cartel. Lacing drugs with fentanyl puts the organization's main cash cows like marijuana, cocaine, heroin, and methamphetamine at risk. Traditional narcotics lines of business would lobby the Sinaloa C-Suite to shutter any new business practice that jeopardized their reliable revenue. Both the chief executives of the organization and lowly subcontractors should avoid a new business venture like fentanyl that risked collapse of the narco-corporate empire's established pillars. They should instead prefer to traffic contraband that has reliably turned profits for decades.

The dons of Sinaloa are operating a business that would likely equal a Fortune 50 company if it was ranked by *Forbes*. They are ruthless killers but also shrewd corporate executives who devise strategic business plans to maximize profits. True, they live opulent lifestyles, but they also maintain frugal financial management of their enterprise and above all are reluctant to waste time with unprofitable ventures. The narco-tycoons of Mexico are not only rational actors but ruthless businessmen driven by profit alone. For decades, Sinaloa's top commodities had been marijuana and cocaine.[3] Marijuana is directly linked to very few deaths.[4] Cocaine kills only a tiny fraction of users.[5] To be sure, drugs like cocaine and heroin have destroyed millions of lives; however, most users remain alive and thus still customers until they kick the habit.

Fentanyl has demonstrated it will kill off ten times more customers than any other drug and potentially scare off future drug users as well, thus lowering profits. If these cartel tycoons only make business decisions that will maximize profit, and selling fentanyl may lower profits, then why do they deliberately dupe their customers into buying this potentially unprofitable product? Especially when the product kills the user and thus seriously erodes the dons' customer base over time.

Government officials rarely agree on whether these business decisions were intentional or whether the cartel just stumbled into the fentanyl market. Sinaloa dabbled in fentanyl for several years while Chinese chemical companies dominated the market.[6] After a People's Republic of China (PRC) government crackdown, the Chinese chemical industry vacated the fentanyl distribution racket. This huge shift presented a market opportunity. Eventually Sinaloa filled the void. Nevertheless, for now, only Sinaloa leaders know how they came to dominate fentanyl trafficking.

In the meantime, it is instructive to assess how Sinaloa has drastically transformed its business model. Mexican cartels have faced significant market disruptions since 2000. Their adaptations to these disruptions have come largely since around 2015. Most significantly, Mexican organized crime's two main commodities have been decimated since the new millennium began. For decades, Sinaloa accumulated the lion's share of its revenue from marijuana and cocaine markets. Then those two markets collapsed.

Monopolizing Marijuana

Americans love to smoke marijuana. Even before the hippies in the 1960s, many Americans inhaled weed as a pathway into the counterculture scene. After the 1960s, ganja was normalized as a rite of passage for millions of American adolescents transitioning into adulthood. We may believe society has changed significantly from indigenous tribes who hold rituals with mind-altering plants for adolescent transition to adulthood. In fact, we have not.

Outside of a tribal setting, these rituals still take place in a dorm room, house party, or deserted parking lot surrounded by classmates and accompanied by chest-thumping music. Aside from the location and religious aspects, the rite of passage continues. Americans normalized weed to such a degree since it hit mainstream culture in the 1960s that no president since Bill Clinton has had to spend time explaining whether they inhaled or not.

Obviously with every action there is a reaction. The U.S. government's reaction to reefer madness in the 1960s and 1970s was swift and fierce. The anti–Vietnam War protesters could be seen openly smoking marijuana on the nightly news at events like Woodstock. Flower Power turned to chaos in the late 1960s as Martin Luther King Jr. and Robert F. Kennedy were assassinated. Drug culture was scapegoated by mainstream society. President Richard Nixon declared a "war on drugs" after taking office in the 1970s, but his "war" did little to curb America's seemingly insatiable appetite for pot.[7]

This war on drugs, however, successfully created a market dynamic with unparalleled economic opportunities for any criminal organization that could capitalize on the new market. The war on drugs imposed costs too high for any domestic distributor of marijuana to scale up production and meet demand in the United States. Anyone who tried would be caught and jailed for many years. Their crops would be destroyed and equipment confiscated. Marijuana simply required too much farmland for an American producer to reliably serve the market. Thousands of small-scale domestic producers served local markets using hydroponics or secluded plots of land. These growers were routinely discovered and arrested. It didn't take the cartels long to realize the American market could not be serviced by a domestic producer. They had been dabbling in ganja smuggling since the 1937 criminalization of the plant.

The smugglers had none other than the U.S. government to thank for eradicating all its American competitors. Inevitably the Golden Triangle dons scaled to serve this vast market of users with seemingly unlimited resources to expend on ganja. However, the pot provider required several critical assets. It required significant financial resources, a vast, inexpensive labor pool; a distribution network in the United States; and the ability to operate outside the reach of U.S. law enforcement. Enter the Sinaloa cartel. Sinaloa and its forebears met all requirements in spades. Most important, they possessed one more crucial attribute no other criminal organization in the world could boast: they and their main competitor, the Cartel de Jalisco Nueva Generación (CJNG), controlled land directly on the southern side of the U.S. border.

The cartel's plaza boss network controls every inch of the Mexican side of the U.S.-Mexico border.[8] The plaza boss network consists of a series of dons who, operating as free agents, each control specific turf in Mexico.[9] Market consolidation forces the plaza bosses to work closely with senior cartel executives. At the same time, they demand a voice in major decisions on Sinaloa business strategy. In exchange, a portion of their profits go to the corporate structure. Paying into the corporate structure reaps benefits in several ways. Dues-paying plaza bosses are allowed to participate in bilateral strategic business-to-business (B2B) relationships that Sinaloa B2B managing directors develop. In fact, plaza bosses affiliated with Sinaloa collected billions in profits from the cocaine distribution deal Sinaloa cut with the Colombian cartels in the 1990s.

Gaining access to Sinaloa's favorable government regulatory regime in Mexico is even more appealing for the plaza bosses. Sinaloa government relations managers design pliant national, state, and local policies via a corruption racket. This corrupt government architecture is achieved through the notorious "silver or lead" dilemma, a term coined decades ago in Colombia.[10] It is a pithy way to sum up the deadly quandary government officials find themselves in when approached by the mob. Gangsters offer the bureaucrats an option to "choose" bribes (silver) from the mafia or they could "choose" a bullet (lead) to the head. This isn't much of a choice at all, especially as the lead option extended to an individual's family as well. The silver or lead policy or "*plata o plomo*" ensures any official who needs to be corrupted can be corrupted. The compromised officials sustain a reliable protection umbrella of government institutions that ensure safe passage of whatever contraband the plaza boss seeks to traffic.

The plaza bosses operate somewhat like a franchise model.[11] But far fewer cartel franchises exist than, for example, the McDonald's empire. Also, franchise head honchos exert influence over corporate decision-making. Unlike the McDonald's franchise owner, plaza bosses maintain small militias and can oppose decisions from corporate headquarters in ways a McDonald's store owner can't.

Controlling the Mexican side of the U.S. border ensured these Mexican cartels would have the lowest supply chain costs of any global competitors seeking a cut of the action. Supply chain efficiencies compounded their advantages with the benefit of a locally sourced product and an inexpensive labor pool. These competitive business advantages guaranteed that in the United States narcotics market no other industrious criminal organization in the world could outcompete the Mexican cartels that controlled the northern border of Mexico.[12]

As we have seen, over the course of the twentieth century, a few ragtag local mafias in northern Mexico bribed, murdered, and consolidated their rivals. A perverse free-market economic battle for monopoly ultimately catapulted the Sinaloa cartel into the kind of corporate stratosphere occupied only by Fortune 50 companies. After monopolizing the marijuana market, the narco-corporate titans exercised their competitive advantages elsewhere in the illicit trafficking market. Sinaloa orchestrated a hostile corporate takeover of adjacent markets dominated by competitors to the south.

Cornering Cocaine

Colombian cartels, most famously helmed by Pablo Escobar, served up cocaine as a staple of the American disco scene in the 1970s. *Time* magazine iconically deemed cocaine an "all-American drug" in its July 1981, edition.[13] Unfortunately for Escobar and other Colombian capos, the Ronald Reagan administration dusted off Nixon's "war on drugs" playbook. At Reagan's direction, Vice President George H. W. Bush oversaw Operation Hat Trick II,[14] which closed Caribbean Sea routes from Colombia to Miami. The legendary effort was reflected in popular culture with TV series like *Miami Vice* in the 1980s. "War on Drugs 2.0" led to Escobar's ultimate demise. To this day, agents who worked on coke and Colombia in the 1980s wax nostalgic about this "golden era" of the Drug Enforcement Administration (DEA). They regale colleagues with epic tales of confiscating seemingly endless lines of white powder crisscrossing the Caribbean.

Yet, solving one problem often simply creates new problems to tackle. Mexican nationals regularly refer to cartel members as "cockroaches" for a reason.[15] As the saying goes, it doesn't matter how many you arrest or kill, more will always scurry out of the woodwork to take their place. So as Reagan closed one door to the Colombian mafia in the Caribbean, he inadvertently propped open another one on the Southwest Border.

Reagan left the door ajar, and the Mexican dons kicked the door wide open. They deftly conquered the adjacent cocaine market where the Colombians desperately cast about for a new means of distribution.

Reagan provided the Sinaloa tycoons a market disruption so severe it was sure to produce paupers and princes. In response, the Mexican mafiosi corporate executives outmaneuvered the Colombians, who were increasingly risk averse as extradition to U.S. prisons became more common. Consistent, predictable delivery of nose candy to loyal U.S. customers drew the Colombian dons further into Sinaloa's web until any escape from the arrangement was futile. Through brilliant supply chain management, strategic subcontractor partnerships with plaza bosses, dexterous handling of government regulators (via silver or lead), and a ruthless penchant for violence, the Mexican cartel corporate leadership shaped the cocaine ecosystem until they owned it. They relegated their Colombian competitors to the low-margin, commodity production end of the market. The Mexican kingpins confiscated the higher-value end of the supply chain: delivery to the customer.

By the time Clinton took the White House from George H. W. Bush, the predecessors of Sinaloa had successfully abducted the white lady from the Colombians. This corporate takeover, combined with their multibillion-dollar marijuana business, positioned Sinaloa among the most massive criminal enterprises in the world. No doubt they had engineered an unbeatable formula. Sinaloa and its main competitor, the CJNG, monopolized the Mexican side of the two-thousand-mile border with the largest economy on earth. They employed inexpensive local labor to package and distribute product to customers in the United States. They sourced high-margin commodities through downward price pressure on offshore producers and designed a pliant government regulation regime via bribes and violence. These foundational corporate advantages became closely guarded pillars of their narco-corporate empires. The business strategy was so sound it could have been penned by the authors of NAFTA. It seemed Sinaloa would reap soaring profits indefinitely.

Market Disruptions

Then fate dealt two catastrophic blows to the cartel business model. The hits were completely out of their control yet still eroded the foundations of the narco-corporate empire. They faced collapse of cocaine demand in the United States and legalization of marijuana. First, inexplicably, cocaine use plummeted throughout the United States. Fortunately for the Colombians, cocaine stayed popular in Europe and became fashionable in countries like Brazil.[16] The end of the Cold War birthed a global middle class. Like the Americans before them, the new middle class in places like Brazil delighted in flaunting their disposable income with piles of blow. Unfortunately for the Mexican mafiosi, their proximity to the United States, inexpensive local labor, and reliably corruptible local officials do not give them any competitive advantage or even relevance in selling coke to Europe, Brazil, or anywhere besides the United States and Canada.

Maybe the collapse of U.S. demand for powder was a result of the Nancy Reagan–style *DARE* messaging to keep kids off drugs. Her pithy ads like the iconic egg frying in a skillet with the narrative "this is your brain on drugs" are seared into every 1980s kid's psyche. Maybe the collapse in demand came from better law enforcement techniques to dismantle criminal distribution networks in the United States. Maybe the recent U.S. middle-class obsession with health and wellness simply translated into more people taking Pilates classes instead of coke to engender an upbeat state of mind. Maybe it's all of the above or something else altogether. Whatever the cause, demand for the white lady collapsed dramatically.

The most recent report from the White House Office of National Drug Control Policy (ONDCP) lays out Sinaloa's predicament in stark terms. At the height of the cocaine craze around 1985, about 5.68 million Americans reported ingesting cocaine in the previous thirty days. In 2018 that number was 1.94 million.[17] So monthly users dropped 66 percent in about thirty years. If the average user spends about $100 on a gram of coke in a month, that is about $586 million a month versus $194 million *per month*. So that 66 percent drop in users equals nearly $4.5 billion in lost revenue annually. Sinaloa is estimated to control about 50 percent of cocaine distribution in the United States. That equals about $2.3 billion annual lost revenue for their narco-corporate empire.[18] Sinaloa can do nothing to solve the problem. They can't send gangbangers to clubs in Chicago and force revelers to snort cocaine. If your product falls out of fashion with your customers, you have two options: go out of business or adapt.

We will get to how they adapted in a moment. Next let's turn to the second catastrophic blow to Sinaloa's business model: legalization of marijuana in the United States. The cartels were largely founded on running alcohol during Prohibition and then marijuana to the United States. Gradually a few states legalized pot, and then in rapid succession, voters in state after state ripped the carpet out from under the cartels. The effect was dramatic. It would be akin to forbidding Ford from participating in the passenger vehicle market or preventing McDonald's from selling hamburgers. Neither company would survive under those restrictions.

Some states still haven't legalized ganja. Yet most people in those less-permissive states obtain their stash from someone who buys it legally in another state, not from a cartel.[19] In 2012, Colorado and Washington became the first states to legalize marijuana. Up to that point the illicit marijuana market was estimated around $45 billion a year.[20] If Sinaloa maintained a 50 percent share of the marijuana market as it did for cocaine, then the Sinaloa corporate empire lost nearly $22.5 billion a year in income.

So as marijuana and cocaine sales decreased over the last thirty years, Sinaloa and its competitors lost nearly $24.8 billion *per year* in revenue.[21] Losses like these would be akin to purging french fries and hamburgers out of McDonald's revenue forecasts or the F-150 and Mustang out of Ford's.

No Good Options

The veritable extinction of the weed business line confronted the Mexican dons with another Darwinian capitalist "adapt or die" inflection point. These were dire circumstances for one of the largest criminal networks in the world. It must have been particularly jarring for these titans of narco-industry to witness both marijuana and cocaine crater on them almost simultaneously. The titans followed sound corporate stewardship and balanced their portfolios through varied offerings in the market. Via extortion they diversified into verticals ranging from the avocado industry, to mining, tourism, and fishing. However, the revenue generated from these industries paled in comparison. The extortion business in avocados or fish would be comparable to the share of revenue Ford makes on mud flaps or McDonald's makes from McCafé macchiatos.[22] Sure, they generate reliable profits. Yet such profits alone cannot sustain a Fortune 50 company.

The extortion business posed a strategic problem for the cartels as well. In the cartel's "hometown" the gangster warlords hold Robin Hood–like status. They evade the cops and shower riches in the form of jobs and philanthropy down on Friar Tuck and the townspeople. They are viewed as ruthless banditos for sure. Nevertheless, they are viewed as *the people's* ruthless banditos. They sling drugs to the gringos and pay off the doltish Sheriff of Nottingham while they parade into town driving Bugattis and doling out $1,000 tips to taqueria waiters.[23]

Like Al Capone in Chicago and the Five Families in New York, the "benevolent" mafioso delivers presents at Christmas to the poor. They fund town pastors to install soccer fields near the church. They even administered COVID-19 vaccines when the government failed to distribute them.[24] Sinaloa cultivates astute corporate philanthropy that time and again wins the local population's hearts and minds. Any Madison Avenue PR firm would be jealous of the goodwill Sinaloa's marketing executives engender.

Unlike dealing marijuana or cocaine to Americans, the extortion business is conducted locally. Those being extorted are the very same hearts and minds Sinaloa seeks to win. The fate of the Zetas cartel exemplifies the extortion business perils. The Zetas syndicate is a particularly ruthless group of assassins who terrorized local communities while constructing a sweeping extortion enterprise across parts of Mexico.[25] The Zetas were former military personnel and thus not schooled in the Darwinian capitalism of narco-business. Consequently, they received a swift and fierce education in unsound business models.

The local population and federal government quickly undermined Zeta extortion ventures. The Zetas were arrested or killed by law enforcement or their competitors. A Mexican official was asked about Zeta complaints that the government was playing favorites. The Zetas whined they were targeted by law enforcement to the exclusion of other cartels like Sinaloa. In a moment of candor, the official agreed the government targets certain cartels over others. He said those choices are made by which gangsters are imposing more harm on Mexican citizens. The official implied that extorting Mexicans is looked upon with greater ire than dealing drugs to Americans. Soon after the Zetas launched their domestic extortion racket, they were out of business.[26]

Sinaloa was in a box. Americans refused their weed and coke. Extorting Mexican citizens could only go so far. What were the capos in Mexico to do? There are no government bailouts for narco-cartels. Despite ranking as Mexico's fifth-largest employer,[27] cartels survive only through astute navigation of the illicit free market. The dons were no doubt scouring the black market for new lines of illicit business to keep them afloat. Enter Osama bin Laden.

The Migration Market

Before 9/11, the federal government housed two agencies, U.S. Customs and, separately, the Immigration and Naturalization Service (INS), which were tasked with enforcing border regulations. U.S. Customs, in fact, is one of the oldest departments in the federal government. It was initially proposed by Alexander Hamilton in 1789 to collect tariffs. In 1891, the federal government took over regulation of immigration from state regulators. This agency ultimately merged with others to become the Immigration and Naturalization Service.[28]

These agencies deterred people and goods from crossing the border illegally and investigated border-related crimes. Still, the border before 9/11 was more a desolate unmonitored expanse than the flawed gatekeeping system it is today.[29] Migrants on both sides largely came and went at will. For example, the migrant farmworkers Cesar Chavez organized to protect from labor abuses generally walked, sometimes ran, but were seldom prevented from crossing the border. Further, if an unlucky fellow got nabbed, he would certainly cross at a subsequent attempt, often the same day. By 2000, the economic boom of the 1990s compelled businesses to depend on low-wage migrant labor. Immigration levels across the Southwest Border surged nearly as high as their peak today.[30]

After 9/11, security experts frantically tried to locate where the next attack could originate. Their gaze immediately turned to the Southwest Border. Any terrorist with a map could easily ascertain that a flight to Mexico City and a bus pass would land them in a U.S. city with scant chance of detection. Consequently, since 9/11, the Southwest Border has witnessed the installation of a surveillance technology web and accompanying ground forces rivaled only by Israel and countries in the Middle East.[31] Early on after 9/11, border passage was still attainable by simply walking across it. Over time a surveillance apparatus quickly enveloped the border, and thousands of border sentries were positioned there. As a result, more migrants than ever solicited aid from experienced "coyotes" familiar with optimal routes and times to cross. Those early coyotes were little more than specialty travel agents—albeit travel agents who often exploited poor, downtrodden migrants. But they were decidedly not organized at the level of a cartel.

As the migration industry picked up on the border, the cartels took notice. Profits lagged from the decline in weed and coke sales. This new migration market appealed to their foundational business model. They were already in the business of moving contraband across the Southwest Border. Whether that contraband was guns, drugs, or humans was irrelevant to the logistics managers at Sinaloa. Soon, the coyotes were required to pay a tax to the cartels. Sometime between 2020 and 2025, the migration market succumbed to a wholesale cartel takeover of the migration distribution networks, customer acquisition, and transportation infrastructure. To be sure, not everyone involved in the supply chain is a card-carrying member of Sinaloa. Rather, now all subcontractors work with and through the cartel network. No one crosses the Southwest Border illegally without buying into the cartel's integrated operations. This network is usually managed locally through the aforementioned plaza bosses. The ruthless plaza bosses enforce compliance through instilling fear of deadly reprisal in the migrants and coyotes.

The migration industry only manifested as a scalable market opportunity in the mid-2010s, after we had implemented much of the post-9/11 border infrastructure investments and dramatically increased the number of border patrol agents. Migration was not even an ancillary line of business for the cartels before 2001.[32] Between 2021 and 2024, however, an estimated two million migrants annually crossed the Southwest Border.[33] Passage costs about $5,000 a person.[34] That provides an estimated $10 billion a year in revenue. If that $10 billion is split evenly between Sinaloa and CJNG, it makes up $5 billion for El Chapo and his Sinaloa contemporaries. Hopefully some industrious economist will study how brilliantly the corporate transformation from running dope to trafficking humans was executed by the narco-entrepreneurs. It certainly requires further study.

Sinaloa adapted to replace its marijuana business by capitalizing on the Western Hemisphere's most acute manifestation of the global migration crisis. Estimates show that this line of business for the cartels is generating handsome sums and generous profits. Adept at identifying new market segments to service, cartels have even diversified to accommodate higher-end customers.

They now offer luxury migration packages replete with air-conditioned buses at $10,000 per person.[35] This incredibly lucrative human trafficking business is only dependent on two variables for the capos to reap their ill-gotten profits. First, the U.S. economy must maintain a low unemployment rate to ensure demand for inexpensive labor. Second, the cartel must control the Mexican side of the border. Most corporate titans would kill for business lines with these competitive advantages if it were not decidedly illegal. Yet, Sinaloa executives still have a significant hole to fill as their marijuana and cocaine business have atrophied. The estimated $5 billion Sinaloa reaps from the migration industry only fills a portion of the $24.8 billion hole left by the losses from marijuana and cocaine. Yet $5 billion wasn't enough. The narco-corporate empire required more to survive.

As noted earlier, Sinaloa's cocaine business has been slowly falling off a cliff for since the 1990s. Cocaine has been trending toward the fate of station wagons for Ford and Fish McBites at McDonald's for a long while. Plugging cocaine's multibillion-dollar hole in its balance sheet is no small task for Sinaloa. The Colombians largely cut Sinaloa out of the blow business in Europe and other places with a middle class and disposable income like Brazil. The Mexican cartels' competitive advantage of controlling the land on the Mexican side of the Southwest Border and U.S. distribution networks is irrelevant to selling coke in Europe or Brazil. Hope seemed to be lost on Sinaloa's second-biggest moneymaker.

China Leaves a Vacuum

In 2018 when the business forecast was its bleakest, none other than President Donald Trump came to the rescue. Trump is not to blame for the current fentanyl crisis. In fact, he achieved an admirable goal at the time. He pressured the Chinese government to shut down sales of finished illicit fentanyl to the United States. These illegal goods were mostly transported through the U.S. Postal Service or other legal shippers to customers in the United States. Also, in the early days of fentanyl, before Trump barricaded this new Silk Road over the Pacific, cocaine and heroin were far less likely to be spiked with fentanyl. Unfortunately, as with so many societal problems, we solve one problem only to create new ones. Trump successfully wrangled an agreement from President Xi Jinping to ban the sale of illicit fentanyl to the United States. Excess fentanyl precursor chemicals piled up overnight at the chemical companies. Relations between Mexican organized crime and Chinese drug distributors date back to the opium trade more than a hundred years ago. Even before Trump inked the deal with Xi, Sinaloa sourced precursors for their toxic synthetic elixirs like methamphetamine from China.

When the Chinese supply of finished fentanyl dried up, Sinaloa executives identified a vacuum in the market and pounced. As any Business 101 class will instruct would-be entrepreneurs, there are two ways to increase profits. The business must either sell more product or increase its product's profit margin. With cocaine sales plummeting decade after decade, it appeared that increasing product sales was tilting at windmills. Fentanyl provided a new opportunity to increase margins.

Sinaloa executives deeply value three key characteristics of fentanyl. First, fentanyl is dirt cheap compared to other drugs. It only costs $1,000 per kilogram[36] to produce and turns a hefty profit for the cartels.[37] Second, fentanyl is a hundred times more powerful than even heroin, which is still more potent than cocaine. Even if the drug lords cut a batch of cocaine with a miniscule amount of inexpensive fentanyl, it would still pack a punch. Thus, cartel executives could stretch the batch of blow or heroin to serve many more users. Third, fentanyl ensnares users far more efficiently than cocaine. Some victims become addicted to fentanyl after just one or two uses.

Fentanyl appeared to be a perfect morbid combination of a low-cost, more potent, and more addictive substitute to cut into cocaine and other drugs like heroin and meth. But there is one more heart-wrenching characteristic of the new fentanyl-spiked cocaine business model: the fatality rate.

The dons remain sanguine about overdose homicides associated with their business model. As discussed earlier, however, fentanyl is several times more deadly. Unlike pharmaceutical fentanyl used in hospitals, batches of cocaine spiked with fentanyl require zero quality controls. A bad batch can lead to dozens or hundreds of deaths in a short period of time. So here again arises the central question for U.S. government leaders grasping to understand Sinaloa's strategy. If Sinaloa's cocaine customer base shrinks every year, why sell a product that will shrink it even faster by murdering a higher percentage of users?

A New Pool of Customers

The underground nature of the illicit drug market obfuscates fentanyl's product development history. Clearly, however, three key strands evolved in concert. Eventually a completely new business model—or at least a new target customer—emerged. First, using foundational business school principles, the cartels shored up profits from cocaine and other drugs by stretching the white powder further with fentanyl. Second, a small market of hardcore narcotics addicts emerged that sought out stand-alone fentanyl until their early demise. Third, and most disastrously for the United States, the cartels expanded their toehold in the fake pharmaceutical market.[38]

The third strand became Sinaloa's most insidious line of business. The new product offering unlocked a market containing tens of millions more customers than anything the narco-executives had ever dreamed. Tragically the narco-tycoons expanded their illicit pharmaceutical line of business just as another historic market development unfolded. The United States ceased the freewheeling prescription opioid–slinging practices at the height of the late 1990s / early 2000s painkiller crisis. After years of overprescribing opioids like oxycodone, the prescription opioid industry installed far stricter guardrails.[39]

Doctors were weaning patients off oxycodone and other legal prescription painkillers. Many of those addicted to the pills flailed about for an alternative. Illicit prescription painkillers became ubiquitously available via an endless series of websites advertising the pills as legitimate. Also, street dealers proffered all manner of illegal pharmaceuticals. Often the pills were clearly illicit, like the rainbow-colored fake oxycodone pills featured in drug bust news clips. Worse, unwitting dealers offered what they believed were real prescription pills to friends and family. Users were scarcely aware the pills contained fentanyl as opposed to pure oxycodone, Adderall, or Xanax, among others.

One may ask, "Why not just manufacture illicit oxycodone or other prescription opioids without fentanyl?" The answer is simple: the Sinaloa cartel is not a pharmaceutical company. Oxycodone, Adderall, and Xanax are complex medicines to produce. They require expertise and a precise combination of chemicals with strict quality controls. Unlike real medicines, illicit prescription pills are often concocted in a kitchen blender with a few easy-to-purchase binder chemicals and fentanyl.

Oxycodone and Xanax are absent from the fake pills. These are not oxycodone pills laced with fentanyl. The pills are just fentanyl and binder chemicals pressed together to look like an oxycodone.[40] In fact, the hardest aspect of producing the drug is often sourcing a pill press that will fashion the illicit drug to appear like a real oxycodone or Vicodin or Adderall. Also, while these drugs can be addictive, none of them are nearly as addictive as fentanyl. So, by adding fentanyl to the mix, they can make any fake drug hopelessly addictive.

As Ernest Hemingway wrote, this shift happened "Two ways . . . gradually, then suddenly."[41] For law enforcement and victim families, a deadly new threat gradually appeared online, on the streets, and in dorm rooms. Illicit prescription drugs of all kinds, even those with very different effects than fentanyl, were spiked with fentanyl. To increase margins and addicts, the cartels cooked fentanyl into the illicit prescription drug recipes they concocted. Then suddenly it appeared in every illicit pharmaceutical. Drugs made to look like Xanax, Adderall, Vicodin, and Viagra were spiked with fentanyl. Corpses began piling up.

This diabolical new business model explains the gangster warlords' blasé attitude toward killing off the customers that fill their pockets with cash. For years, cartels dabbled in fake prescription pills; however, these pills had not been central to their business model. The pills were not central to their business model largely because producing them was incredibly difficult.

What better way to replace the few million American noses not snorting the white lady or lungs huffing Sinaloa ganja than with tens of millions of potential illicit prescription drug users? Moreover, this sadistic new business plan removed an age-old impediment to the narco-trafficker's customer acquisition strategy. In previous eras, customers had to make a psychological leap to illicit drugs. The new business model removed that hurdle. They now proffered pills to unwitting users otherwise averse to illicit substances. Rather, these customers believe the drugs originated from a legitimate website or friend with a real prescription. Obtaining a pill from someone other than your pharmacist skirts the letter of the law. However, psychologically, it is a far cry from seeking out a dealer at a nightclub or shopping for heroin on the Dark Web.

If they survive the first dose, the naive victim is hooked after a few pills. They suddenly display characteristics of hardcore addicts with little chance of recovery. At this point, every new pill is a game of Russian roulette. This risk is compounded because the narcos aren't chemists. They disregard precision, leaving every batch of fentanyl or fentanyl-laced drugs different than the one before it. Some pills may have zero fentanyl, while others will contain ten times the lethal amount.[42] This is why the Russian roulette comparison is quite apt and why some unwitting users don't always die with the first use but perhaps the second, fifth, or tenth use. Regardless, the narco-corporate tycoon is slowly but surely achieving his goal of transitioning those on the periphery of the U.S. prescription drug market into hopelessly addicted customers.

While we all stared endlessly at whiteboards with consultants, military personnel, agents, and physicians, one question persisted: Why would Sinaloa's corporate titans, driven by profits rather than ideology, provide their customers a product that caused a tenfold increase in overdose fatalities? Previously the two most deadly drugs, cocaine and heroin, removed about ten thousand paying customers from the illicit narcotics market every year. Fentanyl removes nearly one hundred thousand paying customers from the illicit narcotics market every year.

Pushing into the expanding fake prescription drug market was possibly the only way Sinaloa could avoid bankruptcy. Therefore, murdering one hundred thousand people a year to enter a market with tens of millions of net new users was an acceptable price of entry—especially since many of the dead users are not from the traditional illicit narcotics market, nor were they likely to ever become narcotics customers in the first place. People who were fatally duped into taking a fake prescription medication don't reduce the number of coke, heroin, or meth users for the cartel. So, their murder by fentanyl was irrelevant to the profit and loss (P&L) sheet of the narco-executives.

The blood-soaked cartel logic calculates that these people are expendable because the pool of victims taking fake prescription medication is a net additive to the cartel customer base. Further, cartel executives likely did not initially realize how high the fatality rate jumped. One key difference between the unbridled capitalism of the cartel versus mainstream capitalism is that the narco-tycoons do not store and analyze the petabytes of data legitimate corporate tycoons obsess over. Wall Street CEOs view databases with customer information as critical to making informed business decisions. The cartel bosses view that data as potential evidence that could be used against them in court. So, to our knowledge, they don't collect it. In the early days of fentanyl, corpses mounted up. However, the cartel executives likely only heard about fatalities via occasional anecdotes. Without a McKinsey-style analysis of customer data, the tycoons didn't ponder fentanyl death rates. Their minds were otherwise occupied pushing into the vast new market vacated by the likes of Purdue Pharma.

Many of the fatalities that piled up in the process of acquiring new customers did not equal lost revenue. New users quickly became addicted. Compelled by addiction, they scrounged for all manner of narcotics to satiate the newfound monkey on their back. These new slaves to the molecule are net newly acquired customers.

The cartel's prescription drug market gains were doused with jet fuel. Their dumb luck was that the U.S. pharmaceutical industry was simultaneously weaning the population off many prescription opioids, which had become ubiquitous in American households. Had fentanyl presented itself thirty years earlier or perhaps thirty years from now, it would not uncover so fertile a market. Consequently, the narco-business line executives of the nascent illicit prescription drug operation at Sinaloa witnessed an uptick in demand. At some point, it must have dawned on these criminal masterminds how vast the illicit prescription market had become and, accordingly, how many millions more customers could be acquired by trafficking fentanyl via pills that look like real pharmaceuticals.

The Answer

Why does the fentanyl business model make such morbid sense? This is the most likely dystopian answer: to fill the hole in their P&L sheets from the decline of cocaine, marijuana, and other drugs, cartel executive decided to take over the illicit migration trade and fentanyl market. To recover profits from decreasing narcotics sales, they increased margins of those products by cutting them with fentanyl. They then eyed an opportunity to expand into the massive illicit prescription drug market and pounced. Whether or not they were aware of fentanyl's deadly effects is irrelevant. Every death of a new pill user was the death of an otherwise unlikely customer. Every new addict produced a net new user they otherwise wouldn't have captured in the illicit narcotics market. Later, Sinaloa corporate strategists calculated that if significant loss of life was required to transition tens of millions of new users from the licit prescription drug market into the illicit narcotics market, so be it. The judgment was sound from a P&L perspective, especially in light of their cratering marijuana and cocaine markets. In the unbridled capitalism of narco-corporate greed, Sinaloa's business decision was based on horrifyingly perfect logic.

When dozens of agents and intelligence officers around the country first heard this theory at a meeting in early 2023, they were stunned. We had all hoped in the recesses of our collective minds that fentanyl was a fluke. The one thing we could always count on was the profit motive of cartel tycoons. We assumed the cartels would realize how many paying customers they were killing. To maximize profits, they would either make the drugs less deadly or stop selling them altogether. When our experts realized fentanyl was a sound business strategy, everyone was devastated. There was little hope that the narco-corporate executives would ever conclude that fentanyl endangered their business model. The fentanyl line of business would persist.

Notes

1 "Safety Topics." National Safety Council Injury Facts, last accessed January 29, 2024. https://injuryfacts.nsc.org/home-and-community/safety-topics/drugoverdoses/data-details/#:~:text=In%202021%2C%2098%2C268%20people%20died,%2C%20homicide%2C%20and%20undetermined%20intents.

2 "Safety Topics."

3 "Sinaloa Cartel." InSight Crime, November 7, 2024. https://insightcrime.org/mexico-organized-crime-news/sinaloa-cartel-profile/.

4 "Marijuana." Drug Enforcement Administration, n.d. https://www.dea.gov/factsheets/marijuana.

5 Qureshi, Adnan I., Saqib A. Chaudhry, and M. Fareed K. Suri. "Cocaine Use and the Likelihood of Cardiovascular and All-Cause Mortality: Data from the Third National Health and Nutrition Examination Survey Mortality Follow-Up Study." *Journal of Vascular and Interventional Neurology* 7, no. 1 (May 2014). https://pmc.ncbi.nlm.nih.gov/articles/PMC4051909/.

6 "Illicit Fentanyl and Mexico's Role." CRS Reports. Congressional Research Service, December 19, 2024. https://crsreports.congress.gov/product/pdf/IF/IF10400.

7 "What Percentage of Americans Smoke Marijuana?" Gallup, November 14, 2024. https://news.gallup.com/poll/284135/percentage-americans-smoke-marijuana.aspx.

8 "Treasury Designates Sinaloa Cartel Plaza Bosses." Drug Enforcement Administration, May 7, 2013. https://www.dea.gov/press-releases/2013/05/07/treasury-designates-sinaloa-cartel-plaza-bosses.

9 "Treasury Designates Sinaloa Cartel Plaza Bosses."

10 "Plata O Plomo." Dictionary.com, 2021. https://www.dictionary.com/e/slang/plata-o
-plomo/.

11 "Treasury Designates Sinaloa Cartel Plaza Bosses."

12 "The Expansion and Diversification of Mexican Cartels: Dynamic New Actors and
Markets." International Institute for Strategic Studies, 2024. https://www.iiss.org
/publications/armed-conflict-survey/2024/the-expansion-and-diversification-of
-mexican-cartels-dynamic-new-actors-and-markets/.

13 Demarest, Michael. "Cocaine: Middle Class High." *Time*, July 6, 1981. https://content
.time.com/time/magazine/article/0,9171,922619,00.html.

14 Gerstenzang, James, and Ronald J. Ostrow. "U.S. Launches Massive Caribbean Drug
Drive." *Los Angeles Times*, November 2, 1985. https://www.latimes.com/archives/la
-xpm-1985-11-02-mn-1072-story.html.

15 Sandoval, Juan Esteban Arratia. "The New Hideout of Cockroaches? The Expansion of
the Mexican Organized Crime in Northern Triangle of Central America." *Usach*, June
2016. https://www.academia.edu/25787161/The_new_hideout_of_cockroaches_The
_expansion_of_the_Mexican_Organized_Crime_in_Northern_Triangle_of_Central
_America.

16 Hernandez-Roy, Christopher, Rubi Bledsoe, and Andrea Michelle Cerén. "Tracking
Transatlantic Drug Flows: Cocaine's Path from South America across the Caribbean
to Europe." Center for Strategic and International Studies, September 19, 2023.
https://features.csis.org/tracking-transatlantic-drug-flows-cocaines-path-from-south
-america-across-the-caribbean-to-europe/index.html.

17 For 1985 data, see "National Drug Control Strategy: Data Supplement 2020." Office of
National Drug Control Strategy, February 2020, 34. https://trumpwhitehouse.archives
.gov/wp-content/uploads/2020/02/2020-NDCS-Data-Supplement.pdf. For 2018 data,
see "2018 NSDUH Detailed Tables." Substance Abuse and Mental Health Services
Administration, August 20, 2019. https://www.samhsa.gov/data/report/2018-nsduh
-detailed-tables.

18 Felbab-Brown, Vanda. "Hooked: Mexico's Violence and U.S. Demand for Drugs."
Brookings, May 30, 2017. https://www.brookings.edu/articles/hooked-mexicos
-violence-and-u-s-demand-for-drugs/.

19 Finklea, Kristin. "Illicit Drug Smuggling between Ports of Entry and Border Barriers."
R46218. Congressional Research Service, February 7, 2020, 2, fig. I. https://crsreports
.congress.gov/product/pdf/R/R46218/2.

20 "What America's Users Spend on Illegal Drugs." Executive Office of the President of
the United States, February 14, 2014, 58. https://obamawhitehouse.archives.gov/sites/
default/files/ondcp/policy-and-research/wausid_results_report.pdf.

21 "What America's Users Spend on Illegal Drugs."

22 Sheridan, Mary Beth, Lorena Ríos, and Fred Ramos. "How Mexico's Cartels Infiltrated the Tortilla Business." *Washington Post*, May 23, 2024. https://www.washingtonpost.com/world/2024/05/23/mexico-cartels-tortilla-exortion-crime/.

23 Graham, Dave. "Even behind Bars, El Chapo's 'Robin Hood' Luster Glows in Mexico Drug Capital." Reuters, January 30, 2019. https://www.reuters.com/article/world/even-behind-bars-el-chapos-robin-hood-luster-glows-in-mexico-drug-capital-idUSKCN1PO2CT/; Obafemee. "See the Amazing Multi-million Dollar Car Collections Seized from Mexican Drug Lord, El Chapo." AutoJosh, July 18, 2019. https://autojosh.com/see-the-amazing-multi-million-dollar-car-collections-seized-from-mexican-drug-lord-el-chapo/.

24 Felbab-Brown, Vanda. "Mexican Cartels Are Providing COVID-19 Assistance: Why That's Not Surprising." Brookings, April 27, 2020. https://www.brookings.edu/articles/mexican-cartels-are-providing-covid-19-assistance-why-thats-not-surprising.

25 Burnett, John. "Mexico's Ferocious Zetas Cartel Reigns through Fear." NPR, October 2, 2009. https://www.npr.org/2009/10/02/113388071/mexicos-ferocious-zetas-cartel-reigns-through-fear.

26 Corcoran, Patrick. "Evaluating the Zetas' Legacy in Mexico." InSight Crime, June 18, 2014. https://insightcrime.org/news/analysis/evaluating-the-zetas-legacy-in-mexico/; Archibold, Randal C., and Ginger Thompson. "Capture of Mexican Crime Boss Appears to End a Brutal Chapter." *New York Times*, July 17, 2013. https://www.nytimes.com/2013/07/17/world/americas/capture-of-mexican-crime-boss-appears-to-end-a-brutal-chapter.html.

27 Irwin, Lauren. "Mexican Cartels Rank as Nation's Fifth-Largest Employer: Study." *The Hill*, September 21, 2023. https://thehill.com/policy/international/4217279-mexican-cartels-rank-as-nations-fifth-largest-employer-study/.

28 "CBP History through the Years." U.S. Customs and Border Protection, n.d. https://www.cbp.gov/about/history.

29 "CBP History through the Years."

30 Baker, Bryan, and Robert Warren. "Estimates of the Unauthorized Immigrant Population Residing in the United States: January 2018–January 2022." U.S. Department of Homeland Security | Office of Homeland Security Statistics, April 2024, 1. https://ohss.dhs.gov/sites/default/files/2024-06/2024_0418_ohss_estimates-of-the-unauthorized-immigrant-population-residing-in-the-united-states-january-2018%25E2%2580%2593january-2022.pdf.

31 Pupkin, Ethan. "Police Claim US-Mexico Border Has 'Eerie Parallel' to Israel-Gaza." Jewish Institute for National Security of America, November 30, 2023. https://jinsa.org/police-claim-us-mexico-border-parallel-to-israel-gaza/.

32 "'Now Nobody Crosses without Paying': Senior Border Patrol Agents Describe Unprecedented Cartel Control at Southwest Border." Committee on Homeland Security, December 14, 2023. https://homeland.house.gov/2023/12/14/now-nobody

-crosses-without-paying-senior-border-patrol-agents-describe-unprecedented-cartel
-control-at-southwest-border/.

33 "Nationwide Encounters." U.S. Customs and Border Protection, n.d. https://www.cbp
.gov/newsroom/stats/nationwide-encounters.

34 "Mesoamerican Migration Project (MMP)." Brown University and El Colegio de
Mexico, 2025. https://mmp.research.brown.edu/news/12-10-2024.

35 Fisher, Steve, and Alfredo Corchado. "Mexican Cartels Offering Pricey VIP Package
for Migrants Trying to Get into US." *USA Today*, June 20, 2024. https://www.usatoday
.com/story/news/investigations/2024/06/20/mexican-drug-cartels-migrant-vip
-package/74154061007/.

36 "PPB Releases New Podcast on Dangers of Fentanyl (Photo)." Portland Police Public
Information Office, n.d. https://www.portlandoregon.gov/police/news/read.cfm?id
=412335.

37 "Two Kilos of Fentanyl Seized by Gang Impact Team." Office of the District Attorney,
County of Riverside, February 5, 2021. https://rivcoda.org/news/two-kilos-fentanyl
-seized-gang-impact-team.

38 "The Expansion and Diversification of Mexican Cartels: Dynamic New Actors and
Markets." International Institute for Strategic Studies, n.d. https://www.iiss.org/
publications/armed-conflict-survey/2024/the-expansion-and-diversification-of
-mexican-cartels-dynamic-new-actors-and-markets/.

39 "Laws Limiting the Prescribing or Dispensing of Opioids." Network for Public Health
Law, May 14, 2021. https://www.networkforphl.org/resources/laws-limiting-the
-prescribing-or-dispensing-of-opioids/.

40 "DEA Laboratory Testing Reveals That 6 Out of 10 Fentanyl-Laced Fake Prescription
Pills Now Contain a Potentially Lethal Dose of Fentanyl." Drug Enforcement
Administration, n.d. https://www.dea.gov/alert/dea-laboratory-testing-reveals-6-out
-10-fentanyl-laced-fake-prescription-pills-now-contain.

41 Hemingway, Ernest. *The Sun Also Rises*. New York: Scribner, 1926. Reprint, New York:
Simon & Schuster, 2006.

42 "Summary and Key Findings." Fentanyl Profiling Program Report. Drug Enforcement
Administration and Special Testing and Research Laboratory, 2022. https://www.dea
.gov/sites/default/files/2022-05/FPP%20Report%20January%202022.pdf.

8

Byzantium

There was no reasoning with the Sinaloa narco-tycoons. Their plan to hook unwitting fake prescription medicine consumers and recreational drug users on fentanyl until their untimely demise was not a fluke but a calculated business strategy. Every instinct of U.S. national security leaders was to attack. Attack the kingpins. Attack the Sinaloa network. Attack the Chinese chemical companies, and attack anyone aiding or abetting the gangster warlords poisoning Americans. But we first needed to get our own house in order so the subsequent attack could maximize impact on cartel operations.

Consequently, in August 2022, the National Security Council (NSC) kicked off an interagency plan to marshal all the power of the U.S. government behind a coordinated assault on fentanyl and the Sinaloa cartel. Few of us foresaw that this process would accentuate rivalries, within our own government, that had been at slow boil for years. Deep fissures fueled by decades-long conflict over who was in charge of fighting drugs versus who was in charge of fighting transnational criminal organizations turned the process into an all-out interagency knife fight.

Fortunately, the NSC wasn't starting from scratch as most agencies relevant to the campaign had assembled bespoke counterfentanyl or counter-Sinaloa operations. Some parts of the intelligence community recently initiated operations dedicated to fentanyl and the cartel. The NSC and other agency leaders, like John Tien, clamored for any intelligence related to fentanyl or Sinaloa to be routed to agencies pursuing fentanyl. As a result, key pieces of intelligence now snaked their way through the behemoth U.S. intelligence apparatus to agents who could action it. Additionally, Homeland Security Investigations (HSI), the Drug Enforcement Administration (DEA), Customs and Border Protection (CBP), the Central Intelligence Agency (CIA), the National Security Agency (NSA), and several other agencies were actively investigating Sinaloa for fentanyl. Some of these cases had been initiated years earlier. Key operations targeting precursor chemicals or pill presses had been kicked off months or years in advance as well. All this activity, however, contributed to the problem of organizing a coordinated assault instead of solving it.

Under normal circumstances, all manner of agencies pursue any case within their remit. Deconfliction between agents inevitably pursuing criminals naturally occurs at multiple steps in an investigation along the way. However, aside from deciding who receives credit for the collar, and whose case is brought in front of a judge, agencies are largely free actors. They can pursue cases as they see fit. This free-for-all causes conflict. Conflict intensifies especially in the senior ranks when agencies are jostling for credit over a big takedown, like El Chapo and his ilk. Typically, agencies are left to deconflict these issues among themselves. Periodically the Department of Justice (DOJ) senior leadership, like the deputy attorney general (DAG), will intervene to mediate particularly thorny disagreements between agencies. Otherwise, it is up to agents and management in the field offices to hash it out.

Fentanyl was different. President Joe Biden and his top lieutenant on this issue, Liz Sherwood-Randall, insisted agencies work in concert on fentanyl. The White House's role is to lead the coordination of the federal enterprise and, consistent with presidential priorities, rise above petty skirmishes between agencies. Here White House leadership was essential, and Sherwood-Randall convened a series of meetings to ensure that there was full alignment on one coordinated effort to combat fentanyl.

The fentanyl epidemic seemed on its face a narcotics problem. Few considered it a mass poisoning yet. So, DEA naturally insisted it command the interagency effort, and all other agencies report up through it. Other agencies, like HSI, however, perceived the fentanyl issues as primarily a transnational criminal organization (TCO) issue. The fentanyl supply chain unquestionably spanned the globe from China to Mexico and seeped across U.S. borders.

Transnational criminal organizations in general fall under the Department of Homeland Security (DHS) and, in particular, HSI jurisdiction. HSI did not expect to lead the effort. Yet, it certainly did not yield to DEA on something it asserted was also in HSI's jurisdiction. Also, long-standing grievances typical of agencies both working side by side and in competition doomed any agreement that placed DEA at the helm.

Moreover, the NSC wasn't just insisting agencies play nice in the sandbox together. Rather, it demanded we enumerate every key component of the plan. Then we were to negotiate which agency quarterbacked each component and which agencies played a support position. For example, it was obvious the Coast Guard would own interdiction of ships suspected of carrying fentanyl. CBP obviously would direct efforts to leverage artificial intelligence (AI) for enhanced detection of fentanyl at the border. It was not so straightforward to delineate responsibility when it came to investigations into the elaborate Sinaloa financial network. Nor was it clear what agency owned cases against Chinese precursor chemical companies. Nor was it clear who was in charge of cases against corrupt Mexican government officials who provided cover for Sinaloa's fentanyl operations.

These open questions notwithstanding, the NSC insisted agencies agree who owned each line of effort. By extension we assigned who reported to whom on each line of effort. While painful for the participating agencies, it was a standard process that the White House corralled them. The White House identifies what activities each agency executes best. It then delineates who owns each action. This way the White House ensures we put the best team together with the most capable agency playing the position best suited to it.

This process ripped open wounds that had been festering for decades. The fight that unfolded has roots reaching back to the Richard Nixon administration when he established the DEA as part of his war on drugs. Over the next few months, we worked through fifty years of real and perceived slights, botched cases, personal animosities, and turf battles between the DEA and legacy U.S. Customs Service, what is now HSI.

To best understand how we arrived at the counterfentanyl strategic plan, it is instructive to review how these internecine battles arose in the first place and how they are intimately relevant for the fight against fentanyl.

DEA and HSI[1]

Narcotics are governed by parts of Title 21 authority of the United States Code. This authority was assigned solely to DEA in 1973 by President Nixon with the merger of the Office for Drug Abuse Law Enforcement and the Office of National Narcotics Intelligence.[2] The DEA was anointed as sole proprietor of this authority as a result of the first "war on drugs" launched by Nixon in the 1970s. Nixon's "war" was launched in response to the hippie culture of the 1960s. Many in Nixon's "silent majority" perceived weed as the flower powering intoxicated youth. As mentioned in chapter 7, a series of events like the bedlam at Woodstock,[3] the violence at the 1969 Rolling Stones concert at Altamont, and most tragically the assassinations of Robert F. Kennedy and Martin Luther King Jr. engendered a deep sense of unease. Many Americans worried the antiwar movement had spun out of control.

Nixon's decision seemed logical at the time. It was expedient to place authority over enforcement of the nefarious elixirs corrupting our children all in one agency. Nearly a decade later in 1982, sole ownership of narcotics enforcement was split. The attorney general extended elements of the Title 21 authority to the Federal Bureau of Investigation (FBI) as well. Later issues became more complicated. The U.S. Customs Service was historically charged with combating illicit drugs that crossed the border. Customs also agitated for its own narcotics authority.

The U.S. Customs Service's mission was to safeguard U.S. borders and investigate international smuggling organizations.[4] This mission was inextricably linked to drug enforcement. In practice it was nearly impossible to demarcate where drug investigations ended and cross-border smuggling investigations began. Inevitably, conflict among customs agents, DEA agents, and their respective managers arose. Promotion and bonus structures made matters worse by constructing a zero-sum environment. Many agents, who otherwise were happy to collaborate, were disincentivized to do so. A collar gained by one agency was a loss to another. This dynamic persists today in even the most petty manifestations. For example, press conferences held by DHS or DOJ for successful cases worked jointly often leave the supporting agency off the dais and mentioned only in the very last, seldom published, paragraph of the press release.

To make matters worse, in 1973 President Nixon transferred all functions related to narcotics from the Secretary of the Treasury, the then parent department of the U.S. Customs Service, to the Attorney General. Compounding this slight to the Customs Service, the Department of Justice (DOJ) Office of Legal Counsel determined in 1986 that the Customs Service did not have independent authority to carry out any drug investigations. Despite continued protests from Customs, it was relegated to limited authorities to interdict and investigate international criminal organizations. Unbeknownst to Nixon, we had entered an era where marijuana was normalized in youth culture and cocaine was becoming the designer drug of choice in the United States. As a result, a tsunami of weed and mountains of snow overwhelmed border officials in a seeming avalanche of narcotics.

After drowning in drugs for more than a decade, the DEA complied with Customs demands and, in 1944, signed an interagency agreement to "cross-designate" a limited number of Customs agents with the Title 21 drug enforcement authority. Cross-designating an agent means that person gains the authorities of both her home agency and that of the cross-designating authority. So, in this case the Customs agents had both border authorities and narcotics authorities. This compromise, however, was contingent on drugs directly connected to the border. Customs agents could only investigate individuals and organizations implicated in smuggling controlled substances across the international border and ports of entry. This compromise sounds logical. There is little utility in Customs agents chasing gangbangers slinging dope around street corners in the interior of the country. Customs agents have bigger fish to fry. International criminal rings strive to smuggle every horrible thing one can imagine into and out of the United States.

But this cross-designation caused more confusion, not less. Since the vast majority of drugs are smuggled in to the United States, Customs agents claimed most street drug cases fell in their jurisdiction. Further, it was nearly impossible for the DEA to probe drug cases that lacked any international nexus. So yet again, an attempt to clarify roles just created more confusion. These somewhat arbitrary restrictions ensured agents from Customs and the

DEA were constantly pursuing the same leads. They also cultivated the same confidential informants. They targeted the same kingpins. They were ultimately in constant conflict over who claimed credit for marquee convictions.

Once again, 9/11 changed everything. After DHS was created in 2003, the U.S. Customs Service was split into CBP and Immigration and Customs Enforcement (ICE). Both CBP and ICE were named parties to the Title 21 narcotics enforcement agreement. As with Customs before it, Title 21 authority limited ICE agents' ability to investigate drug smuggling. As an agency within ICE, these limitations applied to HSI as well. Some changes were made that allowed more HSI agents to investigate narcotics. However, DHS was created after 9/11, based on the belief that better enforcement of immigration laws could have led to the apprehension of the nineteen hijackers on immigration charges before they boarded the planes.

Most of the relevant authorities for CBP and ICE come from Title 19 (Customs) and Title 8 (Immigration). The bureaucratic solution to bring these agencies together under one roof was conceived to give DHS more investigative authorities. George W. Bush administration officials estimated that the more investigative authorities an agency maintained, the better positioned it was to use whatever tool necessary to take down terrorist networks.

As we face a new threat that is killing nearly as many people as 9/11 every few days, leaders at HSI argued the same logic should apply. DHS has unique authorities, unmatched numbers of agents, highly relevant expertise, and geographic primacy along the Southwest Border. DHS alone possesses these competitive advantages. Thus, adding the authority to pursue narcotics cases in this time of crisis seems a no-brainer. The American people surely expect we use all the relevant tools at our disposal in the most effective way possible to stop the flow of fentanyl into the United States.

It only follows that the largest federal law enforcement agency in the United States,[5] with thousands of personnel on the border, billions of dollars in equipment, and authorities to investigate the transnational criminal organizations producing and smuggling drugs, should have all the relevant tools at its disposal to stop the flow of fentanyl into the United States. This is how HSI viewed the matter. By contrast, the DEA has traditionally opposed the proposed expansion of HSI authorities into their turf.

There are several functional reasons why DEA seeks to remain sole proprietor of the narcotics authority. First, DEA can shutter HSI narcotics investigations if they see fit. Second, DEA approves all HSI narcotics investigations.[6] This may sound self-serving on the part of DEA; however, squelching insignificant cases in conflict with more consequential ones is a key aspect of law enforcement. Also, HSI is not allowed to utilize state and local law enforcement task force officers (TFOs) for drug smuggling investigations. State and local officers are crucial to these investigations as they know their communities better than anyone and act as a significant force multiplier. The DEA has had no incentive to relinquish its Title 21 drug enforcement authority because Title 21 maintained control of all drug cases for them since 1973.[7]

Regardless, White House leadership implored HSI to significantly step up its efforts around fentanyl. This delivered HSI the ammunition it needed to grouse about being excluded from Title 21 authority.

War on Terror Era

The changes 9/11 brought about, like merging ICE (legacy U.S. Customs special agents and legacy Immigration and Naturalization Service [INS] special agents) and CBP (U.S. Customs and INS inspectors) under DHS, impacted DEA, too. From its creation in the 1970s through the crack-cocaine epidemic in the 1980s to the early 1990s, DEA enjoyed status as one of the most high-profile law enforcement organizations in the world. In its heyday, innumerable movies and TV shows celebrated the harrowing travails of DEA agents including *Scarface* and *Miami Vice*. However, the crack-cocaine epidemic ebbed in the later 1990s.[8] After 9/11, public safety and national security concerns turned toward terrorism.

DEA plays a far less obvious role in counterterrorism. Some terrorists sold drugs to finance their terrorist activities.[9] For example, proceeds from the poppy farms in Afghanistan financed the Taliban.[10] So those investigations required DEA attention. DEA also had a global network of informants and wiretaps it pulsed incessantly in the years after 9/11 to support counterterrorism efforts.

Otherwise, drugs were relegated to a backwater issue immediately after 9/11. I witnessed this firsthand working in politics since 2001. In the first twenty years after 9/11, I never saw even one poll that ranked drugs in voters' top five concerns. This runs in stark contrast to the 1980s, when drugs were cited among voters' top concerns far more frequently.[11] Lack of relevance to the single most important national security challenge of an era has direct impact on an organization. During the war on terror, DEA was less involved in national security strategy sessions at the White House. Thus, DEA found itself out of the loop on key initiatives. It meant the DEA's brand wasn't as sexy as before. Top recruits applied to agencies more directly involved in the war on terror. Budget requests became difficult to justify to both DOJ leadership and Congress. As the war on terror raged, DEA prominence waned. More than a quarter of the public (27 percent) ranked drug abuse as the most important issue in 1989, but by 2004 that number had fallen to 1 percent. The drug issue largely faded from the zeitgeist of America.[12]

In stark contrast after 9/11, CBP and HSI were injected with steroids. Sealing the border from would-be terrorists was a top concern of the national security establishment and the American people. In the decade after the 2003 creation of ICE (which houses HSI), the agency's annual budget had increased by nearly 80 percent. CBP experienced a similar level of growth during that same period (77 percent). These growth rates were nearly double the rate of budgetary growth DEA was appropriated during the same time.[13] As one can imagine, terrorism ranked in the top five issues of every national poll I saw, and in every election I did, after 9/11 for at least ten years.[14] During the administrations of George W. Bush and Barack Obama, the denizens of the West Wing were laser focused on taking down transnational terrorist networks like al-Qaeda and the Islamic State of Iraq and Syria (ISIS). The two agencies' ranks swelled to officers in the tens of thousands. HSI alone grew to nearly double the size of the DEA.[15] It also received billions to build out an international footprint that spanned the globe. CBP received billions in funding to erect an unprecedented data analytics network across air, land, and sea. It also was allotted massive sums to build the National Targeting Center (NTC).[16] The NTC was built to monitor billions of people and packages traveling around the world every day. Once completed it was a peerless law enforcement tool.

So while HSI chafed at DEA recalcitrance to grant it Title 21 authority, DEA had been wandering in the bureaucratic wilderness for nearly twenty years. DEA watched its sister law enforcement agencies get showered with all the recognition and resources 9/11 brought with it. Fentanyl provided DEA an opportunity for resurgence. However, 9/11 and its aftermath provided HSI with the swagger to insist it would not revert to the days it played second fiddle to DEA. The stage was set for a brawl over who was in charge of fentanyl.

Never Let a Crisis Go to Waste

The NSC convened dozens of interagency meetings with DOJ, DHS, Department of Defense (DOD), and other key departments and agencies enlisted in the fight against fentanyl. NSC worked to address differences and secure agreement on a comprehensive plan that leveraged the whole U.S. government to disrupt the illicit fentanyl supply chain and reduce soaring deaths in the homeland. To maximize impact and opportunity for success, the plan focused on four lines of effort: precursors, pill presses, commercial shipping, and illicit finance. Persistent prodding from the NSC eventually brought everyone to the table. Homeland Security advisor Dr. Liz Sherwood-Randall applied constant, intense pressure on the federal bureaucracy to finalize a plan. Had it not been for pressure from President Biden and his senior leadership team, like Dr. Sherwood-Randall, the whole-of-government fentanyl plan may never have launched.

One key question, though, is why the DEA would adamantly insist on its litany of terms and conditions. Their actions went far beyond typical turf battles. I have no way of knowing for sure. I would hazard to guess that there are a few related factors at play.

First, as stated earlier, until fentanyl arrived on the scene, narcotics had been relegated to a third- or fourth-tier issue in public policy. Also, HSI can claim jurisdiction over any crime that crosses national borders.[17] Fentanyl was produced in Mexico and smuggled into the United States, which gave HSI claim to initiate the lion's share of fentanyl cases. However, fentanyl blew new life into the DEA. DEA was positioned front and center in policymaking again. But DEA's eminence would only materialize if HSI didn't initiate the bulk of the cases against fentanyl peddling criminals by using its cross-border authority, massive resources, and nearly seven thousand agents. DEA could anticipate the enormous opportunity looming for itself. However, one massive potential obstacle was in their way: HSI.

If DEA was installed as the interagency commander directing the entire U.S. government campaign against fentanyl, then it could stake a claim to significant budget and personnel increases. Years of back benching counterterrorism meetings in the Situation Room would cease. As commander in the fight against fentanyl, it could sit at the head of the table leading briefings for the NSC in the Situation Room. DEA again could receive the bureaucratic recognition it once possessed. DEA could be the one briefing the president in the Oval Office about progress against fentanyl.

To be fair to DEA, it also insisted it lead the effort because it believed, rightly, that no agency excelled at the narcotics game better than them. As far as they were concerned, precluding the DEA from running the fentanyl effort was like precluding the Secret Service from protecting the president. Narcotics is their business. They understand their business better than anyone in the world.

Also, DEA would not want to chair meetings in the Situation Room, brief the president, and receive platitudes simply to stroke its collective ego. Like all law enforcement organizations, DEA's ranks at all levels are composed of dedicated professionals who have committed their lives to making America safe and putting those who would do our families harm behind bars.

They staked out a position not petty or nefarious. It is consistent with an aphorism followed from time immemorial, "Never let a good crisis go to waste." All those who thrive in Byzantine bureaucracies, like federal law enforcement, follow this maxim or perish. DEA was not behaving unlike any other agency given the same set of circumstances. It would be bureaucratic malpractice for leadership at DEA to not leverage the fentanyl issue and maximize their budget position, standing in the interagency and recruiting.

Foregoing the mantle of command on fentanyl would amount to even more egregious bureaucratic malpractice because DEA believed it was right on the substance. In Washington, it's rare that one is both right on the substance and its agency stands to benefit bureaucratically in terms of increased budget and personnel. If one finds themselves in that position and they don't fight the bureaucratic knife fight, then they are not worth their salt.

Leadership at DEA was proving they were worth their salt.

Monroe

While the DEA was fighting the interagency knife fight, we pulled together our team internally and quietly kicked off DHS's campaign to combat fentanyl in November 2022. As mentioned earlier, most relevant agencies at DHS, like CBP or HSI, had their own bespoke efforts and dozens of cases and seizures on fentanyl. However, we had yet to form a departmentwide coordinated strategy. At Tien's request, I ping-ponged back and forth between leadership at the three most relevant DHS agencies in the fentanyl fight. My mandate was to ensure our plan was acceptable to all parties. Troy Miller was the acting CBP commissioner. Despite being constantly under siege from dealing with the flow of migrants at the border, Troy was one of the most consistent voices at DHS demanding we up our game on fentanyl. P. J. Leichlieter also insisted we enhance our counterfentanyl efforts department wide. He was a former navy officer turned county cop in Virginia. P. J. rose in the ranks to become the head of HSI and deputy director of ICE. Finally, Ken Wainstein, who was former DOJ and homeland security advisor to President Bush, now served as our undersecretary for intelligence and analysis. He also consistently advocated that fentanyl must be a top priority. All three were incredibly good-natured leaders who spent their lives putting away bad guys. They woke up in the morning and went to bed every night with one thing on their minds: keeping America safe. There wasn't an ounce of ego among the three of them.

Troy and P. J. tapped their top CBP and HSI lieutenants, Jorge Comas and Mathew Brodman, respectively, to prosecute the counterfentanyl campaign. We could not tout the effort publicly. The NSC was still wrangling DEA, HSI, and other agencies to come to agreement on the government-wide plan. However, Tien, Troy, P.J., and Ken were not likely to stand by and watch while Americans were dying. With tacit approval to proceed from the Front Office, Comas, Brodman, and I convened over steaks and drinks at Guerra Steakhouse in Arlington, Virginia, to unofficially launch the effort. Over dinner, I learned why P. J. and Troy picked Brodman and Comas. During the war on terror, the two worked as a tag team targeting (Jorge) and arresting (Brodman) terrorists across Europe and the Middle East. Brodman was stationed in Europe to take out bad guys with foreign law enforcement. Jorge found terrorists for Brodman by mining the massive data holdings and sophisticated analytic tools at CBP's National Targeting Center. They were teamed up again employing much of the same tactics developed to take out ISIS foreign fighters across Europe and the Middle East a decade earlier. Both Comas and Brodman were respectable leaders within the federal law enforcement community who were able to navigate the bureaucratic obstacles and build relationships especially with DEA.

As we washed down our steak with beers, Jorge explained he was adding seventy analysts to his team just to produce targeting packages for Brodman and his agents to action. Jorge also had already recruited people from DOJ and the Mexican government for his targeting nerve center. These officials would inform packages of intelligence developed to target Sinaloa affiliates. Brodman recruited several of his colleagues from his days of gumshoeing in New York. These agents had direct experience taking down key members of Mexican cartels.

Jorge entered CBP shortly after 9/11. He was from Virginia and knew people who were in the Pentagon when it was hit on 9/11. Jorge enlisted immediately. He spent the next twenty years with a team of analysts, technologists, and data wizards building the National Targeting Center (NTC) into a global nerve center to combat terrorism. The NTC contains petabytes of data that monitor the flow of billions of people and cargo across the planet at any given nanosecond. This nerve center is peerless at ingesting and analyzing more data than any other system like it in the world.

Brodman was straight out of central casting from the *Sopranos*. He was about six feet two and 250 pounds and looked like an NFL linebacker. An Italian American, he was born in Brooklyn and joined law enforcement straight out of college. Despite residing in Virginia for decades and being stationed abroad frequently during the war on terror, he maintained a thick New York accent. After being tapped as campaign manager for HSI in the fight against fentanyl,

Brodman swung into action. As the NSC Strategic Implementation Plan (SIP) was still being excruciatingly negotiated with the interagency, we could not make Brodman's role public. So, he quietly built his team and knit together hundreds of cases and other initiatives that somehow touched fentanyl or the Sinaloa cartel. Brodman and his go-to guy, Anthony, drafted detailed engagement plans that were ultimately delivered to Tien and me. Using the campaign plan we developed, we immediately reached out to the CIA, NSA, and other intelligence agencies. Brodman's goal was to illuminate how Sinaloa managed its fentanyl vertical within the overall corporate structure.

We were shocked at how little the U.S. government knew about the Sinaloa cartel. The gangster warlords have massacred more than four hundred thousand people[18] in myriad battles right across our border in Mexico.[19] Their bloody turf wars have spewed blood across Mexico since the mid-1980s. Moreover, Sinaloa had poisoned more than two hundred thousand Americans with fentanyl in the last three years since 2020. Surely we must know everything about them. We don't.

In one meeting with leaders from the military, intelligence community, and law enforcement we received an overview of what we collectively knew about Sinaloa and fentanyl. We were not impressed. I interjected that Ford understands more about Toyota as an enterprise than the U.S. government does about the Sinaloa cartel. I hoped this provocative statement would induce the briefers to interject with more insightful analysis. They did not. I assumed everyone in the room would disagree. They would chastise me as a neophyte completely ignorant of the subject.

Instead, my provocative comment was met with a room full of nodding heads. As we walked out of the room, Brodman snorted, "My high schooler could have done a better brief on Sinaloa than that with a few hours on Google."

After the meeting, he often reiterated that we were so in the dark about Sinaloa: "We need to get smart about the questions we should ask before we can illuminate anything about the cartel network," much less its global fentanyl supply chain. After the meeting Brodman, Comas, and I concluded we could not twiddle our thumbs while the leviathan U.S. government got its act together. So, Morgan Ryan worked with Jorge to organize a weekly meeting with all the intelligence players as well as military and law enforcement partners. We sought to ascertain what everyone knew about Sinaloa and fentanyl. Jorge hosted the call as the NTC was accepted by DEA as a more neutral player than HSI. Understanding the bureaucratic obstacles allowed the three of us to stay one step ahead.

Attendees requested new analysis on specific targets from the intelligence community. They also assessed what targets to pursue. The call was deemed "Fentanyl Friday." It thrust Comas into a position as a nerve center in the fight against fentanyl. That positioned us perfectly. He and Brodman worked hand in glove. They also knew the counterterrorism playbook like the back of their hands. Further, the duo had just drafted our DHS-wide fentanyl campaign plan with a team of more than fifty experts.

We dubbed the plan "Monroe," named after the Monroe Doctrine. I conceived the name one night over a glass of wine. That night I reviewed aspects of the plan related to China's involvement in precursors for the cartels. The next day I was grousing to Morgan, "Honestly, how the fuck can we let the Chinese do this? What about the Monroe Doctrine? We don't let anyone muck around in our hemisphere. We will crush them." After that she just started titling all memos and meetings on fentanyl "Monroe." The name stuck.

Brodman and Comas rallied the interagency and our Mexican counterparts. Jorge tuned our massive data holdings to ID targets for HSI to hunt down. We were firing on all cylinders. Then I got an exasperated call from the NSC. Several agencies were still nitpicking individual words in the implementation plan and holding up agreement.

The NSC staffer asked if I could get a group of DHS people on Zoom with DOJ and "sit in a (virtual) room until there is agreement." I gave them my sympathies, and we commiserated as to how intractable agencies can be. So, in February 2023, I put a group of DHS subject matter experts on the phone with DOJ headquarters leaders who were also lead for their agency's fentanyl plan. We collectively rolled our eyes at the nits-and-nats agencies dug in over. Thankfully, the DOJ Front Office had assigned some real pros to help wrangle all our aggrieved agencies and marshal the combined resources of DOJ, DHS, and the rest of the federal government. Michael Ben'Ary and Hilary Hurd locked arms with us as we aimed the collective firepower of our two agencies at Sinaloa and fentanyl.

However, one key question remained: What exactly were we "aiming" at Sinaloa? Our Transnational Criminal Investigative Units (TCIUs) were a start. We also had parts of the Mexican military and others who would take the fight to Sinaloa on a limited basis. Once henchmen crossed the border with fentanyl, CBP could aim its thousands of personnel and resources at the traffickers. Unfortunately, aside from those assets, there was little else kinetically we could aim at Sinaloa. The United States had similar challenges foiling terrorists who lived outside the theater of war in Iraq or Afghanistan. It could not deploy a predator drone to off a jihadist in Indonesia or Egypt. Like Mexico, they are sovereign nations and allies. As with the war on terror, we did what Americans always do when confounded by physical limitations like geography. We look to technology to conjure a solution.

Notes

1 Information under this section heading draws heavily on a 2022 U.S. Senate policy report by the office of Senator Rob Portman. Readers may access the report in full using this information: "Addressing the Supply Chain of Synthetic Drugs in the United States." Fentanyl Synthetic Drugs Report 63. U.S. Senate Committee on Homeland Security and Governmental Affairs, February 28, 2023. https://www.hsgac.senate.gov/download/fentanyl-synthetic-drugs-report-63-.

2 Richard Nixon. Message to the Congress Transmitting Reorganization Plan 2 of 1973 Establishing the Drug Enforcement Administration. March 28, 1973. The American Presidency Project. https://www.presidency.ucsb.edu/documents/message-the-congress-transmitting-reorganization-plan-2-1973-establishing-the-drug.

3 Shook, Rachel. "Woodstock '69: Catalyst for Counterculture?" Misericordia Digital Commons, 2024. https://digitalcommons.misericordia.edu/research_posters2024/20/.

4 "Agencies—Customs Service." Federal Register, n.d. https://www.federalregister.gov/agencies/customs-service.

5 "DHS Law Enforcement Overview." U.S. Department of Homeland Security, n.d. https://www.dhs.gov/dhs-law-enforcement-overview.

6 Barr, L. "DHS Looking for Increased Authority to Investigate Drug Crimes." ABC News, February 23, 2024. https://abcnews.go.com/amp/Politics/dhs-increased-authority-investigate-drug-crimes/story?id=107457403.

7 Barr. "DHS Looking for Increased Authority."

8 "Prevalence/Trends." Monitoring the Future, n.d. https://monitoringthefuture.org/data/bx-by/drug-prevalence/#drug=%22Crack%22;"Prevalence/Trends." Monitoring the Future, n.d. https://monitoringthefuture.org/data/bx-by/drug-prevalence/#drug=%22Cocaine%22.

9 "Drug Trafficking and the Financing of Terrorism." United Nations Office on Drugs and Crime, n.d. https://www.unodc.org/unodc/en/frontpage/drug-trafficking-and-the-financing-of-terrorism.html.

10 Landay, Jonathan. "Profits and Poppy: Afghanistan's Illegal Drug Trade a Boon for Taliban." Reuters, August 16, 2021. https://www.reuters.com/world/asia-pacific/profits-poppy-afghanistans-illegal-drug-trade-boon-taliban-2021-08-16/.

11 "Public Opinion about Drugs." Bureau of Justice Statistics, n.d. https://bjs.ojp.gov/drugs-and-crime-facts/public-opinion-about-drugs.

12 "Public Opinion about Drugs."

13 "Staffing and Budget." Drug Enforcement Administration, 2021. https://www.dea.gov/data-and-statistics/staffing-and-budget; "The Cost of Immigration Enforcement and Border Security." American Immigration Council, September 23, 2024. https://www.americanimmigrationcouncil.org/research/the-cost-of-immigration-enforcement-and-border-security.

14 Riffkin, Rebecca. "Americans Name Terrorism as No. 1 U.S. Problem." Gallup, December 14, 2015. https://news.gallup.com/poll/187655/americans-name-terrorism-no-problem.aspx.

15 "Our Offices." U.S. Immigration and Customs Enforcement, March 7, 2025. https://www.ice.gov/about-ice/hsi/our-offices; "Staffing and Budget."

16 "CBP National Targeting Center." U.S. Customs and Border Protection, n.d. https://www.cbp.gov/frontline/cbp-national-targeting-center.

17 "What We Investigate." U.S. Department of Homeland Security, n.d. https://www.dhs.gov/hsi/investigate.

18 Puiu, Tibi. "The Math behind Why Mexico's Cartel War Is a Never-Ending Nightmare." *ZME Science*, December 20, 2024. https://www.zmescience.com/feature-post/pieces/the-math-behind-why-mexicos-cartel-war-is-a-never-ending-nightmare/.

19 Breslow, Jason M. "The Staggering Death Toll of Mexico's Drug War." PBS, July 27, 2015. https://www.pbs.org/wgbh/frontline/article/the-staggering-death-toll-of-mexicos-drug-war/.

9

The Digital *Arsenal of* Democracy

Much like the private sector, the government rarely innovates new technology from scratch. Instead, we identify a desired capability and search for existing components that could be combined in new ways to achieve the goal. Consider Uber. The goal was to disrupt the taxi industry by seamlessly matching amateur drivers with riders. Uber did not create a new type of car or mapping program to enable untrained chauffeurs. It did not invent the mobile phone to connect riders and drivers. In fact, Uber was unthinkable before the car was invented *and* before the iPhone was invented *and* before GPS was invented *and* before the internet was invented *and* before apps like Google Maps were invented. Instead, the gargantuan success of Uber, Lyft, and others stems from combining all these technologies. The rideshare services arose from a visionary idea. The service harnesses technology to connect a driver via the internet on their phone with a passenger seeking a ride. Then it employs GPS and simple user interfaces like apps to enable a driver to navigate from point A to point B.

The U.S. government has developed myriad technologies to fight bad guys. For our purposes, there are two relevant technological advancements since the early 2000s. Neither was built from scratch. Both were constructed by combining existing capabilities. Both will enable the fight against Sinaloa by adding yet more capabilities to them. Further, neither of these technological developments were built for fentanyl or Sinaloa. One was built for counterterrorism, and the other was constructed to combat child exploitation as it moved online when the internet spread. Both will be harnessed together to attack the Sinaloa fentanyl network.

One is the National Targeting Center (NTC) at Customs and Border Protection (CBP), founded in 2001, and the other is the Cyber Crime Center (C3) at HSI, founded in 1997.[1]

Targeting Terrorists

First let's turn to the National Targeting Center (NTC). Congress appropriated funds for the development of these tools to fight all types of bad guys. The NTC, however, would never have grown as big and as fast as it did if not compelled with an intense sense of urgency driven by the war on terror. As mentioned in chapter 8, the NTC contains petabytes of data that monitor the flow of billions of people and cargo around the planet at any given nanosecond. As Jorge Comas, director of the Counter Network Division at NTC, describes it, the function of NTC is to pinpoint humans or cargo targets for interdiction. Once a target is identified, the NTC illuminates the network of individuals and cargo associated with that target. Next it extrapolates the tactics and techniques used by the target's network to transport people and cargo around the world. Finally, once the NTC identifies a target and builds a model of its network and tactics, it can collaborate with other law enforcement or military partners to neutralize the threat.

The NTC is capable of these data analytic feats through access to incredibly unique data sets and what at the time was referred to as "big data analytics" but has now evolved into artificial intelligence (AI). It is unlikely anyone flies into Mexico or from Mexico to the United States without the NTC tracking it.[2] We gather a lot of information about people flying to Mexico because of 9/11. After 9/11 national security experts worried about potential terrorists flying to Mexico in hopes of crossing the Southwest Border undetected. Once in the United States, the terrorist could carry out attacks in America. Further, due to a transformative overhaul of data collection and integration after 9/11, the NTC can query databases across the intelligence apparatus. In the years immediately following 9/11, those queries enabled CBP to determine if someone was on the famed "no-fly list."[3]

The no-fly list was essential to intercept would-be terrorists before they boarded planes to the United States. The no-fly list failed in some comical, now infamous, ways.[4] Most experts, however, conclude it prevented terrorists from reaching the United States.[5] The no-fly list—all the data collected to create it and the billions in technology spent to analyze that data—had little to nothing to do with fentanyl or the Sinaloa cartel when it was established in 2001. However, today it seems almost purpose-built for Sinaloa.

It turns out all that data and the billions of dollars in tech analyzing the data is not just useful for combating terrorists. The data and tech is useful to combat the Sinaloa cartel, too. In the wake of 9/11, we cut a deal for a tailored data-sharing agreement with Mexico on people flying into Mexico bound for the United States.[6] We added another data-sharing agreement that scans information on anyone flying from Mexico to the United States. This data is relevant to target Sinaloa because it tells us a lot about the person traveling to Mexico or to the United States. We can derive even more information about the person from monitoring patterns in the data. El Chapo may have never taken a commercial flight outside Mexico; however, thousands of cartel affiliates, their children, attorneys, financial brokers, and chemical brokers fly into the United States or into Mexico every day. Through these data-sharing agreements, the NTC is able to capture and analyze detailed descriptions of these people.

After 9/11, we sought to prevent weapons of mass destruction from being disguised as normal cargo in a commercial truck, plane, train, or boat and transported across the Southwest Border. To address this threat, the NTC established several data collection programs on cargo destined for the United States. In the process, it established capabilities to monitor massive flows of cargo coming into the country from all parts of the world in ways never before possible. Here again, the role of these cargo data collection and analysis programs were born out of 9/11. They were designed to stop weapons of mass destruction from arriving in the United States. They were not intended to combat Sinaloa manufacturing and distribution of fentanyl in the United States. However, an enormous amount of the cargo flowing into North America, which includes Mexico, flows through a U.S. transit hub at some point. So in retrospect, it seems these too were purpose built to fight the Sinaloa cartel and the Chinese chemical companies shipping precursor chemicals and pill presses to the drug lords.

What is particularly relevant about the NTC's capabilities is that none of the capabilities were designed with the aim of taking out a kingpin like El Chapo or even Osama bin Laden. The NTC was designed to illuminate and disrupt terrorist networks, not terrorist kingpins. The campaign to disrupt and dismantle Sinaloa's fentanyl business requires the exact same type of tool. A global data integration and analytic capability that can illuminate and disrupt the Sinaloa network, not just Sinaloa kingpins.

A Beautiful Database

In 2011, I was sent by the DIIS Front Office to confer with Mike (not his real name as he still works in the intelligence field and chooses to remain anonymous) about a data integration program he was leading. As I walked into his office, I was immediately struck by its resemblance to a scene in the movie *A Beautiful Mind*. Russell Crowe, who is playing John Forbes Nash Jr., a math wizard obsessed with making breakthroughs in the field, has scribbled line after line of equations on the walls and windows. Crow is beyond flummoxed and on the brink of a breakdown.

Fortunately, Mike was not on the brink of a breakdown. However, he was as obsessed as Nash with making the dots and lines on his walls connect in a way that provided revolutionary insight into the world around us. The dots and lines traversed butcher paper on nearly every inch of the walls in the room. Mike was in the process of devising a plan to integrate some of the most arcane, siloed, and highly classified databases in U.S. government holdings so they could "talk" to one another.

People in the tech industry may scoff at this quandary. Companies like Amazon, Google, and J. P. Morgan, along with the cottage industry of data firms that have emerged to support them, connect and analyze massive data sets daily—far larger than those Mike faced. However, those data firms are not connecting data sets so top secret no one except for the three guys who maintain it know it exists. Also, the databases are built on top of multiple disparate commercial products whose contract terms disallow government alteration of database component parts or underlying structure, making it nearly impossible to alter one of these top secret databases to sync with another. On top of classification and integration challenges, the data is regulated by a patchwork of privacy and civil liberty protections. While these protections are important because we live in a free democracy, not an authoritarian dictatorship, it certainly complicated Mike's life. Further, we were a decade past 9/11. So, the early impetus to just "get it done" after the Towers fell expired long ago. That impetus had been replaced with bureaucratic malaise correcting for mistakes made in the previous ten years.

Mike was unfazed. This project was the culmination of a decade of his life's work using data to thwart terrorists since 9/11. People like Mike who began as analysts, data scientists, and statisticians got recruited into the intelligence apparatus of CBP. After 9/11, he was recruited along with Jorge and others to tackle the monumental task of integrating data sets across U.S. government holdings to spot and alert authorities before another 9/11 transpired. This project was his last foray to connect the most recalcitrant databases that were so siloed and classified they had yet to be fed into the NTC. He was torturing himself with this project that pitted him against deeply entrenched interests in the government because he had seen firsthand the power of data. He lived and breathed data and databases. Since 9/11, he kicked off the covers every morning with a drive to unlock data that uncovers terrorists and illuminates their support networks.

He also knew full well that we had not yet won the war on terror. In those days, people questioned whether we would ever "win" the war on terror. Terms like "the forever war" were now used to describe the war in Afghanistan.[7] Despite dire predictions of a never-ending war, Mike persisted. Just a couple years earlier he had a front-row seat to witness how this data analytics tool could stymie terrorists and save American lives.

The Needle in the Haystack

Najibullah Zazi was an Afghan-born U.S. resident. In 2009, a confidential informant tipped off the Federal Bureau of Investigation (FBI) that he had just packed a van in Colorado with explosives.[8] But we had no idea if the tip was accurate, where he was headed, or what he planned to incinerate. It's important to note here that after 9/11 authorities were flooded with a deluge of "tips" about terrorist plots daily. One of the most challenging parts of the job was determining which plots were real and which were bogus.

The FBI had little to go on except the tip. With only this information, the data wizards at NTC sprang into action. First, through a scan of his travel history, they found out that he had trekked to Pakistan.[9] Neighboring Afghanistan was at war, and many Afghans had fled to Pakistan. Zazi was born in Afghanistan. So, it's possible the guy just went to visit family. If the FBI chased down every Afghan who traveled home to visit family and whose nosy neighbors suspected him of being a terrorist, all the FBI would have the capacity to do is chase Afghans who posed no threat. So, the details of his travel weren't enough alone to make this tip rise to the top of all the tips the FBI and NTC were investigating that day. The NTC query received a few more hits, however.

Zazi ventured with two other people to Pakistan. The NTC only knew Zazi and the other three traveled together because of network analysis they had developed since 9/11.[10] Before that innovation was conceived, authorities would have no idea if he was traveling alone or with others on the plane. They certainly could not ascertain who those co-travelers were. But now, because of Mike and his colleagues' painstaking effort over the last seven years since 9/11, they were able to connect dots from Zazi's network.

Some of his coconspirators on the trip to Pakistan popped. They turned out to be suspected terrorists. Once the NTC pinpointed his coconspirators, Zarein Ahmedzay and Adis Medunjanin, it expanded its network analysis out further. Soon they knew the trio traveled to Pakistan to train in terrorist training camps.[11]

Immediately the FBI established surveillance. It blared "be on the lookout" (BOLO) advisories to all law enforcement. It scanned biometric indicators like facial recognition, fingerprints, and voice records of the three for any trace left in their wake. Consequently, the three were fingered in New York City. British intelligence intercepted email traffic with al-Qaeda operatives describing bomb-making techniques. Once authorities uncovered the three were in New

York, they raced against time. At any moment, their chase could terminate in a plume of smoke.

Then authorities located Zazi's van. Bomb-making plans had been downloaded on his laptop. The terrorists planned to bomb the New York subway.

Via wiretaps, biometric surveillance, international cooperation, and NTC data targeting, they snatched Zazi and his conspirators before they could harm anyone. The trio did not go down in a blaze of glory. Instead, they languished in a maximum security prison.

Mike knows they sat in prison, terrorist aims foiled, in part because of what he and his colleagues built at the NTC. Back in Mike's office in 2011, the scattered dots connected by zigzagging lines on endless streams of butcher paper was dizzying. Mike pointed and scribbled and paced and lost sleep. Unlike a Silicon Valley data start-up company executive, he wasn't losing sleep because he was stressed about missing a quarterly earnings goal. He lost sleep because he obsessed over connecting even more dots to reveal the next Zazi. He, like so many other unsung heroes at the NTC, believed deeply that we could illuminate the al-Qaeda network. Data was a religion. If we could gain better fidelity on terrorist travel patterns, associates, destinations, and communications, we could win the war on terror that so many at the time predicted was an unwinnable "forever war."

Mike's efforts were not in vain. We won.

A Network of Monsters

The other major technological development of the last twenty years at DHS is the HSI Cyber Crime Center (C3). The former chief of C3, Matt Swenson, who directed the organization from 2021 to 2022, spent time with me to explain how it was established and how it evolved. Much of what follows comes from that conversation.

The center was founded to combat the spread of child pornography as it transitioned from print and VHS onto the internet. Before the internet, if you were some scumbag who wanted to stare at naked kids it was incredibly risky to fulfill your deplorable urges. Joe Scumbag would need to somehow identify a distributor of this material—likely someone who abused a child they knew and filmed it. Then you would have to contact this person somehow, and if they didn't live in your city, you had to receive the child exploitation material in the mail. There obviously exists intense societal pressure against child predators. So, receiving child porn in the mail or just possessing it in one's home presents an enormous risk to anyone engaged in the abhorrent behavior.

Consequently, these monsters were some of the first groups to identify the internet as an ideal place to house a morbid content-sharing platform.[12] On the internet they could obtain and share child porn with anonymity. The shift was profound. Now the predators could communicate with thousands of other predators anonymously. They also provided positive instead of negative reinforcement to each other. In chat rooms and dark web marketplaces they normalized child sexual exploitation. In a world where most bad things—from murder rates, theft, starvation, and death from diseases—had plummeted for more than a century,[13] incidents of child exploitation skyrocketed. According to the U.S. National Center for Missing and Exploited Children, there has been a 900 percent increase in the number of credible tips regarding child abuse materials between 2012 and 2021 in the United States alone. The FBI reports a 422 percent increase in the number of federal prosecutions relating to child abuse materials nationwide between 2005 and 2019.[14] Even more confounding to authorities, unlike other criminals, child predators are largely driven by a deranged libido, not money. So, this cast of criminals does not operate in a hierarchy as a normal criminal syndicate. In most criminal enterprises, there is a boss and some top lieutenants who reap most of the profits from their illicit business. Profits flow down from there with the rank and file scraping up crumbs. Child porn is the opposite. There is no hierarchy. Often money isn't even involved. Instead of paying in dollars for the images, the criminals' currency is often more child porn instead of money.[15]

As cybercriminals have become more advanced and sophisticated, law enforcement tries to stay one step ahead. The internet and rapidly sharing information sites made this even more difficult. When law enforcement uses a new technique to catch cybercriminals, the criminals scour law enforcement affidavits that detail how we catch them and publish this information on dark web forums—so that they can learn how to evade authorities. It becomes a constant game of cat and mouse.

Eventually child porn consumers realized that law enforcement isn't allowed to produce child porn, even child porn they confiscated.[16] So child exploitation material serves as the secret password into the chat room. If you could produce your own child porn, they would admit you to the group. You proved you are not a cop.

Over time the whole industry evolved into a hybrid bartering and for-profit economy. It became a free online marketplace on the dark web where pedophiles traded horrific images to fulfill their grotesque fantasies. It spread as a leaderless, amorphous network of monsters. Some of the monsters were quite adept at cybersecurity and erected digital fortresses around their perverted playground. So no cops could obtain access to the creeps unless they broke the law themselves.

This type of law enforcement was alien to most federal agents. Normally an agent pinches a low-level criminal selling drugs or guns or knockoff Gucci bags. The cop arrests that guy and flips him. Under threat of many years in prison, the low-level goon rats out his boss. This continues until an industrious agent works her way up to the kingpin. In a perfect world, she rounds up the kingpin and his entire criminal enterprise.

Take this same agent and assign her to the child exploitation beat. She has all the sleuthing sensibility and training, but it only takes her so far. Maybe she arrests and flips a guy. But that guy just leads to another node in the network, not another rung up the ladder. She feels like she is just treading water. A federal agent wants to roll up a syndicate, not just nab one low-level perpetrator after another.

So she innovates. What if she could hack the digital infrastructure of the monsters' playground? What if she could burn the whole playground to the ground? It didn't take long for some of the most intellectually curious agents to imagine new options.

Soon they were scanning child predator networks for digital holes they could exploit. Once they identified a hole, they secured a court order and could hack their way into the network and everyone in it. Over the past twenty-five years since C3 was created, it produced a different type of cop—one who knew how to work the street and flip a stooge into a confidential informant. But after that agent was later assigned to a rotation at C3, she also learned how to fight criminals on the dark web and how to attack their most critical asset: digital infrastructure.

In short, C3 trained a generation of federal agents at HSI how to deprioritize kingpins and instead target networks: networks of leaderless monsters and networks of criminal assets, especially digital assets. These agents started attending hacker conferences like DEF CON to scout out more digital weapons.

Twenty-five years after C3's inception, its cybercops preside over a digital arsenal purpose built to hunt in networks. It is designed to unmask those lurking in the digital criminal underworld. It tracks contraband and profiles from one far-flung recess of the internet to another. It is built to expose a back door to a digital criminal marketplace and kick it open. Once the back door is pried open, it is hunting season for the agents on everyone inside.

The New Silk Road

The first major instance of a large, secure digital playground for bad guys was the Silk Road. It was not a primary source of child pornography, but its story is instructive to understand the digital criminal marketplaces that sprung up in the last twenty-five years as the internet spread. In 2011, a brilliant grad student from Penn State born in Texas named Ross Ulbricht was a committed libertarian.[17] He believed in a completely free market. Ulbricht saw the internet as a place where his utopian vision of a world with no laws could be realized.

To achieve his dream, Ross established a marketplace like Amazon. However, unlike Amazon, Ulbricht's marketplace was hosted on the dark web Tor network. Tor obfuscates web traffic by directing it through a series of encrypted nodes. Tor's anonymity makes it incredibly difficult for law enforcement to uncover the identity of users, their activities, or locations. Like Jeff Bezos, once his market platform was in place, Ross began recruiting customers and vendors. Unlike Bezos, however, Ross wasn't recruiting avid readers and bookstores eager to reach a global market. Ross was recruiting users and accomplished drug dealers. Like Bezos, Ross was drawn to names that evoked ancient places and mystical imagery. Amazon was taken. Instead, Ross chose the Silk Road. Of course, the Silk Road between China and Europe had the added benefit of being known over the centuries as an ethereal trade route traversing lands that seemed lawless to the Chinese and European merchants bent on fortune.

As Amazon took off, so, too, did the Silk Road.

Ulbricht's professionalism and cybersecurity prowess gained him success recruiting vendors. Through a series of Ross's clever technical decisions, vendors and customers felt secure buying and selling all manner of drugs, guns, and any other illicit contraband imaginable. Like Amazon, he established a rating system that enabled users to rate their experience with a vendor. They could opine whether narcotics purchased got them high or made them sick or never arrived. Bezos famously toiled countless hours on customer support and disputed claims. Similarly, Ulbricht administered an expansive customer support system and even devised a method to hold payments in escrow until consumers were satisfied with their purchase.[18]

Also, like Amazon, the Silk Road was constantly under attack from hackers trying to rob the platform. Bezos could turn to law enforcement to pursue thieves. Ross had to fight them off himself. Thus, Ulbricht became a cybersecurity wizard able to lock down identities and fortify anonymous payments. In a couple of years, Ulbricht's Silk Road transformed from little more than a secure blog, where a few tech-savvy college kids bought and sold weed, to a multibillion-dollar enterprise that housed tens of thousands of consumers and vendors.[19] It provided refuge to some of the most unscrupulous characters in the world. Cartels, mobsters, and hit men all roamed the Silk Road in search of fortune.

Maybe Bezos's and Ulbricht's most striking similarity was that neither one made or sold anything. They simply built an online network facilitating the exchange of goods and commerce. As stated earlier, HSI agents had developed a penchant for attacking criminal networks online.

Enter the Mongols

The Mongols are largely known for their brutal conquests of Central Asia, China, and Eastern Europe. Yet they don't receive nearly enough credit for their enlightened stance on religious tolerance, internationalism, the pursuit of scientific inquiry, and a rules-based free market. As such, they were also early proponents of the legitimate Silk Road. In fact, they were the self-proclaimed police of much of the land the Silk Road traversed.[20] It was nearly impossible for Genghis and his relatives to police every inch of such an expanse as the sprawling empire. Once they found systemic criminal behavior, however, they brought the hammer down and crushed roving bandits.

With tens of thousands of people engaged in the marketplace, authorities were bound to discover Amazon's evil twin. Like the Mongols before them, HSI agents and other federal law enforcement colleagues could not police every inch of the internet. However, when large-scale, systemic criminal behavior was identified, they too brought the hammer down on the criminal market.

Additionally, Ulbricht inevitably made mistakes. His mistakes were highly technical. He used the same fake username and email address across several platforms. He poorly configured a few of his networks. He also failed to grasp law enforcement's ability to track cryptocurrency.[21] Ulbricht innovated brilliantly. But he knew he was on borrowed time. He just miscalculated how little time it was.

The FBI, DEA, and others began to chip away at his facade of 1s and 0s. HSI agents aimed their digital arsenal at the Silk Road. They also gumshoed it, flipping one buyer and seller after another.

Agents at C3, like Jared Der-Yeghiayan, attempted to sow distrust in the dark web marketplaces. He accomplished this with a two-pronged approach. First, he infiltrated the Silk Road as an undercover agent. He ensured dark market criminals didn't know who they could trust. Second, he hacked the technology that offered a layer of anonymity for the criminals. All technology contains bugs, glitches, and insecure software code. Jared scanned the network for vulnerabilities to attack.[22] Once he found a vulnerability, he pulled back the veil of anonymity. Ulbricht had to be perfect all the time. Jared just had to find one flaw.

In fact, the first breadcrumbs that led to Ross were a few mistakes he made several years earlier. Just before he launched the Silk Road, he posted on a niche drug website about the need for a site like the Silk Road. Soon after, he posted on the same site directing people to the Silk Road. That mere fact of being the first user on an arcane narcotics blog to recommend people check out the Silk Road was a clue.[23] Cyber investigators refer to it as a digital bread crumb.

Digital breadcrumbs never go stale. C3 agents exploit similar digital breadcrumbs all day. Even breadcrumbs left decades in the past can be attributed back to criminals. Now that they had a lead, the hunt was on to unmask the first person to post about the Silk Road.

Next, by flipping customers in the exchange and exploiting security configuration flaws, C3 agents used their digital tools and undercover authorities to impersonate criminals in the Silk Road. By the time Ulbricht was cuffed, Agent Der-Yeghiayan had risen to a full-fledged moderator of the Silk Road. Unbeknownst to Ulbricht, he communicated to Agent Der-Yeghiayan several times a day about strategies to manage the site, improve user experience, and increase profits.

Authorities followed the digital breadcrumbs that ultimately revealed his true identity. Agent Der-Yeghiayan was undercover, conspiring directly with Ross's digital persona and collecting evidence to put him behind bars. Investigators were closing in.

Relying on Bitcoin may have been his most dire mistake. Cryptocurrency changed the game for Ulbricht. Before Bitcoin, criminals operating online were forced to use centralized systems of payment that functioned like PayPal but were operated by criminals instead of legitimate businesspeople. Systems like E-gold, Liberty Reserve, and others operated without any anti–money laundering or know-your-customer requirements.[24] The problem with these systems for Ulbricht was that a buyer or seller had to provide some form of unique identifier. Also, their personal information was stored in a centralized location like a server. If these central servers were seized by law enforcement, the cops could snoop through all their information. The criminals also had to trust people running the server. Ulbricht trusted no one maintaining these servers.

Bitcoin offered another option. It purported to provide total anonymity to buyers and sellers. Bitcoin transactions are recorded on a public ledger (the blockchain), but they are pseudonymous. Addresses are not directly linked to real-world identities.[25] Ulbricht revolutionized online criminal behavior in his expansive use of Bitcoin. Ultimately, though, C3 and others were able to track and map transactions. This enabled agents to pinpoint buyers, sellers, and Ross.

Authorities ultimately took down Ulbricht in 2013 with a clever ruse at a library in San Francisco, California.[26] Ross was a new kind of criminal who, like Jeff Bezos, does not make or sell anything. He provided an online criminal marketplace and got rich off commissions.[27] This new type of criminal called for a new type of agent. C3 produces those agents in spades. They were adept at wielding cyber tools to churn through cryptocurrency records. They honed unique skills to operate undercover online. They also trained with expert hackers to probe cybersecurity flaws in online marketplaces. Once they obtained a court order, they could exploit those flaws to hack away at bad-guy operations on the dark web.

The Full Package

When the NTC and C3 were established, fentanyl was still an obscure pharmaceutical product. No one at the time imagined it would be an insidious poison ripping through communities across the country. Certainly, the Sinaloa cartel existed back then; however, neither the NTC nor C3 were built specifically to attack a regional cartel in Mexico trafficking marijuana and cocaine. Instead, these state-of-the-art technology assets were built to target all types of criminals. Yet both were put on steroids to dismantle terrorist and child pornography networks as those threats loomed.[28]

Twenty years later the two assets have emerged as juggernauts unto themselves. Both were instrumental in prosecuting the war on terror. Both required a new type of agent who thought in terms of networks not kingpins. Moreover, these new agents thought beyond human networks. They thought about IT networks, transportation networks, and cargo networks. Consequently, these new agents demanded the government buy or build tools to run counternetwork operations.

Today CBP has the ability to track detailed travel patterns of people traveling into the United States via any mode of transportation. They know where cargo around the world originates and terminates at any moment. Through data and advanced analytics, they can gather intricate details about travelers and cargo for criminal or investigative purposes.

These global shipping and travel insights are coupled with HSI's fidelity on individuals and assets across the internet. They are adept at investigating cryptocurrency. They operate undercover digital personas on the dark web, and they scan, probe, and ultimately hack digital infrastructure online.

Combining these capabilities engineered an unprecedented suite of tools, none of which were designed for countering Sinaloa. However, Sinaloa's mass poisoning of Americans has ensured that these tools, once aimed at the defeated al-Qaeda and the Islamic State of Iraq and Syria (ISIS), are now aimed squarely at the Sinaloa cartel, the Chinese chemical companies that supply them, and anyone aiding and abetting either.

Notes

1 CBP National Targeting Center. U.S. Customs and Border Protection. January 2002. https://www.cbp.gov/frontline/cbp-national-targeting-center. DHS unveils major expansion of ICE Cyber Crimes Center | Homeland Security. U.S. Department of Homeland Security. July 2015.https://www.dhs.gov/archive/news/2015/07/22/dhs -unveils-major-expansion-ice-cyber-crimes-center

2 "Fact Sheet: APIS Preventing Terrorists from Boarding International Flights and Vessels Destined for or Departing from the U.S." U.S. Department of Homeland Security, n.d. https://www.cbp.gov/sites/default/files/documents/apis_factsheet_3.pdf.

3 "Fact Sheet: APIS Preventing Terrorists from Boarding International Flights."

4 "Declassified FBI Documents Suggest Shoddy Management of 'No Fly' List, Fail to Show How Innocent Americans Can Get Names Cleared." American Civil Liberties Union, September 13, 2005. https://www.aclu.org/press-releases/declassified-fbi -documents-suggest-shoddy-management-no-fly-list-fail-show-how.

5 "The Progress and Pitfalls of the Terrorist Watch List." U.S. Government Publishing Office, November 8, 2007. https://www.govinfo.gov/content/pkg/CHRG -110hhrg48979/html/CHRG-110hhrg48979.htm#:~:text=According%20%0Ato%20 Customs,during%20today%27s%20hearing.

6 "Smart Border: 22 Point Agreement—U.S.-Mexico Border Partnership Action Plan." U.S. Department of State, March 21, 2002. https://2001-2009.state.gov/p/wha/rls/fs /8909.htm.

7　Donati, Jessica. "The Hidden Cost of America's Forever War." *The Atlantic*, November 14, 2022. https://www.theatlantic.com/international/archive/2021/01/america-forever -war-afghanistan/617776/.

8　"Najibullah Zazi Pleads Guilty to Conspiracy to Use Explosives against Persons or Property in U.S., Conspiracy to Murder Abroad, and Providing Material Support to Al Qaeda." Federal Bureau of Investigation, n.d. https://archives.fbi.gov/archives/ newyork/press-releases/2010/nyfo022210.htm.

9　"Three Arrested in Ongoing Terror Investigation (2009-09-20)." Wikisource, November 23, 2021. https://en.wikisource.org/wiki/Three_arrested_in_ongoing _terror_investigation_%282009-09-20%29.

10　Dignan, Larry. "How Internet Surveillance, IT Sleuth Work Helped Indict Suspected Terrorist Zazi." *ZDNET*, September 25, 2009. https://www.zdnet.com/article/how -internet-surveillance-it-sleuth-work-helped-indict-suspected-terrorist-zazi/.

11　Dignan. "How Internet Surveillance."

12　Stanley, Janet. *Child Abuse and the Internet*. New York: Wiley, 2001. https://popcenter .asu.edu/sites/default/files/problems/child_pornography/PDFs/Stanley_2001.pdf.

13　Matthews, Dylan. "23 Charts and Maps That Show the World Is Getting Much, Much Better." *Vox*, October 17, 2018. https://www.vox.com/2014/11/24/7272929/global -poverty-health-crime-literacy-good-news.

14　"National Strategy for Child Exploitation Prevention and Interdiction." U.S. Department of Justice, June 12, 2023, 2–3. https://www.justice.gov/psc/national -strategy-child-exploitation-prevention-and-interdiction.

15　Liggett, Roberta. "Commercial Child Sexual Abuse Markets on the Dark Web." Research article. School of Criminal Justice, Michigan State University, 2021. https://cj .msu.edu/_assets/pdfs/cina/CINA-White_Papers-Liggett_Commercial_Child_Sexual _Abuse_Markets_Dark_Web.pdf.

16　"Child Sexual Abuse Material." National Center for Missing and Exploited Children, 2021. https://www.justice.gov/d9/2023-06/child_sexual_abuse_material_2.pdf.

17　Lim, Naomi. "Who Is Ross Ulbricht, the Prison Inmate Who Could Be Key to Trump's Libertarian Support." *Washington Examiner*, May 26, 2024. https://www .washingtonexaminer.com/news/campaigns/presidential/3017931/ross-ulbricht -prison-inmate-key-trump-libertarian-support/.

18　"Manhattan U.S. Attorney Announces Seizure of Additional $28 Million Worth of Bitcoins Belonging to Ross William Ulbricht, Alleged Owner and Operator of 'Silk Road' Website." U.S. Attorney's Office, Southern District of New York, October 25, 2013. https://www.justice.gov/archive/usao/nys/pressreleases/October13/ SilkRoadSeizurePR.php.

19　"Ross Ulbricht, aka Dread Pirate Roberts, Sentenced to Life in Federal Prison for Creating, Operating 'Silk Road' Website." U.S. Immigration and Customs

Enforcement, November 18, 2024. https://www.ice.gov/news/releases/ross-ulbricht
-aka-dread-pirate-roberts-sentenced-life-federal-prison-creating.

20 Haozhou, Zhang. "The Mongol Empire and the Prosperity of the Silk Road." *Journal of Education, Humanities and Social Sciences* 8 (2023). https://doi.org/10.54097/ehss.v8i .4393.

21 "How OSINT Took Down the Dark Web's Silk Road." Skope Now, June 9, 2023. https://www.skopenow.com/news/how-osint-took-down-the-dark-webs-silk-road.

22 "Inside the FBI'S Search for the Dark Web Kingpin of Silk Road." WTOP News, November 11, 2020. https://wtop.com/national/2020/11/inside-the-fbis-search-for -the-dark-web-kingpin-of-silk-road/.

23 Zbrog, Matt. "Forensic Accounting: Cracking the Silk Road & Capturing Darknet's DPR." Forensics Colleges, March 6, 2024. https://www.forensicscolleges.com/blog/ forensics-casefile/silk-road.

24 "Liberty Reserve Founder Pleads Guilty to Money Laundering." U.S. Immigration and Customs Enforcement, November 18, 2024. https://www.ice.gov/news/releases/liberty -reserve-founder-pleads-guilty-money-laundering.

25 "Is Bitcoin Anonymous?" River Learn, n.d. https://river.com/learn/bitcoin-privacy -and-anonymity/.

26 Mullin, Joe. "Sunk: How Ross Ulbricht Ended up in Prison for Life." *Ars Technica*, May 30, 2015. https://arstechnica.com/tech-policy/2015/05/sunk-how-ross-ulbricht -ended-up-in-prison-for-life/.

27 "Silk Road: How Ross Ulbricht Sold $183 Million Worth of Hard Drugs in 2 Years | Brain Labs." *Medium*, November 28, 2024. https://medium.com/brain-labs/silk-road -how-ross-ulbricht-sold-183-million-worth-of-hard-drugs-in-2-years-5b9880537232.

28 "HSI Combats Child Exploitation at Home and Abroad." U.S. Immigration and Customs Enforcement, February 10, 2025. https://www.ice.gov/features/child -exploitation.

10

Operation Gallant Phoenix

Another more subtle aspect of attacking Sinaloa online was that it required us to map and disrupt the Sinaloa network, not just one individual at the helm. This subtle shift in approach marked a wholesale departure from how the U.S. government typically would have pursued a criminal outfit. Normally, agents would assess a criminal group and target key people in order to topple the kingpin. Nabbing the top don was important for promotions and bonuses. Little favor was shown to those agents who simply took down the don's flunkies. Alternatively, our agents and intelligence officers who cut their teeth on the war on terror, consistently cited something called Operation Gallant Phoenix (OGP) as a model for what we sought to accomplish.

As we based so much of our strategy on counterterrorism, it's instructive to understand a cornerstone program of the global war on terror, around which we patterned much of our strategy. That program is the aforementioned Operation Gallant Phoenix (OGP).

Gallant Phoenix first seeped into our conversations as a result of John Tien's focus on improving our intelligence. His frame of reference was the wars in Iraq and Afghanistan. There an intense focus on accelerating the intelligence-to-action cycle evolved dramatically since the early 2000s. Tien visited the person who had helped educate him on how to create actionable intelligence in a war zone: General Stanley McChrystal. McChrystal had been the commander of NATO's International Security Assistance Force (ISAF) in Afghanistan when

Tien was the National Security Council (NSC) senior director for Afghanistan for President Obama. As General McCrystal has described,

> When an operation was set in motion, information was continuously communicated to and from the combat team, so that intelligence specialists miles away could alert the team on the ground about what they could expect to find of value at the scene and where it might be. Intelligence recovered on the spot was instantly pushed digitally from the target to analysts who could translate it into actionable data while the operators would still be clearing rooms and returning fire. This knowledge was immediately cycled back through the loop to our intelligence and surveillance forces following the results of the raid in real time.
>
> The intelligence recovered on one target in, say, Mosul, might allow for another target to be found, fixed upon, and finished in Baghdad, or even Afghanistan. Sometimes, finding just one initial target could lead to remarkable results: The network sometimes completed this cycle three times in a single night in locations hundreds of miles apart—all from the results of the first operation. As our operations in Iraq and Afghanistan intensified, the number of operations conducted each day increased tenfold, and both our precision and success rate also rose dramatically.[1]

Customs and Border Protection (CBP) and Homeland Security Investigations (HSI) commanded robust intelligence operations. However, they were siloed to each one's discrete purposes. Worse, when it came to fentanyl and Sinaloa, they were largely disconnected from the broader intelligence community (IC) of the U.S. government. So, Tien harangued the IC for more intelligence that could be actioned, meaning an agent could extract useful information from it to take down a bad guy. I groped around the department for a Sherpa who knew the U.S. intelligence apparatus. More important, I needed someone who could call bullshit on anyone feeding me creative reasons why the IC could not help us with Sinaloa.

I called John Cohen, an old friend who had overseen the Intelligence and Analysis (I&A) agency at the Department of Homeland Security (DHS). The explicit reason I&A exists at DHS is to serve as our liaison to the vast U.S.

intelligence community, made up of eighteen intelligence agencies,[2] each possessing its own capabilities and raison d'être. However, I&A is a relatively new intelligence agency established after DHS was erected in the ashes of 9/11. Also, I&A doesn't live in the military or other intel agencies. It lives in DHS, a sprawling law enforcement and emergency response department with amorphous and shifting needs. Thus, I&A exists as somewhat of an anomaly in the IC. I didn't expect Cohen would conjure some intel silver bullet provided by I&A. In some ways, he gave me the next best thing: Phil Groven. Cohen said, "Look, if I tried to spin up an internal program for you on this it would take forever and be a huge waste of your time. Also, most of what you want is with the broader IC. They will just give you and I&A the run-around for months on end until you get sick of asking and give up."

John went on, "But I know a guy. He is someone we recruited from the IC a few years ago. I don't want to go too much into what he does. His background is highly relevant for what you are trying to do." Moreover, John said, "He can find the nooks and crannies of the IC that have the capabilities or types of info you are looking for. Most important, he can go with you to meetings with the IC and tell you whether they were bullshitting you or not."

Somewhat put off, I responded, "Yeah, OK. Sure. I will talk to your guy. I will take what I can get, I guess."

I asked for his contact information, and Cohen said, "No, I will have him call you."

Shortly thereafter, I received a call from Phil Groven. Like so many others in this world, his career was born out of 9/11. He had been working in finance in New York on that day. Immediately after the attack, he quit his lucrative private-sector job and joined the intelligence community. Over the last twenty years, he cut his teeth on the intel ropes in various three-letter agencies. He literally and virtually chased terrorists around the world so they could be "found and fixed" abroad before they could harm the homeland. In the symbiotic relationship the IC and military were developing, his task was the "find" part of the equation. Once the terrorist was found, the intelligence on him was handed to his counterparts in the military to lethally "fix" the guy before he attacked the homeland or U.S allies.

Groven's winding career path led him to DHS, where he liaised with the Central Intelligence Agency (CIA) for I&A. Around the time we connected, the aforementioned fifteen thousand Haitians under the bridge appeared out of nowhere. I queried Groven about how we can push the IC to ensure we don't miss major developments just miles off our southern border. He referenced a program in Jordan called Operation Gallant Phoenix.

Later, I suggested we could not wait for the whole government to rally around fighting Sinaloa and fentanyl. Rather, I argued for mobilizing a "coalition of the willing." Tien and others were in agreement. Groven again resurfaced Operation Gallant Phoenix as a potential model for our efforts.

Tien alternated glad-handing and haranguing National Security Agency (NSA), CIA, Treasury, Southern Command, and Special Operations Command to eventually become eager participants in our coalition of the willing. Unbeknownst to me, these entities all participated in Operation Gallant Phoenix. So when we offhandedly suggested OGP may provide a model for our efforts, a surprising number of heads nodded on screens in front of us.

Gallantly Fighting Terrorists

Operation Gallant Phoenix was a welcome innovation in the war on terror that sprouted from an atrocious war crime committed by the terror group Islamic State of Iraq and Syria (ISIS). In January 2015, ISIS burned a Jordanian fighter pilot alive. This rightly incensed the Jordanian people and, most consequentially, the king of Jordan, Abdullah II bin Al-Hussein. As a result of the atrocity, the king led a raid into Syria and Iraq to attack ISIS and its sympathizers.[3] The ISIS attack created the political space for the United States to persuade Jordan to host a new operation. The operation knitted together intelligence across the region to stymie ISIS operations.

A global intelligence network monitoring al-Qaeda and ISIS already existed. However, operations to date were largely focused on a lethal "finish" in Iraq or Syria. ISIS had stepped up efforts to recruit so-called foreign fighters from countries outside the Levant.[4] Many of these countries, especially in Europe, were places where the United States could not just drop a bomb on a target. Further, counterterrorism officials were concerned particularly about the uptick in foreign fighters that traveled to fight with ISIS in Syria or Iraq and then returned to Europe. These militants posed a significant risk to launch attacks on their native soil.

The unique threat required a new approach. Soon the military's top brass broadened the concept of "finish" to include law enforcement actions and other disruptions to the terrorist networks. Operation Gallant Phoenix was born. OGP was housed in a sprawling facility sitting at the tip of Iraq and Syria in Jordan. It was in the middle of nowhere. A junkyard was its sole neighbor. Those assigned to the operation had literally nothing to do but hunt terrorists. The participants hailed from most U.S. intelligence agencies, dozens of military organizations, and every major law enforcement agency, including Secret Service, CBP, HSI, the Federal Bureau of Investigation (FBI), and the Drug Enforcement Administration (DEA).[5]

It also included foreign partners from across Europe and elsewhere. OGP committed to a foundational principle instrumental to its early success: leads were protected for the originator of the lead. For example, French law enforcement may provide information on a foreign fighter trekking from France through Syria to Iraq. If the U.S. Army knew where the militant was in Syria, the army would not automatically take out the ISIS foot soldier. The army would let the French agents work their case against the militant. Ideally, the French would pick up several of his coconspirators in France before he got "finished" by a Predator drone in Syria.

In this way, participants of OGP achieved enhanced insight into the whole network of ISIS. It was conceived with just eight countries as part of the effort. As the chairman of the Joint Chiefs of Staff, General Joseph Francis Dunford Jr., said, "Three things make these terror groups interconnected and transregional: the flow of foreign fighters, the flow of resources and their message."[6] So the effort began to focus on the ISIS network. The network disseminated messages to recruit foreign fighters from Europe and around the world. The network employed complicated financial and logistics programs to ferry individuals to the front in Iraq or Syria. OGP watched how the foreign fighters maneuvered around the globe and into the main theater of war. OGP was novel because it broadened the scope of its focus beyond foreign fighters. It tracked the narratives, digital platforms, and online influencers the foreign fighters followed. It mined data on finances paid from individuals to transportation vendors or hotels or training camps in theater.

OGP surveilled the whole network transferring foreign fighters, and other contraband, to ISIS. Military leadership's key innovation was that sometimes intelligence was best deployed in the hands of law enforcement. An HSI agent in Chicago could seize a bank account of an ISIS broker paying for bus tickets. A Belgian agent could take down a vocal religious leader recruiting foreign fighters online or whose facilities are used as a makeshift hostel for foreign fighters. Tunisian authorities could indict corrupt border officials producing fake passports for would-be foreign fighters.

Moreover, the most effective use of intelligence might be to sequence law enforcement activities *and* execute a lethal finish on the logistics operator receiving foreign fighters at Syria's border. In some ways, this strategy may appear patently obvious. To those on the outside, the opaque war machine conducting the war on terror may seem a monolith. In reality, the war machine is composed of distinct countries, departments, and agencies. Each brings its own strategies, budget, and personnel to the fight. Further, individuals operate within the unique incentive structure of their organization's priorities.

In December 2024, I conducted a brief interview with the former U.S. ambassador to NATO, General Douglas Lute. During that interview, he explained that in the wars that followed the 9/11 attacks began as conventional operations and transitioned to counterterrorism and counterinsurgency operations. After initial success in both Afghanistan and Iraq, counterterrorism and counterinsurgence dominated the U.S. military approaches for the next two decades. Initially many military operations focused on eliminating enemy leaders. For years the counterterrorism campaign featured a "top 10" list of al-Qaeda leaders, which was refreshed repeatedly as individuals were killed or captured. After the fall of Baghdad in Iraq, U.S. troops sought "former regime elements," collected as a deck of fifty-two playing cards with Saddam Hussein as the lead target. This decapitation approach led to years of frustration as enemy leaders were quickly replaced. Yet their movements proved resilient. For example, even after the iconic leader Osama bin Laden was eliminated in the 2011 raid in Pakistan, al-Qaeda as an organization remains. Therefore, U.S. strategy shifted gradually to address the roots of the terrorism and insurgencies they faced: political, economic, ideological, and sectarian motivations. This broader, more comprehensive approach acknowledged that simply eliminating leaders was insufficient, and "it takes a network to defeat a network." By 2014 and the rise of ISIS, this network approach proved relatively effective in eliminating the so-called geographic caliphate in northern Syria and Iraq.

Under the new paradigm of OGP, the commander and chief lieutenants broadened their view to the entire network feeding foreign fighters, resources, and propaganda to the enemy. Then the chief lieutenants' job performance was measured by how they disrupted and degraded the entire network. This was all geared, as General Dunford said, toward "total annihilation" of ISIS.[7] The military learned in Vietnam that success cannot be measured by body counts. During the war on terror, it also learned that wars cannot be won by simply cutting off the head of the snake. OGP was a manifestation of that realization.

The OGP juggernaut swelled its ranks to more than 250 staff from around the globe—all of whom collected, analyzed, and shared information in ways unheard of before. If 9/11 was the catalyst that propelled U.S. agencies to share information in ways unthinkable before that fateful morning, then foreign fighters were the catalyst that compelled the United States and its allies to share information across law enforcement in ways never before attempted.[8]

Gallantly Fighting Sinaloa

One can understand how Groven and others who worked at OGP immediately gravitated toward that model to combat Sinaloa. U.S. and Mexican law enforcement employed a kingpin strategy for decades to no avail. Most recently the J. J. Abrams–esque saga with El Chapo was the quintessential example of these efforts. Backed by his own heavily armed militia, El Chapo was captured, escaped, recaptured, incarcerated, escaped, chased, recaptured, extradited, and reincarcerated. These dramatic events were punctuated with endless gangland firefights against police and military officials. Sometimes the firefights even included corrupt local police fighting against the military. The saga was replete with bizarre cameos by none other than star power like Sean Penn and Mexican starlet Kate del Castillo.[9]

Thousands of U.S. and Mexican military and law enforcement officials were dedicated to taking this kingpin down. Yet Sinaloa didn't miss a beat[10] after El Chapo was finally extradited. Licking their wounds from this effort and so many others like it, our men and women in uniform yearned for another approach. We raised Groven's suggestion that we implement an OGP model. Several senior officials at HSI and CBP not only agreed but had direct experience with OGP. They had intimate experience in counterterrorism and all benefited from the OGP intelligence.

They also recognized the similarities between challenges we face with both Sinaloa and ISIS. The United States could not simply drop bombs in France, Belgium, or Tunisia on would-be foreign fighters headed to the front. Similarly, we could not simply bomb Sinaloa fentanyl labs in Mexico or fentanyl precursor chemical plants in China. Like foreign fighters, the flow of cartel foot soldiers was also international. Seamlessly interconnected networks of sicarios, brokers, and financiers endlessly ebbed and flowed between the United States, Mexico, and China to keep gears of the massive Sinaloa enterprise churning.

Sinaloa financial entanglements in the United States were deemed a particularly high-value target for our agents. The labyrinthine holdings of the cartel executives was legendary, and an enormous portion of this financial web was invested in the United States. American real estate, front companies, planes, and yachts were only a few assets the dons used to shroud their money.[11] Several agencies—and, critically, Mexican intelligence—were required to uncover and seize the ill-gotten funds.

OGP constantly scanned the whole ISIS distribution network for vulnerabilities in flow of foreign fighters. Similarly, our agents were keenly interested in Sinaloa's recruiting efforts and process. Our agents fixated on transportation experts, real estate brokers, chemists, lawyers, accountants, and weapons distributors.

Unlike ISIS, Sinaloa isn't motivated by ideology. It is solely motivated by profit. Despite that difference, here, too, our operation drew inspiration from OGP. OGP sought to monitor, infiltrate, and disrupt the propaganda machine of ISIS that recruited foreign fighters. Sinaloa didn't have an ideology; however, it maintained a brand similar to the aforementioned Robin Hood. It also had thousands of young aspiring banditos who, like other people their age, can't help themselves from documenting every minute detail of their lives on social media.[12] Sinaloa astutely cultivated its Robin Hood brand for years to both win over the local population and instill fear in rivals. The kingpin strategy put little effort into challenging that message or exploiting the endless deranged social media posts from Gen Z cartel members.

The Campaign Plan

Tien recruited his friend and former army colleague, Colonel Fernando Lujan, from the National Defense University to assemble a campaign plan. Colonel Lujan took lessons learned in the twenty-year war on terror and applied them to the fight against fentanyl and Sinaloa. Most important for us, he was part of the early team that oversaw OGP.

CBP and HSI alternately hosted Colonel Lujan in hours of whiteboarding sessions with the best and brightest from their organizations and the interagency. Gallant Phoenix served as a template for the planning sessions.

Colonel Lujan was a career military officer with humble beginnings in a small predominantly Hispanic town on the west side of San Antonio, Texas. He toiled away in school and work until securing a spot at West Point. Later he served in the Special Forces and spent three years at the National Security Council in the White House. Colonel Lujan was born in the United States but maintained close ties to family members who had immigrated here. He was initially wary of taking on an operation he thought could be used to persecute migrants. The migrants in his view, like many from his own family, were just people striving for a better life. The last thing he wanted to take part in, much less lead, was a military planning process targeted at migrants.

I laid out our goals over lunch at the Homeland Security Executive Dining Room. The Executive Dining Room (EDF) is where the seniormost leaders at DHS dine and host special guests when we want to impress them. Unlike other executive dining facilities at departments like State and the Pentagon, DHS's appeal isn't owed to its museum-esque ambiance. The DHS facility is ideal to wow visitors because the Coast Guard chefs are the best in the military. They routinely best their adversaries in the other branches of the military in culinary contests.[13]

So while the Coast Guard chefs dazzled our palates, I attempted to woo Lujan for our cause. I laid out the prospect of developing a campaign plan that targeted the very criminal organization oppressing migrants: Sinaloa. I also sprinkled in some facts about China's role in the fentanyl trade to sweeten the pot. Finally, the Coast Guard served up one of their decadent chocolate desserts. With Lujan fully satiated, I flatly interjected that fentanyl was killing the equivalent of one 9/11 a week. This factoid always made counterterrorism warriors stand up and take notice. Colonel Lujan was on board.

Colonel Lujan shepherded a plan for DHS's version of Gallant Phoenix through the fall and winter of 2022. The operation consisted of three main lines of action inspired by efforts against ISIS and al-Qaeda. Our shorthand for the lines of action was: "illuminate, enable, disrupt." The first line of effort sought to illuminate the cartel network. In the fight against ISIS, the military and intelligence community realized that many parts of the government acquired key pieces of information about terrorist networks; however, no one central entity analyzed all the knowledge of the network in one place. So decision-makers struggled to decide which parts of the network were most vital to ISIS.

We found ourselves in the same place vis-à-vis Sinaloa. There was a lot of information on Sinaloa, but it was diffuse throughout the massive federal government intelligence, military, and law enforcement holdings. Many parts of the government knew something about its small piece of the cartel, but no one understood the entire network.

Groven arranged briefings from a laundry list of three-letter agencies. In every meeting, agents or intelligence officers would regale us with astounding intelligence collection capabilities and astounding insights gleaned from surveillance of Sinaloa affiliates. Two aspects of the intelligence became clear. First, except for specific case data held in Organized Crime Drug Enforcement Task Forces (OCDETF),[14] a database maintained by DOJ, none of the intelligence repositories shared information related to the Sinaloa cartel specifically. The CIA data lived in their system, DEA in theirs, HSI in its system, and so on. Second, the data was almost exclusively tied to individuals, not the network as a whole. Any one of the three-letter agencies inspecting Sinaloa could draw a pretty accurate relational map. In presentations, these criminal relationship maps often resemble those on cop shows where the zig-zag connection lines between thugs all lead to the kingpin in the center.

The OCDETF system was a huge step forward years ago when it combined all federal government case data. For example, it enabled anyone who had a case against El Chapo to access information from anyone else investigating El Chapo. This helped officers deconflict competing cases against the same target. But these tools did not indicate which mechanic shops in Tijuana the gangsters employed to install hidden drug compartments in cars, for example. That was the type of network information we sought.

Individual criminal records were useful when building a case against an individual. Building cases against individual criminals had been the raison d'être of law enforcement for centuries. Over time, bespoke databases sprung up holding terabytes of information related to specific criminals. Unfortunately, they proved ineffective in mapping the contours of the broader Sinaloa network. For example, they couldn't answer critical questions: What did their IT systems link to? What financial institutions did they use? Which construction companies built their homes and tunnels into the United States? None of the databases could illuminate such details all in one place. That was exactly the type of information Colonel Lujan pushed our team to uncover and map.

We fixated on the issue and began to make progress. For example, for months we debated on the best way to track Sinaloa capos' finances. Then in one meeting with HSI, we had a breakthrough. A tech program they developed in their Innovation Lab could merge petabytes of Treasury Department financial crime data with HSI case data on Sinaloa gangsters. This data integration illuminated the intersection of financial flows and the Sinaloa C-Suite executives under investigation. This provided one of the few eureka moments in our campaign against fentanyl. It enabled agents to uncover in hours what used to take months of investigation.

If we were not focused on "illuminating the network" as Colonel Lujan suggested, we would never have ascribed such a high priority to connecting these data sets. CBP took a cue from HSI's success with Treasury. CBP integrated some of its massive shipping and international travel data with both HSI's case data and Treasury information. Once complete, HSI's case data and Treasury's financial activity could be cross-referenced with precursor shipments around the globe.

Colonel Lujan's second pillar, "enable," was also derived from the war on terror. Once illuminated, we must enable our U.S. government network of agencies and allies to prosecute a campaign against the cartels. But like our diffuse intelligence, the parts of the U.S. government attacking the cartel were also siloed. Specific individuals or activities were pursued for prosecution. They were not collectively analyzing the network as a whole to determine which nodes presented the most valuable targets for attack. Our next task was to enable our network to attack the Sinaloa network. We had to architect a more powerful and sophisticated good-guy network to attack the bad-guy network.

Enabling the disparate parts of the U.S. government and its international partners, in particular Mexico, to row in the same direction was a mammoth undertaking. Colonel Lujan insisted the "enable" aspect of Gallant Phoenix was crucial. According to him, collocating every relevant agency in the war on terror—from DOD, to the intelligence community, law enforcement, and even dozens of foreign governments at OGP in Jordan—was critical to success.

Conversely, many of our personnel were stuffed in offices across the Washington, DC, area and abroad. They had families. They had to take their kids to soccer practice. Also, post-COVID-19, many people didn't schlep to an office at all. The Gallant Phoenix experience in Jordan was impossible to re-create. We could not trap everyone in a building in the middle of the desert with nothing but a junkyard in sight and no personal life. So we adapted. Jorge Comas at CBP stepped up to provide an office in Ashburn, Virginia, that housed all those willing and able to show up and fight fentanyl and Sinaloa every day. Most important, like OGP, he invited foreign partners from Latin America to collocate in Jorge's Sinaloa Campaign pop-up office. We also leveraged the aforementioned and now global "Fentanyl Friday" meeting that included dozens of leaders across the military, intelligence agencies, and law enforcement to foster the necessary cohesion.

Fentanyl Friday quickly yielded results. Some agencies like DEA kept their cards close to their vest. Others like Treasury, Southern Command, NSA,

CIA, and HSI were eagerly forthcoming. It seemed people welcomed the opportunity to compare notes on otherwise siloed efforts against the gangster warlords and their fiefdoms. We also endeavored to make this a "moveable feast" as Ernest Hemingway mused. Tien went on the road. He visited various secure headquarters in his two-vehicle Suburban security detail, and each key partner would host him at one of the Fentanyl Friday discussions. The presence of a deputy cabinet secretary generally meant that, when we showed up, so did the top brass from whatever agency we visited.

This is an old bureaucratic trick. You force an agency to get its act together by setting up a meeting with your boss and their boss. This ensures their boss demands briefings on the topic in question. Invariably the executive will find the briefings insufficient. As is bureaucratic nature, the other principal expects to demonstrate his agency is excelling at the task at hand. He will demand action to report to his counterpart (Tien) at the meeting. The staff will then scramble to achieve results their boss can tout to Tien. So just by setting up a meeting between principals, we set off a chain reaction that results in Tien's counterpart browbeating his staff until the group in question makes demonstrable progress.

In this way, we used Fentanyl Friday and the corresponding Tien roadshow to create our own version of OGP. While by no means a perfect replica, this effort made the interagency team begin to form bonds over a common enemy. We began rowing, somewhat, in the same direction.

Third, we sought to disrupt the Sinaloa network and specifically dismantle its capacity to distribute fentanyl to Americans. One may wonder why we did not seek to dismantle the network altogether. We certainly desired Sinaloa to be dismantled. Sinaloa, however, has existed in one form or another for nearly a century. It is estimated to be the size of a Fortune 50 company. Collectively the cartels in Mexico account for nearly 3 percent of Mexican GDP.[15] So dismantling Sinaloa could span decades, like the war on terror. With nearly one hundred thousand Americans dying every year from fentanyl, we didn't have decades. We certainly didn't have the twenty years the war on terror was waged. At one hundred thousand dead a year, two million would be in the grave after twenty years.

It was not something people said out loud. But we were content to leave the other lines of business of the cartels to regular order law enforcement investigations. The military, intelligence community, and other parts of the federal government were not necessary to prohibit the cartels from selling stolen tilapia or avocados. Those lines of criminal business weren't killing many Americans. They could be left to run-of-the-mill law enforcement operations. Our priority was to dismantle their fentanyl line of business in the United States.

For example, the cartels knew smuggling terrorists or weapons of mass destruction were a red line the United States would not permit to be crossed without dire consequences[16]—consequences that risked the survival of the cartel itself and everyone associated with it. We needed to demonstrate to the cartels that fentanyl also fell beyond that red line.

Here again, Fentanyl Friday was a key instrument in the program. On the weekly calls, agency leads would learn about other agencies' lines of pursuit. After the call, they would reconvene independently to plot future lines of attack against particular Sinaloa gangsters, Chinese chemical companies, or even parts of the logistics network like the pill presses used to make Sinaloa's fentanyl look like prescription medication.

Also, the planning process—maybe more than anything—helped spur the creative juices of participants to imagine new types of disruption. We even brought in PhDs from DHS's office of Science and Technology (S&T), the department's R&D arm. S&T convened scientists to ideate on novel ways to detect fentanyl, its precursors, or even the location of labs in Mexico.

Colonel Lujan's campaign plan was finalized with three distinct lines of attack. Our intelligence team was to illuminate the Sinaloa networks. Our operators were to enable U.S. and foreign governments to architect a network of assets more formidable than the Sinaloa network we illuminated. Finally, we would disrupt the cartel fentanyl business vertical so dramatically that American fatalities from fentanyl would drop precipitously.

Most important, through Colonel Lujan's planning process, we cobbled together a cohesive group focused specifically on fentanyl and Sinaloa. Fortunately, the National Security Council had finalized the effort discussed in chapter 8 that brought further structure to this whole-of-government approach.

The NSC brought the entire interagency to the table. All this planning by the NSC, Tien, Colonel Lujan, and the rest of us laid the groundwork for a true blitz. The blitz would leverage every aspect of U.S. government power short of dropping bombs.

It was to be the largest onslaught against the Sinaloa network's fentanyl operation in history.

Notes

1 McChrystal, Stanley. "It Takes a Network." *Foreign Policy*, July 30, 2019. https:// foreignpolicy.com/2011/02/21/it-takes-a-network/.

2 "What We Do." Office of the Director of National Intelligence, n.d. https://www.dni .gov/index.php/what-we-do.

3 Ma'ayeh/Amman, Suha. "How Jordan Got Pulled into the Fight against ISIS." *Time*, February 26, 2015. https://time.com/3721793/jordan-fight-against-isis/.

4 Dlewis. "ISIS Foreign Fighters: Why Do Foreigners Join the Caliphate?" Vision of Humanity, November 29, 2022. https://www.visionofhumanity.org/can-economic -conditions-explain-flow-foreign-fighters-isis/.

5 Hummel, Kristina. "Beyond the Conflict Zone: U.S. HSI Cooperation with Europol." Combating Terrorism Center at West Point, January 17, 2019. https://ctc.westpoint .edu/beyond-conflict-zone-u-s-hsi-cooperation-europol/.

6 "Australia, U.S. Discussions Ranged the Globe, Dunford Says." Joint Chiefs of Staff, n.d. https://www.jcs.mil/Media/News/News-Display/Article/1205895/australia-us -discussions-ranged-the-globe-dunford-says/.

7 Woody, Christopher. "The Chairman of the Joint Chiefs of Staff Explains the US's 'Annihilation Campaign' against ISIS." Business Insider, November 14, 2017. https:// www.businessinsider.com/gen-joseph-dunford-on-the-us-annihilation-campaign -against-isis-2017-6.

8 Garamone, Jim. "Dunford Asks Defense Chiefs to Guard against Complacency." Joint Chiefs of Staff, n.d. https://www.jcs.mil/Media/News/News-Display/Article/1664622/ dunford-asks-defense-chiefs-to-guard-against-complacency/.

9 "Timeline: How 'El Chapo' and Kate del Castillo's Relationship Evolved from a Tweet to Their First Meeting." *Good Morning America*, March 21, 2016. https:// www.goodmorningamerica.com/news/story/timeline-el-chapo-kate-del-castillos -relationship-evolved-37697837.

10 "After El Chapo Conviction, Sinaloa Drug Cartel Carries On." PBS News, February 12, 2019. https://www.pbs.org/newshour/world/after-el-chapo-conviction-sinaloa-drug -cartel-carries-on.

11 "Sophisticated Sinaloa Cartel Money Laundering Organization Dismantled." U.S. Attorney's Office, Southern District of California, April 12, 2023. https://www.justice .gov/usao-sdca/pr/sophisticated-sinaloa-cartel-money-laundering-organization -dismantled.

12 Muggah, Robert, and Pedro Augusto P. Francisco. 2020. "Latin American Drug Cartels Are All over Instagram, Facebook, and TikTok." *Foreign Policy*, December 16, 2020. https://foreignpolicy.com/2020/12/15/latin-american-drug-cartels-instagram -facebook-tiktok-social-media-crime/.

13 Pulkkinen, A. J. "Coast Guard Culinary Team 3-Peats in the Joint Culinary Training Exercise." U.S. Coast Guard, April 2023. https://www.mycg.uscg.mil/News/Article /3350094/coast-guard-culinary-team-3-peats-in-the-joint-culinary-training-exercise/.

14 *Annual Report of the Organized Crime Drug Enforcement Task Forces*. U.S. Drug Enforcement Administration, 2018. https://www.dea.gov/sites/default/files/2018-07/ dir06515.pdf.

15 In 2006, a high-end estimate of cartel earnings was $48.4 billion annually; it is likely higher now. Seelke, Clare Ribando. "Mexico: Organized Crime and Drug Trafficking Organizations." Congressional Research Service, December 20, 2019, 4. https:// sgp.fas.org/crs/row/RL34215.pdf. Nominal Mexican GDP is 1.82 trillion, meaning cartel drug revenue is equivalent to 2.78 percent: "IMF DataMapper." International Monetary Fund, n.d. https://www.imf.org/external/datamapper/profile/MEX.

16 "Transnational Organized Crime: A Growing Threat to National and International Security." White House, n.d.. https://obamawhitehouse.archives.gov/administration/ eop/nsc/transnational-crime/threat.

11

The Agent

Before we delve into the sting operation, we should take a closer look at the agents who executed it. Drug Enforcement Administration (DEA), Customs and Border Protection (CBP), and Homeland Security Investigations (HSI) agents make up the bulk of the force pursuing the gangsters at Sinaloa. HSI agents in particular are not as well known as other federal law enforcement like the Federal Bureau of Investigation (FBI), DEA, or Secret Service. In late 2024, I interviewed an HSI agent for this chapter. The agent I interviewed is not an anomaly. He was certainly one of the most accomplished agents at HSI. But his story is similar to the thousands of HSI agents who have served our country by dismantling an assortment of global criminal networks that plague our society. His career aligns with the evolution of the global criminal underworld. He began his early career working for the State Department traveling to Africa at the emergence of terrorism as a global threat. Then he confounded Chinese piracy criminal networks seeking to flood the U.S. market with knockoff products. Later as the internet took off and online child exploitation exploded, he hunted down networks of these monsters in the deepest recesses of the dark web. The Islamic State of Iraq and Syria (ISIS) eclipsed al-Qaeda as the deadliest terrorist network on the planet by dramatically expanding the global terrorist network. He then was assigned to thwart terrorism 2.0 by dismantling ISIS networks that inspired foreign fighters to seek jihad in Syria and Iraq. So, before we go into the blitz against Sinaloa, we should take a moment to understand who some of the key people are that executed the blitz. The following are excerpts from a conversation I had with a senior agent at HSI and how his life and career unfolded. I use a pseudonym to protect his identity because of the sensitive nature of his story.

Elliot: I attended a small law enforcement college. I began my law enforcement career as an NYPD cadet, then did an internship with U.S. Customs.

Jake: How long had you been at NYPD?

Elliot: Probably about a year. I was a police cadet. So, it was a part-time program. No gun, different uniform, and I'd work two days a week.

Jake: Why didn't you stay with NYPD? Why'd you become a customs inspector?

Elliot: I wanted to become a special agent and conduct criminal investigations. I first became a customs inspector whereas six months I went to college, six months I worked. I did that for two cycles. I graduated college, and six days later I was in the academy to become a customs inspector. Sad truth is that my dad died a couple days before college graduation, and I didn't have the courage to let him know that I would be going to the academy while he was on his death bed. So, he never knew I went on to become a customs inspector.

Jake: Was he happy that you were getting in law enforcement?

Elliot: Yes and no. Again, I was still twenty years old. He didn't know the path that laid ahead. He worked for the NYC transit authority and law enforcement did not run in my family.

Jake: By the way, in retrospect, looking at how you grew up and everything, does it now seem obvious that you would have wound up an agent?

Elliot: No way. . . . A local cop in New York, perhaps. The girls become teachers, and the guys become either firemen, cops, or sanitation workers. Like city jobs. My dad worked for the city. My mom worked for the school system. My sister's a teacher.

I became a customs inspector and worked in Newark for three years. As a customs inspector you're always aiming to become a special agent. After the embassy bombings in 1998, State Department diplomatic security was hiring.

Jake: Oh, wow. This is like right before 9/11. You were already working counterterrorism before 9/11 because you got in right around the Kenya bombing?

Elliot: Yes. With State Department, I was doing dignitary protection. Like, here's this: take a kid from Brooklyn that reads the *New York Post* every day, and now you put him in front of Secretary of State [Madeleine] Albright and Ambassador Richard Holbrooke while they're arguing in the armored limousine. It was pretty wild to me. I joke around that my first trip out of Brooklyn was the trip to Bamako, Mali. There was a case of water in my room. I said to my boss at the time, I was twenty-one years old. I said, "Hey, I have water if you're thirsty." He goes, "No, that's not for drinking. That's for showering and brushing your teeth." That was an eye-opener. We did ten African countries in ten days. I did that for a little less than three years.

In 2001 I transferred to U.S. Customs as a special agent. I was assigned to a money laundering task force and all eyes were on the big T: terrorism.

Jake: Was that the first time they had done something like that?

Elliot: For terrorism, finance was now front and center. Of course, money fuels all crimes, right? The money laundering investigations for terrorism were more prevalent after 9/11. At that time, the focus was on following the money for various programmatic areas, just as Customs had done for narcotics investigations.

In 2003 when we merged [with Immigration and Naturalization Service to become DHS/ICE]. That's really when child exploitation kicked off from the internet. So, we started a child exploitation group. That's the group I went to.

In New Jersey, we had an investigation that focused on the illicit funds used to pay for subscriptions to child exploitation websites. Operation Falcon yielded financial transactions for thousands of predators who used their credit card for monthly subscriptions to various child sex abuse material. Every office in the United States had a list of hundreds and hundreds of subjects who paid for child exploitation via credit card.

We did a search warrant on the server that processed the credit cards. So, we got all those leads. By the time we got the leads, many were stale or not as fresh as we would like to use to obtain a federal search warrant. In

Newark, what we did, we had a great team. We would do knock-and-talk at their house. We would go knock on their door at 6:00 in the morning. We would ask them if someone stole their identity because it was being used to purchase illicit items on the internet. They'd say "no."

"Well, have you purchased kids online or anything?"

"No."

"Do you mind if we come in and take a look around? Make sure there's no kids in the house?"

"Yes, no problem."

"Do you mind if we look at your computer?"

"No problem."

They would give us consent. We go through that computer, we find child images, we lock them up.

Jake: Holy shit. How many people did you take down that way?

Elliot: Oh, hundreds. We were doing this for three, four days every week for months at a time, years at a time. Bringing them to the U.S. attorney's office for prosecution. That transitioned us into doing chats online and meeting people. They say, "come have sex with the kids," and then we'd lock them up when they pull up to the site [to meet me]. I did an undercover where I pretended that I was a child predator. Some guy was running a website where he was a sex tourism guy. He was going to take me overseas to have sex with kids and I would pay him a fee for his services. I met him face-to-face in Atlantic City.

Jake: In Atlantic City?

Elliot: In Atlantic City, and the fucker brought his wife.

Jake: Are you kidding?

Elliot: No. She was Filipino. The plan was he's going to take me and my friend overseas to have sex with kids. Weeks later, he flew to New Jersey; we stayed in a hotel. We were going to fly out the next morning. When he flies in, we are in the hotel room, all surveillanced up. Next door is the takedown team. He's telling me how you got to be careful overseas. . .

There was a *Dateline* special once with a doctor that was in the Philippines called "Thailand, to Have Sex with Kids"[1] and he showed me the video. He was showing me what not to do while I'm overseas. In the corner of the room, we had an alarm clock radio that was a surveillance camera. So, that's how we're recording it.

He said: "You see that over there?" He pointed to the alarm clock radio.

He goes: "That could even be a camera."

He walked over to it. He picked it up and he flipped it over.

He goes, "This could even be a recorder."

When you watch the video, you see the video go upside down [because he picked up the clock]. I used this surveillance video many times to teach new undercovers.

Jake: HAHAHA. Holy shit.

Elliot: Then you see me in the background, "Bro, what the fuck are you doing?"

I go, "What the fuck are you doing, man? You're freaking me out. Cut the shit out."

He puts it down. Then a couple of minutes later we arrest him.
Pretty funny.

Jake: That's crazy.

Elliot: We locked up teachers, a priest, a doctor; predators that are actively abusing kids. Arresting a sick fucker that comes to meet you, thinking that he is going to meet an underage child with duct tape and condoms. There's nothing more rewarding than that. A proud moment to be a law enforcement officer.

Matter of fact, in 2004-ish, I started going on chat rooms. I think it was AOL at the time. We had an undercover computer, dial-up. I went to one of the chat rooms. Within like an hour or so, I got a guy to come meet me. I was pretending I was a little girl. One of the bosses walked in and I got yelled at.

He's like, "You can't be doing that."

I'm like, "Why?"

He goes, "Because you just can't. It's not what we do."

I already had a target, but at that time I was forced to let it go. We didn't do anything with him.

Like a year or two later, one day, it was slow and we wanted to work, and I said, "Hey, let's go visit this guy."

Sure enough, we go to that guy's house, and he had child exploitation material on his computer, so we locked him up. Crazy.

Jake: Jesus Christ. It seems like these guys all moved to the internet really quickly.

Elliot: So quickly. Now they don't have to go to a park. They don't have to order DVDs. It's real time. They're impulsive. Now they could do everything from their house. We arrested clowns. You name it, we arrested them.

Jake: Fucking clowns, man.

Elliot: They're all clowns. We arrested a guy who dressed up as a clown for children's parties. He dressed up as a clown, as Santa, anything he could do to spend time with kids. These are the sick folks that are out there. Many times we were actually searching backyards for places where a child could be buried. We would be able to tell how far along the predators were on their path to active molestation, and if we determined that they were actively abusing children, we would take the extra time to search the backyards, garages, alleyways, or any place where a child could be buried. This work was mentally exhausting, yet taking these predators off of the streets was extremely rewarding. You would go home knowing that you made a difference.

Jake: Right. I'm saying all clowns are terrifying.

If I was you guys, I would be taking fucking heroin just to forget what I was dealing with all day.

Elliot: Going into these dirty houses, you felt disgusting. There are times when I would get home and I'd undress by my front door just to go in and shower. I didn't want to even wear the clothes into my house. I'd shower and just let the water run down my face trying to get the images and, more importantly, the guy's confession out of my mind. Talking to a sick man and hearing him talk about getting abused himself at an early age, and how he now abuses little children is mentally draining. How the hell can a teacher, a priest, a doctor, anyone, take advantage of the innocent.

I wanted to punch the guy in the face, but if you can talk to him and get an easy confession, you're sealing the deal. Easy conviction and less paperwork.

Jake: It would be all I could do to resist clocking the guy.

Elliot: I think once you've worked child exploitation, it stays with you. My kid was a couple years old, three, four years old. We go to a karate place in the neighborhood, and the sensei is walking around with ten to fifteen kids. One time he pats someone on the back. Another time, he pats someone on the back. The third time, he slapped the kid's ass. I said, "Let's go. We're out of here."

Jake: Yes, right.

Elliot: Even if it was innocent, it just bothers me because there's so many things that you see.

Jake: God, child predator stuff at twenty-five, twenty-six years old. Man . . . that's young to be dealing with such deranged aspects of humanity.

Elliot: Again, I think saving kids and arresting really bad guys was just so rewarding. There's no other feeling putting handcuffs on someone who's victimizing children. Perhaps something that I am most proud of: taking child predators off of the streets.

Jake: I get that.

Elliot: You got to just beat them at their own game and know how to talk to them. You say you think someone stole their identity and they're buying guns off the internet. "Ah, if you have, child pictures, don't worry about it. We want to make sure you're not buying guns or missiles." Eventually, we had to say something in there about child exploitation before we even started looking at the computer. Imagine knocking on someone's door and having them give you consent to search their computers when they know there's child exploitation on it, sick people.

Jake: Well, and it's probably because it's been so normalized in their mind because of these morbid chat rooms they live in that they actually don't think it's as bad as it is.

Elliot: We had the best relationships with the U.S. attorney's office. Our all-star assistant U.S. attorney is still a dear friend to this day. Plus, they loved all our cases. Great relationships with state and locals. We were just runnin' and gunnin' and locking up predators. It was pretty rewarding.

Jake: Well, and plus there's so many other things in law enforcement that there's ambiguity around. With this, it's just so clearly a bad fucking guy. You may have had this horrible childhood but too fucking bad. That doesn't give you a right to do what you're doing. Every one of those guys you lock up and then obviously the subsequent kids that are saved by it. You must feel like fucking Superman. I would.

Elliot: Then they started doing—Chris Hansen, *To Catch a Predator*. Remember that show, *To Catch a Predator*? Where he'd go online and he'd get kids to come to a house. That's how easy it is. It was just easy. We weren't superstars. We were just working hard and locking up bad guys. At one point, the management said, "All right, let's do bigger cases." Then that's when we started focusing on bigger networks for child exploitation. Like the child sex tourism case we did.

Jake: With the bigger rings you were going after, it was the tourism thing, sex tourism?

Elliot: Sex tourism. Yes. Then people starting to trade their kids. Chat rooms for all these different types of things.

Jake: Trading their own kids?

Elliot: Yes.

Jake: What the fuck?

Jake: Right. You just think about all these guys who spent their whole career trying to seize weed. Then thirty years after their career, we've essentially legalized it. You can see how they might be looking back on this going, "Jesus, what the fuck did I do for thirty years?" Whereas with this—

Elliot: It's righteous.

Jake: There's no gray. It's 100 percent black and white.

Elliot: Absolutely. As I said before, my most rewarding work was working child exploitation. Again, locking up bad guys out of victimizing those kids. There's no better feeling. No better feeling.

The Longshoreman

Elliot: Can I back up to when I first started with Customs?

Jake: Yes, of course. Back up.

Elliot: We had a bunch of undercover operations in Newark. We had undercover tractor trailers at the seaport. They asked me, the older guys, "Hey, kid, you want to drive a tractor?"

I'm like, "Yes, I'll drive."

They sent me to learn how to drive a tractor trailer. To pass the road test in New York, you actually had to parallel park a tractor trailer. I failed it the first time after the rear tires hit the curb.

I'm like, "Oh, my God."

I was so embarrassed. I took it again and I passed it. That's how I started doing some undercover work driving a tractor trailer.

Jake: Wait, so then how did being able to drive a tractor trailer help you?

Elliot: Because there were only a few certified CDL undercover agents in the East Coast. They sent me to truck driving school. I got my license and then they put me at the top of the list to go to undercover school. I transport all the loads. I transported dope. I transported counterfeit cigarettes. If you're a bad guy and you need transportation services, we could do it. Also, when

CBP gets a load at the port in a container, we would actually deliver that for them to the [criminals'] warehouse.

All right, so that was 2006/2007, and we got a lead from a cooperating defendant who was an organized crime guy. He has Chinese [mobsters] wanting to get counterfeit goods out of the port. Big forty-feet containers, hundreds of thousands of dollars' worth of merchandise, and they have a container that's stuck, and they want help for it. So it's perfect. Right up our alley, right?

Jake: Wait. How did they find you?

Elliot: The guy was a cooperating defendant. A Jersey-based mobster that was working off some time. He sat down with us, and he tells us that he has some Chinese mobsters who are willing to pay someone to get a forty-foot shipping container released from Port Newark. The container was filled with millions of dollars' worth of counterfeit Nikes, but CBP has it seized.

Here I come, a kid from Brooklyn, sitting down and negotiating deals with a guy who just flew in from China. To be honest, I played a undercover [UC] role that was everything opposite of being a squared-away special agent. I meet with the Chinese [mobster] guy. He has a container that's going to be seized. It's been detained. Counterfeit Nikes. He's willing to pay shitload of money to get the container out of the seaport. I think he originally offered about $20–30K for its release. So, "Okay, no problem." Easy to do. I worked the seaport and know that we can make it happen. This guy thinks I'm a corrupt longshoreman and that I'm paying bribes to CBP.

Yet, on the legit side, we have to work with CBP to get that container released. It's hard to do that. It's not easy. We can't just tell them to release it. We have to write memos, get various levels of authorization.

My undercover persona was a wannabe wise guy that has connections all over the seaport. I have someone from CBP in my pocket that I pay.

After several meetings with the bad guys, I said, "Give me the containers before they even get here, and I'll get them out." Bottom line is that it was easier for me to get approval to have containers released with counterfeit items if I had the information before the container even arrived at the port. It was a pain in the ass if CBP already detained it at the seaport.

Eighteen long months later, we took down the whole organization. From a licensed customs broker, to street thugs, to a so-called general in the Chinese army, as well as an established trucking company that would transport the sea-laden containers with millions of dollars in counterfeit goods.

Once I was able to get the first container out, they really accepted my bona fides. The floodgates just kept opening from this one guy, Michael C. After a few weeks, Mike and I took a trip to Atlantic City. Again, I was a wannabe wise guy gambler. All cashed up and always ready to spend money. We had a great time together, and the plan worked out perfectly. Our office rented a high-end SUV and got me a personal driver. Truth is, it was a good friend who was also an undercover agent. Going to Atlantic City in a [UC] role was entertaining. I had eyes on me at all times, not just from the hotel security team, but many of our agents were on the casino floor. The office gave me $2,000 to go gambling. Turns out first time in Atlantic City, I won. I more than doubled the money. I ordered the most expensive cigars that they had at the Borgata Casino. I executed the [UC] role to the fullest, not knowing where this investigation would take us. After a long night of drinking, gambling, and staying focused, I head to my room at about 2 a.m. I'm exhausted, and mentally drained. I'm starving and wanting to decompress. So I ordered room service—a turkey and bacon sandwich, a soda, and a small desert. It cost like $150. Keep that in your mind. One of the best turkey sandwiches ever.

On the way back from Atlantic City, Michael starts telling me about a customs broker that is involved with his organization. For us to get a customs broker that's licensed and certified to move containers is pretty significant. You don't get that all the time. He put me in touch with the customs broker.

Jake: You mean you don't normally find corrupt customs brokers?

Elliot: No, we don't. It's hard to find one that's dirty because it's a highly reputable occupation. You have to be licensed as a customs broker and the test is somewhat intensive. They also make good money and are usually upstanding citizens. That whole trip was worth it. But I come back to the office and now I have more money than I started with. I had to write five different memos on why I had more money. I had to document and justify dollar for dollar, how I spent the money and how I won more money. Then when I documented that I bought $150 in room service. My bosses at the time were like, "Are you serious? You just spent $150 on food?"

"Yes, motherfucker, because I just made $4,000."

Jake: What does that have to do with the winnings? Do you have to turn it over?

Elliot: As part of our undercover operation, we have various funds that we can utilize for undercover operations. As part of undercover proceeds, we can use those funds to offset undercover expenses. My blackjack winnings, the cash that I was paid for releasing containers with counterfeit goods, all those funds went back into our undercover accounts.

Jake: Oh, but still the government gets the money you legally won at the blackjack table. You don't get to keep it?

Elliot: I don't get to keep it, no. I would get paid anywhere from $5,000 to $80,000 per container to get it out of the seaport. These are forty-foot containers with counterfeit Nikes.

So, a few days later I am meeting with the customs broker across from ground zero. As we are eating a nice lunch, the view out of the window has me looking over the devastating effects of 9/11. It hit me; I had to refocus for a minute. This customs broker is exploiting the U.S. trade system right in front of our faces. Although most of the containers had counterfeit products inside, what if one container had a dirty bomb? This was serious shit, and we couldn't take anything for granted. This fucker knew the customs system, the databases, better than I did. So, there's no way we can bullshit this guy, and I had to actually do research to know what I was really talking about because I couldn't lie to this guy.

He would see the containers in the systems before we would see them. He could probably teach customs inspectors how to use the system better than many folks we knew. That's how good this guy was. He also tracked what type of customs holds were being placed on each container. We couldn't bullshit this guy that much. He was spot on in his game.

Jake: He thinks you're a longshoreman?

Elliot: He thinks I'm a mobbed-up longshoreman that's paying off a customs inspector. As he is a customs broker, he knew many of the same folks I did. I had to be extremely careful of saying too much to him about my UC persona. He can see who's putting holds on these containers. If Jake puts in a customs hold on this container all the time, he'll think that I'm paying you off. We had to stay one step ahead of him.

After several months, we identified that this lady, Grace, was running logistics for the crew. Grace was involved in every container that we had identified as being dirty, I finally had the chance to meet with Grace and started working with her. Well, after working hand in hand with her, I recruited her to work directly for me.

Grace was like my executive assistant. Every morning I go to the bagel store. I have coffee. I read the paper and I call her, "What do we have on the plan?" She'd send me daily spreadsheets and updates. She'd go out and collect money for me. She was extremely loyal. Grace managed the daily and weekly forecasting of which containers we needed cleared. She kept me organized and out of trouble as an undercover who was handling hundreds of thousands of dollars each week. In fact, I used her spreadsheets that she created as a way to keep track of how much payment I received for each specific container. I was nowhere near as organized as she was. Grace also provided me with further insight into the organization as she knew all of the players. She was well liked and trusted with the business guys, street thugs, trucking company, and our customs broker.

Jake: Holy shit.

Elliot: Yes. With Michael, Grace, and the customs broker in my pocket, the floodgates started to open even more. My name was out there and word spread amongst the counterfeit importers. Grace and Michael would offer up meeting new bad guys who were looking to use my services. Grace connected me with a local trucking company that dealt with transporting sea-laden containers loaded with illicit goods. Now we were able to identify even more bad guys and the business names that they used. I'd like to mention that many times we would seize the containers that transported illicit contraband.

We kept close track of how many containers we would let walk, compared to how many containers we ultimately seized. For every one container that we let walk, we would be sure to seize many more. At first I was hesitant to have to explain why containers were being seized, but the fact is that we would come up with some good reasons why some containers were seized. It turned out that this played right into my [UC] role—some were trying to evade paying me $50–$80K per container.

If I found out, I would ensure that it was going to get seized. You can imagine how these bad guys needed me more than I needed them. It was a game of cat and mouse. If our team identified containers that were not on my spreadsheet of payments that Grace organized, they would forfeit millions of dollars' worth of counterfeit goods. So, in reality, utilizing my services were more beneficial to them than not. And, as a result we kept identifying additional throw down business, further exploitation of the customs importer system, and additional individuals who were involved.

While working with Grace, we often spent many days together and I got to know her well. She was a nice person who really cared about people. We grew closer and I always treated her with the utmost respect. She asked me to serve as her best man at her wedding. Her partner was another really nice lady, who I had also befriended. Turned out, her wedding was scheduled just a few weeks before we had planned the takedown.

Jake: Oh my God, that's amazing.

Elliot: I gave the best man speech, the toast. I walked her down the aisle. I sat in the front row at the reception. I danced with her. It was legit! I was the best man at a wedding, while portraying myself as a wise guy.

Jake: Holy shit. Man, so they really didn't see it coming? That's unbelievable. How was your best man speech?

Elliot: Oh, it was great. Of course, I was nervous; but I crushed it. Kinda mushy, but I was really proud of Grace for marrying her longtime partner.

Jake: That's unbelievable. You must be what, thirty years old?

Elliot: Something like that.

Jake: That's remarkable.

Elliot: It's funny. I probably gave her more money as a wedding gift than my mom gave me for my wedding. It was all perfectly planned because she was holding a lot of money for me, but I knew that we were going to hit her house in a few short weeks and the money would still be sitting in her safe at her house. We would eventually get it back as evidence.

Here's something funny. My [UC] role was a wannabe mobster, so I portrayed myself as a big-time gambler. So, for another wedding gift, I told her that I'm going to give her a suite at the Borgata Hotel, which was one of the fancy Atlantic City casinos back then. After the wedding, her entire bridal party was going down to the Borgata, except for me.

Well, two o'clock in the morning she calls me, she says, "Hey, Elliot, I'm at the front desk. They're asking me for government ID."

I go, "What do you mean asking me for government ID?"

She said, "Because it's a government rate so they want me to show ID."

When they booked it, of course, the knucklehead from hotel security blocked the room for government rate. So, the desk clerk is asking for government ID.

I just said, "Just pay for it and I'll pay you back."

When we arrested her two weeks later, she goes, "Ever since that night, I thought you were in law enforcement." I felt bad about locking her up because she was a nice person.

If I go back and think about it, my undercover persona was a wannabe wise guy. Always going out and drinking. The truth is my kids were one, two, and three. At two o'clock in the morning when I'm waking up to change diapers, I would call and leave messages on their phones pretending that I'm out drinking. Really, I'm home changing diapers. Hahaha.

Jake: Were you worried about them following you home or something like that?

Elliot: Yes, I had access to several law enforcement sensitive items at my disposal. Every few weeks, I'd get a new rental car and would ensure that I wouldn't take it to my legit office. I always carried my gun. I was always cognizant of driving, especially noticing who is taking more than two turns with me. At my house, I had a surveillance system installed and was always attentive to my surroundings.

Jake: I bet you were.

Elliot: Looking back now, I realize how stressful the undercover work was. Inherently dangerous, yes, but just dealing with the adrenaline, stress of being in a [UC] role. The daily chaos of handling undercover work with life as a dad was a lot. The night before the takedown, I went to urgent care because I was having bad chest pains. The doctor did some tests and advised that I should go to the local emergency room for additional testing. Well, as a wannabe mobster, with a big enforcement operation coming, I handled it as a tough guy and just went back home. Needless to say, I survived and the chest pains were likely from the stress, anxiety, and sense of relief that tomorrow is the big day.

The day of the takedown, we arrested like fifteen people. Our team identified and executed a search warrant at another warehouse which was the mother lode. At the time, it was one of the biggest takedowns ever, that warehouse was filled with about forty or so forty-foot containers which were all filled with counterfeit items. Millions and millions of dollars' worth of counterfeit goods from China. [Elliot holds up newspaper clipping.]

Jake: "Fed Smash Massive Fake."[2] Wow. One of the largest international counterfeit smuggling rings ever uncovered.

Foreign Fighters

Elliot: Shortly after that undercover investigation, I received a promotion and served as a group supervisor. After an eighteen-month stint in Washington, DC, I was offered a position in Frankfurt, Germany.

Working overseas was the first time I saw an all-hands-on-deck government approach between law enforcement and the intelligence community (IC). Intrigued with the IC, I was always willing to work together and share information. The law enforcement community has so much to offer the IC. Working hand in hand with intelligence professionals was the key to taking down networks: executing disruptions, and dismantling transnational organized syndicates.

Jake: How did you provide more?

Elliot: Just with law enforcement, criminal intelligence or criminal investigations that the IC would be interested in, or interest in folks we were dealing with in country. I'm not talking about source development or anything. I'm just talking about the ins and outs of people who want to travel to the United States and what investigations we have domestically that touched Germany or the ten countries in our area of responsibility. As a regional attaché office, we were responsible for international liaison with about ten countries in and around Europe. Going country to country, meeting with the embassy people, really showing that you can work together was just awesome. A lot of times there's so much infighting between the DEA, FBI, HSI, and on and on.

In Germany, we worked well with the Department of Defense folks who were out there trying to keep our war fighters safe, not only downrange, but the thousands of troops that we have stationed in and around Europe.

There was this all-star analyst that is one of the best out there. Super smart, super competent, and simply gets it. We worked together trying to identify foreign fighters and the exploitation of the financial system used to fund real bad guys. As the foreign fighters were moving throughout Europe, we identified their financial flow and then illuminated that network so the IC could see who's who. This DOD analyst was highly respected within the German intelligence and law enforcement community and was known to build out illicit networks using his connections and putting the pieces all together. So many times, criminal intelligence is still so compartmentalized not getting into the hands where it can add value. Well, this guy was the fixer to get people together and he did some amazing work.

Jake: How? In a way you can actually tell me that's not classified.

Elliot: Simple, through financial transactions we would illuminate the network. If a subject was identified as a bad actor, we would work on the financial side of things. Tracing funds to/from the subject was key. Other folks would work their magic, and HSI would focus on the illicit funds being transferred from one person or business to a known or suspected bad guy. One of HSI's programmatic expertise is tracing illicit funds, basic money laundering. This is value added for any type of criminal investigation. As most illicit financial transactions touch the U.S. banking system, we were fortunate enough to expand the networks, highlight the key players, and illuminate key information to our partners.

Jake: What about the Hawala networks often used in terrorist finance operations?

Elliot: Yes.

Jake: Could you exploit those or no? Were they too closed off?

Elliot: Yes, we did. In Germany, one of our significant cases that we worked with DOD and the German law enforcement authorities was taking down a high-value Frankfurt cell that supported and hosted foreign fighters coming in to Germany. Although limited on what can be said, this network based out of Frankfurt, Germany, was facilitating real bad guys who were attempting to do harm in and around Germany. We were able to illuminate the network and identify several foreign fighters who were setting up shop to facilitate and execute recruiting operations. We executed several enforcement operations in Germany and disrupted foreign fighter activity that was a credible threat. Some years later, we actually received an award on behalf of the U.S. intelligence community for that investigation. Sitting hand in hand with intelligence professionals, receiving an award for righteous work just proved to me that there is so much more to be done.

Jake: DOD is basically saying, "Hey, we need your help going after these guys, but we can't because we're the military; but you guys can because you are law enforcement." Then you guys track what's happening, identify the network, and then German police goes in. Then I assume the military and the intelligence agencies at some point are like, "Oh, yes. Of that network, those guys are the ones we see in Syria or Iraq or whatever."

Elliot: Exactly.

Jake: Okay. Can you explain?

Elliot: Yes. A fusion center downrange hosted IC and law enforcement partners. This operation was consolidating intelligence information and law enforcement information to provide actionable leads for partners to work. The information was then used to disrupt and dismantle foreign fighters, terrorist organizations, and, once again, the exploitation of the financial system. It was a very successful operation called Operation Gallant Phoenix (OGP).

Jake: Ah, so the basis of OGP intelligence analysis on foreign fighters was electronic media, like cell phones and laptops?

Elliot: Yes. Anything and everything that can be exploited and turned into valuable information.

Jake: OK.

Elliot: Over the years of OGP, there was some amazing information sharing, and the best of it, I think that law enforcement really showed their value added to the IC folks. Illuminating the flows of money really proved useful to identify the bad actors.

Jake: I thought you guys had done that forever.

Elliot: Criminal enterprises revolve around financial gains, but having an ideology to conduct terroristic acts is not really about financial gain. Old-school money laundering was sending illicit proceeds back to Colombia, Mexico, and the cartels. Drugs come in, and money goes out. Foreign fighters were different. They are not sending large sums of money back home. Many of their small transactions wouldn't raise to a typical suspicion level.

Jake: So you guys would find a foreign fighter and then track what he thought were innocuous financial transactions to illuminate his network of coconspirators. After you had the network, you worked with the IC and local authorities to pounce on the whole network at once?

Elliot: Exactly. People don't always think of HSI this way. But we kept a lot of foreign fighters out of Syria, and we and our local partners took a ton of terrorists off the street in Europe. As a result they never made it to America to do us harm.

As referenced in chapter 8, HSI agents have an amorphous mission. Their raison d'être is combating transnational criminal organizations. During the war on terror, that mission had a clear target: terrorists. The mission persists, but the target is less clear. Further complicating attempts to sharpen the focus of HSI is the march toward globalization in every part of our society. Every crime seems to have some aspect to it that crosses borders. In fact, even something as hyperlocal as domestic abuse cases may be inspired by online content emanating from abroad or predicated by drugs originating from another country. HSI agents live in a world of squishy definitions. DEA recruits are compelled by a call to combat narcotics. A Secret Service agent is called by the drive to protect our leaders. Even a CBP agent is laser focused on protecting the border. The animating forces and career trajectory for an HSI agent are less linear.

Fittingly the capstone achievement of his winding career was being on the front lines of an all-out assault on possibly the largest international cartel on the planet as we sought to stop it from massacring more than one hundred thousand Americans a year.

Notes

1   "Children for Sale." NBC News, January 9, 2005. https://www.nbcnews.com/id/wbna4038249.

2   "22 Charged with Smuggling Millions of Dollars of Counterfeit Luxury." U.S. Department of Justice, August 16, 2018. https://www.justice.gov/opa/pr/22-charged-smuggling-millions-dollars-counterfeit-luxury-goods-china-united-states.

12

Mexico City

The first step to launch the assault on Sinaloa was securing support from the Mexican president and his National Security Council. As discussed previously, the pesky fact about Mexico is that it's a sovereign nation. We cannot legally deploy the 82nd Airborne Division to drop bombs on Sonora or direct the Fifth Infantry to invade Coyocan. As the team of grizzled agents, soldiers, and spies told Morgan Ryan and me at the U.S. embassy in Mexico a few months earlier, the only way to effectively thwart Sinaloa was with the Mexican military and law enforcement kicking down their doors. So, we boarded a Gulf Stream for Mexico City to elicit support of the Andrés Manuel López Obrador administration.

President Joe Biden had directed Dr. Liz Sherwood-Randall to lead both bilateral and trilateral efforts with Mexico and Canada. During the January 2023 North American Leaders' Summit (NALS), President Biden, President Obrador, and Prime Minister Justin Trudeau committed to launch a trilateral effort to address the fentanyl challenge facing North America. After NALS, President Biden directed the formation of a senior-level Trilateral Fentanyl Committee (TFC) with Mexico and Canada to guide priority actions by the three countries to address the fentanyl threat facing North America. The TFC built on the existing work of the North American Drug Dialogue (NADD); the U.S.-Mexico Bicentennial Framework for Security, Public Health, and Safe Communities; and the U.S.-Canada Opioid Action Plan.[1] To follow through on this commitment, on March 7, 2023, Dr. Sherwood-Randall, John Tien, deputy attorney general Lisa Monaco, Office of National Drug Control Policy

(ONDCP) director Dr. Rahul Gupta, and another half dozen senior national security staff traveled to Mexico City. The next month the TFC met for the first time on April 13, 2023, in Washington, DC. The TFC then met again in Mexico City on July 25, 2023; virtually on December 19, 2023; and in Mexico City on February 7, 2024. In addition, Dr. Sherwood-Randall led a series of interagency delegations to Mexico, often coinciding with TFC meetings, to press for additional cooperation in our fight against fentanyl.

To their credit, the Mexican government had taken down some high-profile drug lords in the last several months. The president had partially abandoned his "hugs not guns" policy. "Hugs not guns" was a departure from his predecessor's war on the cartels. The cartel war cost Mexico more than one hundred thousand lives,[2] with little to show for the carnage in terms of dismantling the cartels. Obrador reduced the homicide rate by instituting a de facto truce with the cartels. However, three years in, he realized that, if left unchecked, the cartels would terrorize the population.[3] The cartels were rampantly kidnapping, extorting, raping, and murdering innocent citizens.[4] In his last two years in office, Obrador attacked the cartels with new vigor. The Mexican government orchestrated a high-profile hit on a key fentanyl cartel leader right before our official visit.[5] This arrest was likely intended to hammer home how deadly serious Obrador was about fentanyl.

Aside from enlisting the support of the military and law enforcement, the primary goal of the Department of Homeland Security (DHS) on the trip was to obtain access to Mexican-held data. That data would enable us to better illuminate the Sinaloa network. We sought to connect Mexico's key arrest, cargo, shipping, and drug seizure databases with our National Targeting Center (NTC) and Homeland Security Investigations (HSI) analytics efforts. Colonel Fernando Lujan's plan called for illuminating the Sinaloa network. As mentioned earlier, the strategy for combating Sinaloa was based on that used to defeat al-Qaeda and the Islamic State of Iraq and Syria (ISIS). That strategy relied heavily on churning through massive amounts of data. The more germane the data to the fight, the more impactful the targets identified. In fact, the counterterrorism war machine spawned an entire data analytics cottage industry with firms like Palantir making billions analyzing terrorist data. We planned to use the same strategy against Sinaloa. To apply the same strategy, we needed highly relevant data. The NTC housed petabytes of data on cargo and travelers from Mexico. Coupling NTC with the trillions of data points the Mexican government collected would dramatically increase our ability to target cartel members, precursor chemicals, fentanyl labs, and transportation infrastructure, among other things.

The other key request we delivered was for the Mexicans to stand up an investigative unit of about seventy additional polygraphed agents: our Transnational Criminal Investigative Units (TCIUs). This request became a point of contention for the delegation. The Mexican government didn't want to allocate the Drug Enforcement Administration (DEA) any more vetted agents as they were miffed at DEA for arresting a corrupt former cabinet official years ago. In DEA's defense, by all accounts, the secretary in question was corrupt.[6] Regardless, because of the secretary's former position, the Mexican government considered the arrest a breach of diplomatic protocol.

In contrast, the Mexicans had increased HSI's vetted units significantly since 2021. It was undeniable that these vetted units were incredibly effective at pursuing the cartels. More vetted units would undoubtedly expand our capacity to combat the flow of fentanyl into the United States. Despite this fact, the interagency delegation vacillated on whether to make the ask. Fortunately, Alejandro Mayorkas and Tien did not buckle under pressure to forgo the request and insisted that more vetted Mexican agents were crucial to the fight against fentanyl. Thus, we resolved to request the units on the diplomatic mission.

Tien and I were puzzled as we boarded a Coast Guard C-37B jet on the way to Mexico. Maybe we were missing something. Possibly there was some other reason we should not lobby for the agents. Maybe we would undermine some other important initiative by making the ask. However, our fears subsided in the initial prep session with U.S. ambassador to Mexico Ken Salazar. He held up a cable from the Mexican Justice Department, Fiscalía General de la República (FGR), proposing a dedicated unit of about 250 vetted agents and analysts to focus exclusively on fentanyl. FGR director Alejandro Gertz Manero expected us to finance the units, a condition we were happy to accommodate. He also wanted President Obrador to approve the unit. FGR floated a wise proposal to co-manage the unit among the military, the Department of Justice (DOJ), and DHS. This suggestion was intended to limit the risk of turf battles between agencies. While it still needed to be funded and approved by Obrador, 250 agents amounted to nearly four times the 70 agents we initially sought. Tien and I glanced at each other suggesting we quickly take "yes" for an answer. Also, we didn't protest when FGR proposed DOJ serve as the main interlocutor with the Mexican FGR as the unit was established. We got what we wanted, which was a commitment to a dedicated unit of vetted agents to target fentanyl. Which agency liaised with FGR over the unit was irrelevant to us.

Better to Be Lucky than Good

Unbeknownst to us, while we were on flights and in closed-door meetings with no phones allowed, a media frenzy ensued. Republicans in Congress unleashed a barrage of attacks against the Mexican government. GOP leadership like Lindsey Graham[7] pilloried Obrador's administration for allowing cartels to operate with impunity across much of the country and funnel fentanyl into the United States. We urged the Mexicans to approve a dedicated a unit of 250 agents and analysts and grant access to their data holdings. Senators like Lindsey Graham threatened military action against the cartels if Mexico failed to halt the flow of fentanyl. Other GOP members of Congress demanded the Mexican mafias be labeled foreign terrorist organizations (FTO).[8] They insisted special forces strike against the gangsters on Mexican soil. Clips of U.S. leaders beating the drums of war against the narco-tycoons blared across news broadcasts throughout Mexico.

Backed into a corner by the Republicans, Obrador lashed out. In advance of our meeting, he delivered a tirade to the Mexican press.[9] Obrador lambasted the United States. He even threatened to lobby Mexican American voters to oppose the GOP in the 2024 election. Obrador espoused patently false claims that fentanyl did not originate in Mexico.[10] These claims contradicted his previous statements. As we arrived to meet with Mexican foreign minister Marcelo Luis Ebrard Casaubón, and later Obrador, they were loaded for bear.

The GOP attacks emboldened Mexican leadership to harp on their go-to gripe. Morgan and I got an earful about weapons flowing south when we traveled to Mexico months earlier. This diplomatic mission was no exception.

Mexican officials delivered identical talking points to those the journalists previewed on our last trip. One hundred thousand Mexicans perished in cartel wars of the last decade. The cartels were armed with an arsenal Made in America. If the cartels weren't so heavily armed with American weapons, they could be defeated. We could have delivered the standard rebuttal that the cartels would get their weapons with or without the United States. However, that argument opened us up to the counterargument that the same could be said of fentanyl and the United States. To avoid this logical trap, we agreed to seize more weapons flowing south.

We anticipated this line of argument. So, in advance of the diplomatic mission, DHS committed to expand a program dubbed Operation Desert Lightning.[11] The operation was a monthly weapons dragnet on the border. Customs and Border Protection (CBP) officers surged to search and seize weapons and ammunition at unannounced ports of entry. The rounds were destined to end up in deceased Mexican citizens caught in cartel feuds. Tien announced this new antiweapons initiative in every meeting. Yet we were still pummeled. In every meeting with the FGR, Navy (Secretaría de la Marina [SEMAR]), Army (Secretaría de la Defensa Nacional [SEDENA]), and State Department (Secretaría de la Relaciones Exteriores [SRE]), they hammered us on unabated weapons flowing south. Further, as we got in our convoy of black armored SUVs back to the Air Force G5 waiting for us, our phones blew up with another screed from Obrador bashing the United States for threatening war on Mexican soil.[12]

On the way to the airport, Tien and I absorbed how surreal and intense the day's events were. The media backdrop unfolding around us. The GOP fusillade against the drug lords. The visceral reaction of Mexican officials. It made for must-see TV on a global scale. I posited to Tien that, while chaotic, it all may work out in our favor. The Mexican government was apoplectic about the GOP attacks. Despite that, in a way, we were lucky that a seemingly unhinged GOP called for extreme measures. They played sociopathic cop as we played reasonable cop offering aggressive but sane alternative proposals. Our proposals appear quite palatable when the alternative emerges as the Fifth Infantry marching into Sonora. Several people cornered me after the trip. They detected a conspiracy afoot. We must have planned all this. I replied truthfully that we are not that good. It took five people to organize a six-pack and two bottles of wine for the plane back to Andrews Air Force Base. Even that got screwed up. There is no way we could orchestrate the GOP attacks to be timed with our diplomatic mission. The scheme would invariably leak or go sideways on us. But sometimes it's better to be lucky than good.

"Showing Up" to the White House

A few weeks after we returned from the diplomatic mission to Mexico, nearly the entire Mexican national security cabinet rolled into Washington. The top officials in the Mexican government trekked to DC to demonstrate just how serious they were about fentanyl. Rosa Icela Rodríguez Velázquez, secretary of public security, led the delegation. She was the minister Obrador appointed as lead for fentanyl. The delegation also included Foreign Minister Ebrard; Attorney General Gertz; the secretary of national defense, General Luis Cresencio Sandoval; the secretary of the navy, Admiral José Rafael Ojeda Durán; and the director general of the National Intelligence Center, Audomaro Martínez Zapata, among others. President Obrador stuck to his public claims that fentanyl was not made in Mexico and that Republicans in Congress erroneously blamed them. Conversely, this delegation was determined to communicate how serious they were about fentanyl. We received them in the Diplomatic Room of the Eisenhower Executive Office Building (EEOB) in the White House complex.[13]

The Mexican delegation delivered several presentations to highlight the scale of their efforts to combat fentanyl and Sinaloa. Thousands of personnel were enlisted in the fight. Law enforcement agents in FGR investigated fentanyl networks. Army and marine personnel pursued and eliminated cartel members. They took down fentanyl labs. They seized precursor chemicals in their ports from China. Since stepping up efforts at Biden's request, the military reportedly lost nearly four hundred personnel due to firefights with cartel militias in 2024 alone.[14] We were clear eyed that corruption from the bottom to the highest levels of government remained a problem. The "silver or lead" dilemma for government officials had not vanished. Still, the Mexican government turned a corner in the last six months. They took down El Chapo's son, Ovidio.[15] Obrador refused to incarcerate Ovidio just a few years earlier. This time he remained under lock and key in a jail cell.

Military Takeover

Many of these recent successes were due to Obrador's militarization of the border, police, and ports. Obrador was fed up with the rampant corruption of Mexican border security forces, port authorities, and local police. The president abandoned reform efforts. Instead, he ordered the marines to assume control of the ports.[16] The army took responsibility for the border and many law enforcement activities.[17] Corruption in the military still proved a problem; however, it engaged in comparatively far less corruption than local law enforcement. Military personnel didn't live among the local community. They resided on a military base. Military personnel could also be deployed to parts of the country far from their hometown. Thus, they didn't have family living alongside the gangsters and easy to threaten. Further, unlike local cops, military personnel could be rotated regularly. So, anyone who had been corrupted could be cycled out quickly. For all these reasons, transferring control for local law enforcement functions to the military seemed prudent.

We welcomed these changes. However, many in Mexico pointed to some disconcerting ramifications of these decisions. First, military personnel are not trained in policing issues like due process. Particularly if shot at, the average soldier was just as satisfied expeditiously killing the cartel militia targets in self-defense as they were achieving a conviction years in the future. The military was considered less corrupted by the drug lords than law enforcement. However, the military was not directly responsible for combating the gangster warlords as it had been in other administrations like Lázaro Cárdenas's.[18] So it was also possible that the military wasn't as corrupted by the cartels because the cartels didn't require it to be corrupted.

Most insiders believed that once the cartels decided they needed the military corrupted, they could do so. In past administrations, the dons proved "lead or silver" was just as effective with the military as with law enforcement.

Now that the military was in the countercartel business, skeptics argued, the cartels would devise methods to corrupt it more thoroughly. A corrupted military would corrode Mexican institutions and present significant dangers for citizens. This proved true in past administrations when a corrupt military was even more dangerous than corrupt local police.[19] These problems loomed for a future president to solve. For now, military control of the ports, border, and major law enforcement activities seemed the best option Obrador had in front of him.

Important for us, the military in Mexico had an incredibly strong relationship with the U.S. military. The ties harked back decades.[20] Senior Mexican military officials often receive extensive training from their U.S. counterparts and billions worth of equipment and aid.[21]

Further, many of the recent successes—taking down El Chapo's son, Ovidio Guzmán López, for example—were executed largely by the military. In fact, nearly all recent successful raids on the capos were executed by the military.[22] Gangsters lucky enough to survive military raids were later indicted by the Mexican DOJ (FGR). FGR had often painstakingly pieced the indictments together over years. Unfortunately, FGR could not rely on local cops to arrest the suspects. Charges developed from FGR's cases must be argued in court to ultimately put the mafiosi behind bars. National and local law enforcement were either outgunned in the case of the former or too riddled with corruption in the case of the latter. Still the unfortunate reality remained that to apprehend key nodes of the cartel, the military was the only option available.

The Mexican military presented another short-term benefit for us. Our intelligence community (IC)—the Central Intelligence Agency (CIA), National Security Agency (NSA), Military Intelligence in Northern Command, and others—had been working with the Mexican military for decades on various threats. Our intelligence agencies cooperated with the Mexican military on cartel issues.[23] The relationship could be traced back to both world wars, the Cold War, and, most recently, the war on terror.[24] From 9/11 onward we viewed our two-thousand-mile southern border as a key area of focus in our security infrastructure. It could be exploited by terrorists seeking to sneak into the United States and carry out attacks on U.S. soil. Thus, we established strong relationships between our intelligence community and the Mexican military.

We wanted to identify potential terrorists in Mexico so that any suspected terrorists could be apprehended before they ever made it to the United States. As one can imagine, the Mexican government was also loath to harbor any terrorist traveling through their country, lest the would-be terrorist blow something up in Mexico or establish a cell in Mexico to attack the United States.

The U.S. intelligence community recently marshaled unprecedented resources against the cartels, making a reliable partner in Mexico essential. But the intelligence collected was only valuable if the dons were not tipped off before their doors were kicked down. So President Obrador's decision to install the military in the ports, on the border, and on counter-cartel raids served this specific objective. It subverted corrupt port administrators, customs officials, and local police. That shift created a far more reliable counterpart in Mexico with whom we could securely share intelligence on Sinaloa vulnerabilities.

During the Mexican national security cabinet's diplomatic mission to Washington, Attorney General Gertz advocated precursor chemicals and pill presses rank as the top targets for our disruption effort. He cited a 1970s U.S.-Mexican campaign[25] against poppy crops as evidence that targeting raw materials is the most effective method to prevent drug production. His focus on precursor chemicals and machine parts like pill presses conjured memories for many of the American former counterterrorism warriors in attendance. Counterproliferation was a massive line of effort in the war on terror. The IC, DHS, and the military were steeped in counterproliferation. Since Hiroshima, intelligence teams had scoured the globe for nuclear materials and other weapons of mass destruction (WMDs). However, 9/11 compelled the United States to focus like a laser on the raw materials necessary to assemble nukes, WMDs, and improvised explosive devices (IEDs) from winding up in the hands of terrorists. Gertz's focus on the proliferation of precursors and pill presses made the looming battle against Sinaloa resemble the war on terror more closely than ever.

The Mexican government, though imperfect, was brought in. Obrador's rhetoric notwithstanding, the proof was in the significant high-level arrests and pitched battles against Sinaloa that had produced more than four hundred casualties of the government's own rank and file. The mere fact that Gertz was devising his own innovative strategies was a sign of their commitment.

Obrador's move to hand over control of so many levers of power to the military was further evidence of support for our cause. With these albeit tenuous and imperfect commitments from our most important ally in the fight, Mexico, we had completed the first step of the blitz on Sinaloa.

The only thing left to do was launch the attack.

Notes

1 "Joint Statement from Canada, Mexico, and the United States Following the First North American Trilateral Fentanyl Committee Meeting." Privy Council Office, Government of Canada, April 14, 2023. https://www.canada.ca/en/privy-council/news/2023/04/joint-statement-from-canada-mexico-and-the-united-states-following-the-first-north-american-trilateral-fentanyl-committee-meeting.html.

2 Breslow, Jason M. "The Staggering Death Toll of Mexico's Drug War." PBS, July 27, 2015. https://www.pbs.org/wgbh/frontline/article/the-staggering-death-toll-of-mexicos-drug-war/.

3 Stevenson, Mark. "Mexico Appears to Abandon Its 'Hugs, Not Bullets' Strategy as Bloodshed Plagues the Country." AP News, November 7, 2024. https://apnews.com/article/mexico-drug-cartels-migrants-hugs-not-bullets-violence-5cf8bbefe68ea9762a0bdd23868029f3.

4 Stevenson. "Mexico Appears to Abandon Its 'Hugs, Not Bullets' Strategy."

5 "Mexico Arrests Cartel Member Suspected of Leading Fentanyl Trade." *Malay Mail*, February 13, 2023. https://www.malaymail.com/news/world/2023/02/13/mexico-arrests-cartel-member-suspected-of-leading-fentanyl-trade/54703.

6 Ahmed, Azam. "Salvador Cienfuegos Zepeda, Mexico's Ex-Defense Minister, Is Arrested in L.A." *New York Times*, October 16, 2020. https://www.nytimes.com/2020/10/16/us/mexico-general-cienfuegos-dea.html.

7 "Graham: 'We Are Going to Unleash the Fury and Might of the U.S. against These Drug Cartels.'" U.S. Senator Lindsey Graham, March 7, 2023. https://www.lgraham.senate.gov/public/index.cfm/press-releases?ID=A86EA474-0423-4160-974D-EBCEB3C8F6E7.

8 "Graham, Senators Introduce Legislation to Designate Mexican Drug Cartels as Foreign Terrorist Organizations." U.S. Senator Lindsey Graham, March 29, 2023. https://www.lgraham.senate.gov/public/index.cfm/2023/3/graham-senators-introduce-legislation-to-designate-mexican-drug-cartels-as-foreign-terrorist-organizations.

9 O'Boyle, Brendan. "Mexico President Rejects 'Irresponsible' Calls for US Military Action against Cartels." Reuters, March 9, 2023. https://www.reuters.com/world/

americas/mexico-president-rejects-us-lawmakers-calls-military-intervention-against
-2023-03-09/.

10 Mann, Brian. "Mexico's Leader Denies His Country's Role in Fentanyl Crisis: Republicans Are Furious." NPR, March 10, 2023. https://www.npr.org/2023/03/10/1162584753/president-obrador-disputes-mexico-fentanyl-crisis-republicans-outraged.

11 "Third Meeting of the U.S.-Mexico High-Level Security Dialogue." U.S. Department of State, April 10, 2024. https://2021-2025.state.gov/third-meeting-of-the-u-s-mexico-high-level-security-dialogue/.

12 O'Boyle. "Mexico President Rejects 'Irresponsible' Calls for US Military Action against Cartels."

13 "Joint Statement from Mexico and the United States on the Implementation of the U.S.-Mexico Bicentennial Framework for Security, Public Health, and Safe Communities." White House, April 14, 2023. https://bidenwhitehouse.archives.gov/briefing-room/statements-releases/2023/04/13/joint-statement-from-mexico-and-the-united-states-on-the-implementation-of-the-u-s-mexico-bicentennial-framework-for-security-public-health-and-safe-communities/.

14 Ferri, Pablo. "Shootouts, Burned-Out Cars and Closed Airports: Los Chapitos Terrorize Culiacán after Ovidio Guzmán Arrest." *El País English*, January 6, 2023. https://english.elpais.com/international/2023-01-06/shootouts-burned-out-cars-and-closed-airports-los-chapitos-terrorize-culiacan-after-ovidio-guzman-arrest.html.

15 Stevenson, Mark, and María Verza. "Mexico Gives Account of Violence after 'Chapo' Son Nabbed." AP News, January 6, 2023. https://apnews.com/article/politics-united-states-government-mexico-drug-crimes-city-d74ba460138c067ca538c862e3f0a5b0.

16 Mahoney, Noi. "Mexico Puts Military in Charge of Nation's Ports." FreightWaves, July 20, 2020. https://www.freightwaves.com/news/mexico-puts-military-in-charge-of-nations-ports.

17 Mahoney. "Mexico Puts Military in Charge of Nation's Ports."

18 Sánchez, Fabiola. "Mexico's Congress Puts National Guard under Military Command Despite Criticism: Why Does It Matter?" AP News. September 25, 2024. https://apnews.com/article/mexico-congress-national-guard-military-b31ab1b6aa165f87012fb93845922b9a.

19 Freeman, Will. "Can Mexico's Next President Control the Military?" *Journal of Democracy*, March 2024. https://www.journalofdemocracy.org/online-exclusive/can-mexicos-next-president-control-the-military/.

20 González Torres, Jonathan Agustín. "U.S.-Mexico Military Cooperation: From WWII to the Merida Initiative." Banderas News, October 14, 2010. https://banderasnews.com/1010/edat-usmexcooperation.htm.

21 Lettieri, Michael. "U.S. Military Training of Mexican Armed Forces and Law Enforcement." Mexico Violence, 2022. https://www.mexicoviolence.org/military-training.

22 For example, see "Mexican Soldiers Kill 19 Drug Cartel Suspects and Suffer No Casualties in Sinaloa State." AP News, October 23, 2024. https://apnews.com/article/mexico-army-drug-cartel-sinaloa-9789a8286055ec01d13497b2a8e3f995; "Mexican Troops Seize a Record Fentanyl Haul in Northern Sinaloa State." AP News, December 4, 2024. https://apnews.com/article/mexico-fentanyl-drug-seizure-76b274660df084d d36e57dc6c000d922; "Mexico Arrests Ovidio Guzmán, a Son of 'El Chapo,' Ahead of Biden Visit." CBS News, January 6, 2023. https://www.cbsnews.com/news/el-chapo-son-ovidio-guzman-arrested-mexico-culiacan-violence/.

23 Several examples of intelligence cooperation are outlined here: "Third Meeting of the U.S.-Mexico High-Level Security Dialogue." U.S. Department of State, April 10, 2024. https://2021-2025.state.gov/third-meeting-of-the-u-s-mexico-high-level-security-dialogue/. The following are some other specific examples: Iaconangelo, David. "Operation 'Lowrider' Sends US Manned Aircraft into Mexico to Track Drug Cartels." *Latin Times*, August 30, 2013. https://www.latintimes.com/operation-lowrider-sends-us-manned-aircraft-mexico-track-drug-cartels-130720; "DEA Operation Last Mile Tracks Down Sinaloa and Jalisco Cartel Associates Operating within the United States." Drug Enforcement Administration, May 5, 2023. https://www.dea.gov/press-releases/2023/05/05/dea-operation-last-mile-tracks-down-sinaloa-and-jalisco-cartel-associates.

24 Arzt, Sigrid. "U.S.-Mexico Security Collaboration: Intelligence Sharing and Law Enforcement Cooperation." Wilson Center, n.d. https://www.wilsoncenter.org/sites/default/files/media/documents/publication/Chapter%2012-%20U.S.-Mexico%20Security%20Collaboration%2C%20Intelligence%20Sharing%20and%20Law%20Enforcement%20Cooperation.pdf.

25 Craig, Richard. "Operation Condor: Mexico's Antidrug Campaign Enters a New Era." *Journal of Interamerican Studies and World Affairs* 22, no. 3 (1980): 345–63. https://doi.org/10.2307/165493.

13

Blue Lotus

All the data we poured into the analytics machine at the National Targeting Center (NTC) and Homeland Security Investigations (HSI) lab yielded results.

Once we combined financial data with shipping data and case data on Sinaloa or fentanyl, the agents could predict where some loads of fentanyl would materialize. They also generated a significant number of high-value leads that had previously gone unnoticed in their database. It was striking how a few conversations several months ago about mundane data integration yielded such significant results. The progress made HSI feel comfortable sharing their case data. That led Customs and Border Protection (CBP) to add their shipping data to the mix. Treasury integrated its data early in the process. Between the NTC and HSI lab, we amassed a potential data analytical juggernaut that could illuminate Sinaloa's network with unique insights otherwise masked from us. A tech entrepreneur once told me that anyone can write code to analyze data. What provides an analytics company competitive advantage is gaining access to unique data. So when the incredibly unique case data, shipping data, and finance data was combined, in Silicon Valley parlance, we had a unicorn on our hands. HSI and CBP, especially via the NTC, had accumulated more relevant data on fentanyl and the Sinaloa network than anyone else on the planet.

This new targeting capability, along with the internal operational planning and diplomatic groundwork we laid with the Mexican government, produced a strong foundation for launching operations against Sinaloa. HSI, CBP, and other parts of the federal government had been pursuing cases against

Sinaloa for years. Until now, many of those cases were worked in silos. Today, the Central Intelligence Agency (CIA), U.S. military, Drug Enforcement Administration (DEA), National Security Agency (NSA), Department of Justice (DOJ), CBP, HSI, and Treasury collaborated to disrupt Sinaloa's fentanyl network. Traditionally, agents in the field routinely assisted their colleagues on cases because of personal relationships. Now that collaboration was mandated from the top and routinized with recurring exercises like Fentanyl Friday. We could swarm multiple aspects of the federal government all at once. The capability to direct data collection, analysis, and diplomacy, which translated to attacks on Sinaloa, had been absent at the seniormost levels of government until now. We were poised to pounce on Sinaloa at a degree not conceivable even a few months earlier.

Department of Homeland Security secretary Alejandro Mayorkas upped the ante at a meeting in early 2023. He directed HSI and CBP to surge forces at the two ports of entry laden with fentanyl on the Southwest Border. San Isidro and Nogales were key ports of entry that fell in Sinaloa plaza boss turf.[1] Those ports were also the most efficient access points for drugs destined for Los Angeles and then shipped around the country. HSI leadership initially committed to surge fifty agents to those ports for fentanyl investigations and seizures. Upon hearing this, the secretary demanded they and CBP increase that number tenfold to five hundred. His strategic bet was that the border surge would not only interdict fentanyl coming across the border. More important, the seizures would generate arrests and the accompanying interrogations to provide our agents with leads. Those leads would enable agents to chase key nodes in the Sinaloa network. Further, Mayorkas insisted we speed up timelines to install additional container scanning equipment at the border. Here again, he had another key insight. As the scanners would still take months and years to fully install, he directed CBP leadership to leverage artificial intelligence (AI) to analyze millions of images of vehicles and shipping containers at once. The AI would then alert customs officers or border agents if a vehicle or package looked suspicious. Massive scanning equipment would take years to install, but AI software could be downloaded with the click of a button.

Mayorkas also knew the visible surge in agents and equipment would deter the cartels from sending fentanyl through those two ports. One may think this is a fool's errand. Sinaloa can just shift fentanyl packages to other ports where we are *not* surging. The Sinaloa logistics executives are well schooled to outmaneuver us by flooding fentanyl wherever the border patrol surge is *not*. It is true that the cat-and-mouse game between customs officials and the cartels is tilted in the cartels' favor. However, the other ports east of Nogales and San Isidro are ruled with an iron fist by other cartels like the Cartel de Jalisco Nueva Generación (CJNG).[2] CJNG is the archenemy of Sinaloa. Forcing Sinaloa east significantly increases the cost of fentanyl. CJNG would levy a hefty tax to run fentanyl through their ports. CJNG would relish extorting an astronomical rate for moving the gringos' most despised poison through their turf. Sinaloa's narco-tycoons could also make a business decision to fight their way into control of one of the CJNG ports. That would likely cost hundreds if not thousands of lives. But with increased pressure from the Mexican military and U.S. agencies, Sinaloa executives needed their foot soldiers focused on smuggling and fighting off the military. The Sinaloa C-Suite could not afford to have its militia bogged down in a pitched battle with CJNG or another cartel. Sinaloa transportation gurus could activate their prolific network of tunnels, drones, and submarines to sneak fentanyl across the border; however, our intelligence network scanned the skies, water, and even underground to stymie the criminal corporate logisticians' best-laid plans.

Despite all these gains, we understood the war on fentanyl would not be won at the border. Inevitably, duffel bags or car trunks full of fentanyl would slip by. Just one of those duffel bags or car trunks could contain enough fentanyl to kill everyone in Chicago. The days of interdicting marijuana were over. Back then the cartels were required to ship in multiple tons just to fulfill demand. Fentanyl was so potent a few kilos was enough to kill millions.[3] Mayorkas was adamant we couple our border surge with increased investigations on the cartels and the Chinese chemical companies supplying them. HSI had implemented pilot programs in select cities like San Diego and Fresno to focus local investigators on fentanyl.[4] At the secretary's direction, those efforts expanded to multiple cities around the country with various degrees of effort, including opioid suppression teams, fentanyl overdose response teams, and state and local law enforcement support.

Mathew Brodman at HSI and Jorge Comas at CBP pulled their teams together for several all-nighters. They meticulously plotted and deployed the operation Mayorkas directed. Both welcomed Mayorkas's directive. They were champing at the bit to take the fight to Sinaloa with the new tech and organizational assets we had painstakingly built over the last several months. Usually, an operation like the one Brodman and Comas executed would take months to plan and deploy. They churned through all the logistics planning in two weeks. Brodman and Comas were men on a mission. They instantiated a fentanyl war room pop-up at the National Targeting Center. On March 17, 2023, just two weeks after the Mayorkas directive to "think through how to surge at the border," they launched the first of several successive waves of federal agents and police.[5] We netted seventy-three people on fentanyl charges and seized nearly one thousand pounds of fentanyl in the first week of the operation alone.[6] This was nearly a 500 percent increase from the same period a year earlier.[7] Comas and Brodman's zeal for the mission clearly transferred to their troops. After Brodman put his agents on conference calls with deceased victims' families, they were fired up. By the time they boarded planes for the border, there was no question how high the stakes were for what they were about to do.

We named the operation Blue Lotus. The name was chosen out of thin air as many of these named operations are. Ultimately, we would surge more than five hundred HSI agents and CBP officers to a handful of key ports of entry on the border.[8] Now that we had full cooperation from the intelligence community (IC), we had the IC watching the operation unfold on the Mexican side of the border. They could monitor how the Sinaloa logistics executives scrambled to adjust their tactics based on our surge. In fact, Troy Miller, the steady hand leading CBP, repeatedly emphasized the most valuable commodity we would gain out of Blue Lotus was not just fentanyl seizures or arrests but, rather, intelligence to illuminate the network and decision-making process of Sinaloa. Despite our dramatically increased intelligence collection and analysis, we still groped in the dark for insights on key parts of Sinaloa's network. Locations of labs, money laundering, and precursor distribution throughout Mexico opaquely drifted behind an unpierceable veil covering the criminal underworld. The illumination tactic of Blue Lotus was informed by the war on terror. When General Stan McCrystal took over the Joint Special Operations Command (JSOC) in 2003, he changed its mission to be one of intelligence gathering as opposed to simply taking terrorists off the field through capturing or killing them.[9] While JSOC still oversaw the capture and killing of scores of terrorists, this paradigmatic shift radically changed how the war on terror was conducted. It also enhanced our understanding of the terrorist network and consequently our ability to defeat the network. The same lessons applied to the fight against Sinaloa.

This intelligence-gathering sensibility was deeply ingrained in both the military and homeland security enterprise. Years of experience hunting terrorists made Miller conclude the intelligence gleaned from the operation was paramount to building out the broader networks, illuminating the entire fentanyl supply chain, and eventually helping save more lives. And it did. The intelligence gathered during Blue Lotus laid the groundwork for future operations. The numbers we touted to the press and Congress were predictably focused on arrests and seizures as those are the catnip metrics reporters and congressmen feed on. What sent Morgan Ryan and me into a giddy frenzy, however, was the intelligence Blue Lotus flushed out for our spies. We queried our IC friends during the operation. We pressed for any new insights into the inner workings of the Sinaloa enterprise during Operation Blue Lotus. They responded, "Oh yes . . . we are already working on a report for you."

Another positive development of Blue Lotus was that DOJ collaborated more closely with HSI than ever. Senior leaders at DHS and DOJ in Washington, DC, had worked out much of what irked them. As a result, their teams worked hand in glove as we planned the operations to combat fentanyl. That reconciliation provided ample running room to prosecutors at DOJ who were aggressively pursuing cases against those HSI and CBP pinched during Blue Lotus. All told, between the results of Blue Lotus and a DEA operation running concurrently that took down several high-ranking gangsters in the Sinaloa network, it was the largest and by far and away most successful counterfentanyl operation in history. HSI and CBP arrested 284 cartel affiliates in less than three months and seized more than ten thousand pounds of fentanyl.[10]

At about the same time as scores of thugs and mountains of fentanyl were nabbed during Blue Lotus, DOJ, State, and Treasury quietly executed other disruption activities. The results of their efforts were announced at the same time as the results of Blue Lotus. The coordinated announcements were explicitly designed to pack a bigger punch in the collective psyche of Sinaloa's C-Suite. We wanted the criminal corporate executives to understand in no uncertain terms that they had made a grave miscalculation. Their decision to conceal poison in the drugs they sold to the United States would result in one unrelenting wave of attack against the cartel after another. The entire U.S. government was now unified in our plan of attack on their narco-empire. We hammered home in the media that the dramatically increased heat they felt from the authorities on both sides of the border was solely due to fentanyl. The criminal executives were rational actors. They were not ideologues like terrorists. They were businessmen at their core. We used the bully pulpit to ensure the cost-benefit analysis was clear as day: "Keep selling fentanyl in the United States and this heat will only increase. Stop selling fentanyl and we will turn down the heat."

Next, the State Department put bounties on the heads of several top mobsters: "The U.S. Department of State, through its Narcotics Rewards Program, offered rewards of up to $10 million for information leading to the arrest and/or conviction of Ivan Guzman Salazar, Alfredo Guzman Salazar, and Ovidio Guzman Lopez, and up to $5 million for information leading to the arrest and/or conviction of Joaquin Guzman Lopez."[11] This incentivized the gangsters' comrades to curry favor with authorities and garner a reward by turning in their nefarious colleagues. Narcos routinely turned in their competimates when it benefited them. Gone were the days these corporate gangsters adhered to the "honor among thieves" mantra. There were billions of dollars at stake. The dons strategically ratted out rivals the federales pinned on the Most Wanted list. Ratting conveniently removed an obstacle to career advancement without being forced to take a rival out themselves. If the heat was too hot on a guy you don't like, just give him up to the authorities and make it look like the Americans' expert sleuthing smoked him out. Adding narcos to the State Department most wanted list was like affixing doomsday clocks to their lapels. Everyone knew the gangsters' days were numbered.

Next the Department of Treasury levied sanctions against multiple Chinese nationals and precursor chemical companies supplying Sinaloa with chemicals requisite to make fentanyl. A description of the charges reads as follows:

The U.S. Department of the Treasury's Office of Foreign Assets Control (OFAC) designated two entities in the People's Republic of China (PRC) and five individuals, based in the PRC and Guatemala, for supplying precursor chemicals to drug cartels in Mexico for the production of illicit fentanyl intended for U.S. markets. OFAC designated Wuhan Shuokang Biological Technology Co., Ltd (武汉硕康生物科技有限公司) (WSBT) and Yao Huatao (姚华涛) (Yao) . . . for having engaged in, or attempted to engage in, activities or transactions that have materially contributed to, or pose a significant risk of materially contributing to, the international proliferation of illicit drugs or their means of production. Yao, a PRC national, is the sole owner of PRC-based chemical company WSBT—an entity responsible for the sale of fentanyl precursor chemicals—and, as its Executive Director, oversees the company's operations. OFAC additionally designated WSBT for being owned, controlled, or directed by, or having acted or purported to act for or on behalf of, directly or indirectly, Yao. OFAC also sanctioned three additional PRC nationals for their association with WSBT. Wu Yaqin (吴雅琴) (Wu) and Wu Yonghao (吴永昊) (Yonghao), sales representatives of Yao's company WSBT, not only negotiated and facilitated the sale of fentanyl precursor chemicals on the behalf of WSBT, but Wu also provided information on efficient preparation methods for synthesizing illicit fentanyl. Wang Hongfei (王洪飞) (Wang), a WSBT collaborator, is the owner of a cryptocurrency wallet that has been used to receive bitcoin payments for illicit drug transactions on behalf of WSBT.[12]

These sanctions represented the culmination of months of painstaking work at Treasury. Treasury officials were now firing on all cylinders. These sanctions were just the beginning. Dozens more would follow.[13] More important, these sanctions put the other three hundred chemical companies supplying precursor chemicals to the cartels on notice. Uncle Sam was coming for them and their ill-gotten proceeds. These sanctions, and many more to come, alerted otherwise legitimate Chinese chemical companies that they should think twice before dabbling in the black market with Sinaloa. Sanction after sanction tightened our grip on the spigot of chemicals streaming into Mexico from China.

Finally, the Justice Department, along with the DEA, unsealed indictments on several Sinaloa tycoons.[14] They also arrested several key dons deep into the Sinaloa network. These arrests had been planned in excruciating detail for months. In the weeks leading up to the operation, we were on pins and needles hoping nothing would go sideways. Many of the perpetrators were hit simultaneously to avoid any one gangster tipping off the others. Much of this was accomplished because the DEA had targeted the highest ranks of the Sinaloa C-Suite. The DEA had unparalleled access to informants, intelligence, and operatives who set their sights on the executive ranks of the organization directing operations for Sinaloa and took them down in unison.

In an unforeseen turn of events, however, we learned the entire Mexican national security cabinet, at the direction of President Andrés Manuel López Obrador, was headed to Washington. The meeting was requested as a follow-up to the diplomatic mission a few weeks earlier; however, they arrived the very same day the arrests, indictments, and sanctions were to be executed and announced. This posed a serious potential problem. If these massive strikes against the Sinaloa tycoons came to light as we were meeting with the Mexican leadership, it could be terribly embarrassing for the Mexicans. We had spent an enormous amount of time and energy cultivating goodwill between our teams. They also took on political and even personal physical risk by partnering with us to oppose Sinaloa. This new trip was a case in point. It turned out they were traveling to the United States to report back on efforts against Sinaloa since our last strategy session. It posed huge risks if we did not alert them to the massive operation unfolding while they were sitting across the table from us. Surely it would come off as a slap in the face to the only people who could take action against Sinaloa in Mexico. Forging a strong partnership with these officials presented our best option at taking down the gangster warlords. But we knew they were imperfect partners. A courtesy heads-up to them could end up as a tip-off to the gangsters we were trying to pinch. We opted to leave the leadership in the dark. Instead, we timed the agenda for the meetings to coincide with the arrests. So during a strategically timed break in the agenda, we pulled a few key partners aside moments after the final apprehensions were made. We came clean on the dragnet. We also gave them time to retire back to Mexico before we announced the operation. This ensured they maintained political distance from the arrests. The officials didn't want to appear as America's lapdogs brought here to eat crow as we announced arrests of Mexican citizens. The day after they left Washington, DHS, DOJ, Treasury, and State made our respective announcements. The facts stared Sinaloa bosses in the face. The entire U.S. government was working in unison to take down their fentanyl operations.

Some petty bureaucratic infighting continued; however, it was muted compared to early planning stages of the operation. Mike Ben'Ary and Hilary Hurd, top lieutenants for Attorney General Lisa Monaco, kept plates spinning as dozens of DOJ component operations converged on Sinaloa at once. While Mike and Hilary were loyal to their agency, they were pros and became great partners for Morgan and me to orchestrate our respective agencies' fight against fentanyl. However, the most important driver of cooperation was constant pressure from the very top. Joe Biden himself was consistently clear with his senior leadership team that combating fentanyl was one of the top priorities of his administration. Consequently, Mayorkas, Liz Sherwood-Randall, John Tien, and Monaco consistently pushed their organizations to do more.

Later in 2023, Sinaloa executives disseminated public messages instructing its subcontractors to cease and desist the production and sale of fentanyl immediately. Just a few weeks later, the *Wall Street Journal* reported Sinaloa's corporate enforcers directed kidnappings and assassinations of the narco-corporations' affiliates involved in fentanyl.[15] My law enforcement colleagues were dubious as to the sincerity of these unprecedented directives. Needless to say, this was atypical public behavior for the gangster warlords. Thankfully, our agents are suspicious by nature of anything the bad guys conjure up. They suspected a lot of the assassinations were astute marketing by the Sinaloa C-Suite to dress up an unrelated Byzantine corporate purge as a bloody fentanyl business line downsizing. In Sinaloa's own unique brand of corporate marketing, these messages were delivered in the form of bloodstained banners draped on highway overpasses. Bodies of insubordinate dealers were left in public places.

Regardless of the motivation, it was unprecedented that Sinaloa leadership would publicly target corporate managers of an otherwise profitable line of business. As mentioned before, to sustain eminence in the local populations' hearts and minds, the criminal corporate philanthropists had to perpetuate the ethos of Robin Hood. Kowtowing to the Sheriff of Nottingham's wishes subverted that narrative. The brand managers at Sinaloa had taken a radical departure from their marketing strategy. It may have been a convenient way to kill two birds with one stone: justify assassinations of internal rivals and give U.S. and Mexican authorities a false sense of progress. While all this may be accurate, the macabre drama unfolding in Sinaloa strongholds was unthinkable when we initiated this effort just a year earlier.

Another blow to the fentanyl trade came from the Joe Biden–Xi Jinping summit in San Francisco, California, on November 15, 2023. Tensions had flared over Taiwan. Relations were at a nadir from the past three years. Most of the summit seemed to be about simply agreeing to reestablish lines of communication as the two nations had severed cooperation on a number of key issues. One issue, however, stood out as tangible progress. Biden lobbied Xi to clamp down on the flow of fentanyl precursor chemicals to Mexican cartels. Xi agreed. We must obviously verify progress on China's enforcement of this ban.[16] Until that summit, China didn't factor precursors into its earlier commitment to ban sales of illicit finished fentanyl in the United States.

Also, federal law enforcement agencies armed with tools like the NTC and C3 have been on a rampage against Sinaloa since Blue Lotus. CBP launched Operation Plaza Spike to disrupt fentanyl operations of the Sinaloa plaza bosses in border towns. Authorities arrested another of the Chapitos and El Mayo, key leaders of the cartel. Further, HSI arrested forty-seven key members of Sinaloa involved in facilitating its fentanyl supply chain. Later, in DEA's Operation Last Mile, more than three thousand cartel henchmen involved in fentanyl distribution were arrested.[17] Leveraging the NTC, CBP has now seized millions of fentanyl pills and mountains of powder. We have also assisted Mexican authorities to strike at fentanyl labs deep in Sinaloa territory. A constant onslaught of successive surge after surge with operations like Four Horsemen, Artemis, Rolling Wave, and Apollo netted 43,000 pounds of fentanyl, 5,600 arrests, and 3,600 of the insidious pill presses. In some cases, this represented a 2000 percent increase in law enforcement actions from the year previous.[18]

The Treasury Department has also continued to pile on and is now sanctioning whole companies like Wuhan Shuokang Biological Technology involved in selling fentanyl precursors to Sinaloa, along with dozens of other individuals and entities involved in fentanyl in both China and Mexico.

This level of focused, tech-enabled, counternetwork campaign is surpassed only by the war on terror. No previous campaign against transnational criminal organizations has had anywhere near the technological and data analytic support as this. None has marshaled this many agents against it at once. None has enveloped the globe as completely as this campaign. Never has the intelligence community devoted this much time and energy to support a counter-cartel operation.

In short, the scale of the counterfentanyl campaign against Sinaloa and its affiliates is unprecedented. No wonder the Sinaloa C-Suite is turning on each other and assassinating those involved. If this pressure holds, we can expect a significant decrease in fentanyl fatalities in the United States. In fact, 2023 saw the first year-over-year drop in overdose deaths in over a decade since the crisis began.[19] Then, in 2024, after the counter-fentanyl campaign effects were realized, overdose deaths dropped a full 37 percent.[20] These drops are unprecedented. Enforcement cannot claim sole ownership of the decline. Public awareness and broader distribution of antidotes like naloxone certainly have had an impact. That being said, it is also true that the decline began at nearly the exact same time as Blue Lotus and the other efforts were launched.

But we have not yet won. Too many people per year are still poisoned to death by fentanyl. While this operation is unprecedented, it is not enough. More must be done if we are going to win the fight against fentanyl as we won the war on terror.

Notes

1   Resendiz, Julian. "DEA: Cartels Now Growing Coca in Mexico." BorderReport, June 14, 2024. https://www.borderreport.com/immigration/border-crime/dea-cartels-now -growing-coca-in-mexico/.

2 Prendido, Sol. "US Congress: Jalisco Cartel Now Has Presence in 28 States." Borderland Beat, August 8, 2022. https://www.borderlandbeat.com/2022/08/us-congress-jalisco-cartel-now-has.html.

3 "Why Is Fentanyl so Dangerous?" Drugs.com, last updated August 5, 2024. https://www.drugs.com/medical-answers/fentanyl-deadly-3569690/.

4 "HSI San Diego Welcomes California DOJ to Multiagency Task Force to Target Fentanyl Trafficking." U.S. Immigration and Customs Enforcement, October 23, 2023. https://www.ice.gov/news/releases/hsi-san-diego-welcomes-california-doj-multiagency-task-force-target-fentanyl.

5 "Fact Sheet: DHS Is on the Front Lines Combating Illicit Opioids, Including Fentanyl." U.S. Department of Homeland Security, December 22, 2023. https://www.dhs.gov/news/2023/12/22/fact-sheet-dhs-front-lines-combating-illicit-opioids-including-fentanyl.

6 "DHS's New Operation Blue Lotus Has Already Stopped More Than 900 Pounds of Fentanyl from Entering the United States." U.S. Department of Homeland Security, March 21, 2023. https://www.dhs.gov/news/2023/03/21/dhss-new-operation-blue-lotus-has-already-stopped-more-900-pounds-fentanyl-entering.

7 "Fact Sheet: DHS Is on the Front Lines Combating Illicit Opioids, Including Fentanyl."

8 "Statement of Katrina W. Berger, Executive Associate Director, Homeland Security Investigations, U.S. Department of Homeland Security, Regarding a Hearing Titled 'Oversight of Homeland Security Investigations' before the U.S. House of Representatives Judiciary Committee." U.S. Department of Homeland Security, September 18, 2024, 8. https://www.ice.gov/doclib/news/library/speeches/240918berger.pdf.

9 Gray, Kevin. "The General Who Led a New Kind of Warfare to Take on Al-Qaeda." *Wired*, December 10, 2014. https://www.wired.com/story/new-art-of-business/.

10 Gray. "The General Who Led a New Kind of Warfare to Take on Al-Qaeda."

11 "Narcotics Rewards Program." U.S. Department of State, January 7, 2025. https://www.state.gov/inl-rewards-program/narcotics-rewards-program/?coll_filter_year=2023&coll_filter_month=&coll_filter_country=244&coll_filter_release_type=&coll_filter_bureau=&results=.

12 "U.S. Sanctions Suppliers of Precursor Chemicals for Fentanyl Production." U.S. Department of the Treasury, April 14, 2023. https://home.treasury.gov/news/press-releases/jy1413.

13 "Treasury Targets Large Chinese Network of Illicit Drug Producers." U.S. Department of the Treasury, January 14, 2025. https://home.treasury.gov/news/press-releases/jy1779.

14 "Four of Chapo's Sons Indicted for Large-Scale Drug Trafficking, Money." U.S. Attorney's Office, Southern District of California, April 14, 2023. https://www.justice

.gov/usao-sdca/pr/four-chapos-sons-indicted-large-scale-drug-trafficking-money
-laundering-and-violent.

15 Weber, P. "Mexico's Sinaloa Cartel Bans Fentanyl, Reportedly under Pain of Death."
The Week, October 17, 2023. https://theweek.com/business/mexicos-sinaloa-cartel
-bans-fentanyl-reportedly-under-pain-of-death.

16 Sevastopulo, Demetri. "China Imposes Restrictions on Fentanyl Chemicals after
Pressure from US." *Financial Times*, August 7, 2024. https://www.ft.com/content
/9e2bcaaf-6acc-4c64-b8c7-99cf58120f97.

17 "DEA Operation Last Mile Disrupts Fentanyl Trafficking Fueled by the Sinaloa and
Jalisco Cartels." U.S. Department of Justice, May 5, 2023. https://www.justice.gov/opa
/pr/dea-operation-last-mile-disrupts-fentanyl-trafficking-fueled-sinaloa-and-jalisco
-cartels.

18 "Fact Sheet: DHS Is on the Front Lines Combating Illicit Opioids, Including Fentanyl."

19 Garnett, Matthew F., and Arialdi M. Miniño. 2024. "Drug Overdose Deaths in the
United States, 2003-2023.

20 CDC, National Center for Health Statistics, Office of Communication. May, 2025.
"U.S. Overdose Deaths Decrease Almost 27% in 2024." https://www.cdc.gov/nchs/
pressroom/nchs_press_releases/2025/20250514.htm.

14

To the Gates of Hell

The administration made significant progress in the fight against fentanyl over the course of 2022 and 2023. It enhanced data collection and analysis capabilities. It honed intelligence operations. It expanded enforcement actions with the Mexican government. It integrated attacks on Sinaloa's fentanyl supply chain across multiple departments. As a result, and likely increased public awareness of the dangers and ubiquity of fentanyl, overdose deaths have finally begun a significant drop.[1] We are also detecting signs Sinaloa has received the message and curbed production.[2]

For example, we are seizing fewer loads of fentanyl at the border while other drug seizures remain high or the same.[3] A drop in seizures of any contraband always begs the question, "Has the cartel just gotten better at smuggling fentanyl? Are we seizing less as a result of better obfuscation tactics?" Possibly. However, normally we find that creative drug stashing leads to an overall decrease in seizures. Not just a decrease in one drug. We have also seen the cartels alter routes they use to smuggle fentanyl.[4] Changing routes generally means the criminal logisticians are under such duress they are forced out of their comfort zones. Also, Sinaloa now recruits minors as smugglers. This is likely in part because it lost so many henchmen due to the massive series of arrests that the Department of Homeland Security (DHS) and other agencies executed in programs like Blue Lotus. Minors generally just get slapped on the wrist and sent home with incensed parents. They are not locked up for years on a drug mule charge. Thus, they can return to driving fentanyl across the border within days of arrest. Sinaloa does not change tactics unless it is forced to do so. Changing tactics adds new variables into their process. Those variables can lead to unforeseen attacks on the organization like loads seized, foot soldiers rounded up, or money and guns confiscated. The fact that Sinaloa has changed its tactics provides a clear indication they are feeling the pinch.

Pinched or not, fentanyl still flows and Americans still succumb.

There are several fronts where we must ratchet up pressure on the gangster warlords for the death toll to drop more significantly.

There are three aspects of the Sinaloa cartel central to its staying power and massive profits. First, Sinaloa is situated next to the largest economy on earth. Thus, it is quite literally uniquely positioned to reap enormous profits from distribution to the U.S. market. Second, it is a narco-capitalist criminal enterprise that is driven solely to maximize profits. It is not ideologically driven. Finally, Sinaloa enables that criminal enterprise through a ubiquitous corruption regime that protects its criminal exploits. If we are to degrade the narco-empire's ability to sustain a business vertical, we must attack all three pillars of its corporate empire.

Each line of attack broadly falls along the same three areas. First, to address the enormous U.S. economic opportunity just across the border from Sinaloa, we must seek to shrink that market. This presents a conundrum as the demand for fentanyl stands close to zero. This should not be done with typical harm reduction messaging. As stated earlier in the book, traditional antidrug messaging is irrelevant for fentanyl. Instead, we must approach consumption reduction as a public service announcement (PSA) to alert Americans that a mass poisoning is happening in America. Fentanyl PSAs to date have been too targeted and do not squarely address the crisis as a mass poisoning as opposed to a narcotics problem. Parents, teachers, social service workers, and nearly everyone in America must be vigilant to shield loved ones from this poison. In short, this is not an advertising campaign to educate kids about the dangers of fentanyl. It is a public service announcement about their risk of poisoning.

Second, we must employ new and innovative methods to find and seize cartel financial assets. Sinaloa has a host of brilliant accountants stashing money for them.[5] One key attribute of the narco-tycoons, however, is that they desire Western assets in the United States and Europe. The dons yearn for U.S.

and European real estate, cars, clothes, and legitimate (and illegitimate) front companies. These assets are hidden under layers of accounting misdirection, but they can be ascertained. Further, we must work with the Mexican authorities to seize their assets in Mexico as well. Investigators do yeoman's work in this area. Through cyber intelligence gathering, we can do more.

Finally, we must disrupt the formidable corruption racket insulating Sinaloa from investigation, capture, prosecution, and incarceration. Here again, the intelligence community plays a pivotal role. The U.S. government still understands less about Sinaloa than Ford knows about Toyota. One may argue that the Ford versus Toyota comparison is unfair. However, the U.S. government also doesn't know as much about Sinaloa as it does about al-Qaeda or the Islamic State of Iraq and Syria (ISIS). Yet Sinaloa's fentanyl kills more than one hundred times as many Americans as al-Qaeda and ISIS have combined. Said another way, it kills twenty-five times as many Americans annually as all Islamic terror attacks since 9/11 combined.[6] Generating a level of fidelity of the Sinaloa network, as Ford has on Toyota, or we have with ISIS, is crucial to dismantling the corruption network that safeguards their business.

Fatality rates are decreasing. But they are not decreasing fast enough. Tens of thousands of people still die from fentanyl every year. As long as deaths remain high, we need to build on the significant achievements to date. The following sections describe six actions that could achieve a broader impact.

1. Shrinking Market for Fentanyl

This effort should ideally shrink the market for all drugs containing fentanyl. Sinaloa's dons must experience a decrease in sales of all drugs as a result of fentanyl being cut into other drugs. We know cartel executives are contraband agnostic. If sales of coke, heroin, meth, and illicit prescription pills *all* decrease because the public is appropriately terrified the drugs conceal fentanyl, then the drug lords will have no choice but to resume selling purer forms of those drugs. Thus, the advertising message cannot treat the epidemic as a run-of-the-mill narcotics crisis. We cannot simply reboot the slogan "This is your brain on drugs." A Gen Z version of "This is your brain on fentanyl" will fail.

Instead, these PSAs need to label this epidemic what it is: a mass poisoning. These ads must convince current and future users that, for the moment, the U.S. government is not preaching to them about living a clean life. Instead, we must make explicitly clear that all unregulated drugs may contain this deadly poison. All drugs, including any prescription pills obtained from a friend or otherwise not purchased from a legitimate pharmacist are highly likely to contain fentanyl. If they consume unregulated drugs, they may perish due to fentanyl poisoning. It should be clear that no dealer will tell them their drugs are cut with fentanyl, and the narco-corporate titans purposely conceal the poison in their drugs. The drug lords obfuscate fentanyl to get victims more high and hooked. Once hooked, the victim will seek fentanyl-laced drugs incessantly until they die. Period.

Further, the ads the government has run are far too targeted at kids and young adults on social media.[7] The federal government must flood every digital and broadcast media platform. To date, messaging has been highly targeted on particular social media platforms. The ads educate youth about the dangers of consuming fentanyl. There is no question we must get the message to the country's youth. However, instead of overly sophisticated targeting, we must blanket the airwaves. Rather than microtargeting, we should ensure no one in the country can escape the poison message. We must sear these ads into the brains of parents, educators, health care professionals, grandparents, and everyone in between. The ads should compel everyone in a current or potential user's life to incessantly remind loved ones that any drug not obtained legitimately could be poisoned.

Most parents and educators have no concept of the scope and scale of the problem, nor that there's no room for error. Parents and educators, those closest to our nation's children and young adults, are blind to the reality that we are living through a mass poisoning. They are oblivious that their loved ones are at risk of being fatally poisoned. Further, most adults consider fentanyl a "hard drug" problem like heroin. Thus, many parents of kids who do not display a tendency toward highly risky behavior may find the problem irrelevant. However, if asked whether their little angel may take a Ritalin from a friend as a study aid for finals, they may rightly assess the risk to their child very differently. Messaging narrowly instructing people to abstain from fentanyl misses the mark. So the messaging should broaden. This messaging has been adopted in New York City.[8] NYC authorities educate residents they should assume all illicit drugs and any pill that did not come directly from their pharmacist contains fentanyl and can kill them. We need to be clear that this is not a redux of the Reefer Madness panics of the 1970s. It's not just the cause du jour of America's temperance movement. Rather, fentanyl has already killed hundreds of thousands of Americans and can and will kill anyone who consumes it.

In short, two key changes should be made to current PSAs about fentanyl. The messaging must shift from a narcotic prevention message to a public alert about mass poisoning. We should forgo narrowly targeting the messaging campaign to kids. Parents, grandparents, educators, nurses, and nearly everyone in between must hear the message. Think Mr. Beast (a YouTuber you have probably never heard of but your kids definitely have), *Monday Night Football*, and *The Bachelor*.

2. Nuevo Gallant Phoenix

We must either fund DHS or task the Department of Defense (DOD) to develop an "Operation Gallant Phoenix" (OGP) for fentanyl. DHS recruited key experts, like Colonel Fernando Lujan, who had experience establishing OGP in Jordan. Those experts generated a plan to reconstruct a similar program for fentanyl. Galant Phoenix was required to coordinate with local governments to apprehend and prosecute foreign fighters, just as we must with Mexico. Also, Gallant Phoenix employs a counternetwork strategy as opposed to a kingpin strategy. Only a counternetwork strategy will defeat the Sinaloa cartel, fentanyl supply chain, and any successor to Sinaloa who may fill the fentanyl void if Sinaloa desists. Yet the government has only partially implemented the recommendations of Colonel Lujan and his team. This is due to several factors, including lack of budget, scattered authorities, stubborn bureaucratic silos, and recalcitrant foreign partners. All these issues plagued

Gallant Phoenix in its inception as well; however, through dedicated, long-term focus and investment, the military overcame those challenges and defeated ISIS and al-Qaeda.

The same could be true for Sinaloa. But we need to evolve past the poor man's version of Gallant Phoenix we have today. We must construct a Gallant Phoenix for fentanyl as robust as that which defeated ISIS. To re-create OGP for Sinaloa, we must designate a single base to house analysts and agents from each relevant agency. Like Gallant Phoenix, this base should not be situated in Washington. It should be located in theater or theater adjacent. For example, the U.S. embassy in Mexico City or Customs and Border Protection (CBP) facilities in Nogales or San Isidro are possible locations for OGP headquarters. Further, Mexican officials, ideally from the Secretaría de la Marina (SEMAR) and Transnational Criminal Investigative Units (TCIUs) from the Mexican Justice Department (Fiscalía General de la República [FGR]), should be stationed there. As with Gallant Phoenix, concerns will persist about leaks that tip off the gangsters; however, DOD dealt with potential leaks at Gallant Phoenix every day. Yet it allowed foreign partners to participate who were no less prone to leaks than the Mexican government. The agency assigned to oversee the new base can arrange for classified office space at the base that is only for American personnel with clearances. They can also instantiate information-sharing processes to minimize the risk of leaks to the Sinaloa capos. All relevant agencies should be represented. Officials from DOD, the Drug Enforcement Administration (DEA), the Department of Justice (DOJ), DHS, CBP, Homeland Security Investigations (HSI), the Bureau of Alcohol, Firearms and Explosives (ATF), Treasury, State, SEMAR, Mexican FGR, and partners from Canada and Guatemala should pursue cases side by side. Only then can we illuminate the Sinaloa corporate structure, network of suppliers, finances, brokers, accountants, chemists, distribution channels, assets in the United States and information technology infrastructure. Not until we establish a program resourced like OGP will we unveil the Sinaloa network and see it like Ford does Toyota or we do ISIS. Not until we understand the entire Sinaloa network will we disrupt it and specifically its two most important assets: its finances and the corruption racket of government officials who protect the gangster warlords and their henchmen from capture and conviction.

3. With Us or against Us

Shuttering Sinaloa's fentanyl line of business requires Mexico's participation. Declaring war on Mexico or dispatching Seal Team Six to eliminate a never-ending series of kingpins is foolhardy. However, we must face the insidious power of the "silver or lead" maxim. Anyone who Sinaloa needs to corrupt will be corrupted, regardless of their integrity. To counter this, we must fully leverage all trade, diplomatic, financial, and political tools. It is imperative to enlist Mexican leadership as an active ally in the fight. There exists a host of reasons, dating back to the Mexican-American War, that the Mexican government does not kowtow to the United States. Hence it does not accept direct U.S. financial assistance for many activities. Regardless of their distaste for appearing too cozy with the United States, their support is essential. The circumstances are too dire. We must insist on this level of cooperation until fatalities drop by 95 percent, to below five thousand a year, under the fatality rate of heroin and cocaine. Then, the issue could be left to regular order law enforcement. This cooperation likely manifests in three forms.

First, Mexico should expand its vetted units by an order of magnitude. That would translate into an increase from the two hundred Mexican agents[9] in vetted units today to two thousand. Regular polygraphs, personnel rotations, and improved physical protection will help stave off widespread corruption. Mexico may lack the resources to sustain such a TCIU cadre; however, DOJ has devised creative ways to source funds more palatable to the Mexican government. For example, funds confiscated by U.S. law enforcement from Mexican criminals and repatriated to Mexico are especially well received. These funds appear as return of Mexican resources rather than hiring Mexican agents as toadies for the United States.

Second, to deal with the notoriously corrupt Mexican court system, the United States should fund separate courts for fentanyl cases. This should be facilitated in a way that protects judges' identities so they don't fear for their families' lives as a result of a conviction. Here again there exist creative ways to fund judicial enhancements through international organizations like the United Nations (UN).[10] If funded through a vehicle like the UN, Mexican judicial leadership would not be perceived as being in bed with the Americans.

Finally, to address the infamously corrupt Mexican prison system that allowed El Chapo to escape prison twice in one decade,[11] we should press for a special extradition policy for fentanyl cases. That policy should mandate those convicted on fentanyl charges serve their time in a U.S. prison. We should also funnel investment from the U.S. private sector into private-sector projects in Mexico via quasi-governmental organizations like the Export Import Bank (EXIM) and the Overseas Private Investment Corporation (OPIC). Like repatriated cartel funds from DOJ or resources funneled through the UN, EXIM and OPIC investments do not bear the stigma direct funding from the United States does. Whether it arrives via repatriated ill-gotten criminal proceeds, the UN, EXIM, OPIC, or any number of other sources, there are sufficient ways to ensure the United States can fully fund the counterfentanyl campaign in Mexico. The United States, however, should be clear to the Mexican government that it *will* accept these funds and will directly support our efforts against the narco-corporate empire's fentanyl business.

Here again the war on terror is instructive. As discussed in chapter 5, after 9/11 and the invasion of Afghanistan, the United States required Pakistani assistance for a host of U.S. operations in Afghanistan. The Pakistani government had ties stretching back decades with al-Qaeda and the Taliban. Corruption ran rampant in Pakistan. Leaders there also faced a silver-or-lead dilemma from terrorist groups. However, through steel-eyed realpolitik, the George W. Bush administration cajoled and coerced the Pakistani government to facilitate much of what Bush sought.

Secretary of State Colin Powell has reflected that the message he delivered to Pakistan at Bush's behest was simple and uncompromising: "You are either with us or against us."

He was dispatched by Bush to ensure Pakistan provided immediate support in the war against al-Qaeda and the Taliban. Powell's ultimatum underscored the gravity of implications for Pakistan in the wake of the U.S. response to the 9/11 attacks. It worked.[12]

Pervez Musharraf, president of Pakistan from 2001 to 2008, agreed to side with the United States. He provided logistical support, intelligence sharing, and access to Pakistani airspace and bases. The Pakistanis also directly helped the United States hunt and capture or kill key terrorists.[13] Musharraf later recounted that Pakistan's decision was driven by the perilously high stakes involved because the United States made it clear that noncooperation could lead to severe consequences for Pakistan.[14]

The United States spent billions in Pakistan during the war on terror. We knew Pakistani government officials skimmed off the top. This was not a bug but rather a feature of the program. Bush's team ensured Pakistani leadership depended on U.S. dollars. This dependency solidified key officials' resolve to keep cash flowing into their coffers. Further, the Pakistanis did not have a choice as to whether they would accept these funds. Pakistani leaders could choose whether U.S. funds would be embezzled; however, they could not choose whether to accept the funds and support the United States in the war on terror.

The Mexican government should be offered the same deal. We will fund the war on fentanyl to the tune of billions of dollars. We will ensure the funding is more palatable politically in Mexico via a litany of financial vehicles like those mentioned above. Invariably, some leaders will devise methods to pocket some of the cash for their own aggrandizement. That is the cost of doing business. Yet we should adopt the same steel-eyed realpolitik approach the Bush administration deployed in the war on terror.

Diplomats should deliver a clear message to Mexico: too many Americans are dying from a mass poisoning event emanating from Mexico. We will not debate as to whether the Mexican government will participate in the fight against fentanyl. In Pakistan, an implicit threat of force compelled assent to this deal. Obviously, we do not want to even implicitly threaten force with our southern neighbor. Geopolitical strategists would argue that, while fentanyl is horrific, bluster that drives Mexico into the arms of China in advance of a potential war with China is worse.[15]

Regardless, the United States has an enormous amount of leverage it can deploy in negotiations with the Mexican government. We have pulled few of these levers to date. Largely we have not employed these levers because they would inflict pain in the United States as well. There are myriad trade penalties that could be implemented. In fact, Trump's tariffs on Mexico as a consequence of fentanyl trafficking is a welcome method to use his bravado and bluster for good.

Yet there are still more levers to pull with Mexico. We could target remittances. Remittances from the United States make up 4.5 percent of Mexico's gross domestic product (GDP).[16] We also provide hundreds of millions in civil society and humanitarian assistance that could be relegated to the chopping block.[17] The family of high-ranking government officials traveling to the United States could have visas revoked. We could sanction senior government officials involved in fentanyl like we do the dons of Sinaloa. We could lobby for international arrest warrants for corrupt government officials aiding and abetting the fentanyl trade. We could seize all U.S. assets of Mexican officials involved with the fentanyl trade. These measures could be topped off by direct marketing to the millions of Mexicans living in the United States who can vote in Mexican elections. These actions or a sampling of them could inflict enormous pain for officials in Mexico. Tough actions like these, particularly around trade as Trump has called for, would certainly cause hardship for some industries in the United States, particularly those in border towns.

Under normal circumstances, these tactics would appear overly aggressive. However, the United States has the moral high ground on this issue as it is not a narcotics issue but a mass poisoning epidemic. Andrés Manuel López Obrador[18] and Xi Jinping like to assert that the United States needs to look in the mirror and deal with the narcotics consumption issue at home. They love to pontificate that America's supposed breakdown in family structures and religion have lured our young people into taking fentanyl. That is an old argument. It may have been applicable in drug heydays like the 1980s when users knew what they were consuming. Instead, this is a mass poisoning. The state of our families or religious participation is irrelevant.

Also, we would offer billions in aid for Mexico to wage the war on Sinaloa and fentanyl. We would not expect the Mexican government to conduct this effort as an unfunded mandate from Washington. Of course, alternating pressure and aid must be applied adroitly. But diplomats, like Secretary Powell, train their whole lives specifically for these types of negotiations. The judicious delivery of respect, aid, and firm consequences should induce Mexican leadership to conclude the prudent decision is to work with us rather than against us.

A key shortcoming of our negotiation package is that we cannot protect Mexican officials from Sinaloa's silver-or-lead policy. Initially we could likely expect leaders would find themselves in a deadly, unwinnable conundrum. Their only rational option is to play both sides. This is the same situation officials faced in Pakistan.

But time may be on our side. We have only begun to execute a coordinated campaign against Sinaloa. Yet already we have witnessed a drop in fentanyl fatalities immediately after the U.S. government launched the assault. It is possible that, if the counterfentanyl campaign described here is executed, we will experience a significant drop in fentanyl deaths quickly. Thus, Mexican officials could be out of harm's way sooner than one would experience with a more traditional narcotics law enforcement effort. If conditions seem too dire, we could even grant visas to the immediate family of key Mexican government officials to live in the United States for protection while the operation is underway. To recap, the request from the United States should include several key components:

- We need a dramatic increase of FGR vetted units to nearly ten times what they constitute now.

- Critical Mexican agencies like FGR and SEMAR must actively participate in Gallant Phoenix Mexico.

- Mexican military organizations like SEMAR should work with our intelligence community and law enforcement to hunt down key nodes of the Sinaloa network.

- Fentanyl cases should be heard in separate courts that protect judicial privacy.

- If convicted on fentanyl charges, prisoners should serve their time in a U.S. prison.

The United States should make clear that it will find politically palatable ways to fund all of these activities in Mexico and anything else operators deem relevant and reasonable. We need to make it very clear, however, that we will accept only one answer for this proposition: yes. If it is not quickly accepted, a litany of clearly enumerated consequences like those above will be implemented.

4. Gunning for Sinaloa

Tough talk aside, a critical path to cooperation is through the hearts and minds of the Mexican people. Recruiting the Mexican people to our side requires careful consideration of the plan's ramifications. A successful campaign against Sinaloa invariably entails significant bloodshed on both sides. This may be akin to the tens of thousands of deaths from the cartel wars in the mid-2000s. The average Mexican citizen will not support a deal that costs thousands of Mexican lives in exchange for saving thousands of American lives.

In exchange for bearing the brunt of this campaign, we must make significant, demonstrable progress to dramatically reduce the flow of arms from the United States to Mexico. Frankly, the United States should be ashamed it has wandered so far astray from Franklin Roosevelt's proclamation before entering World War II. He rallied the American people by arguing that the United States should be the "arsenal of democracy." He mobilized a war machine on an unprecedented scale. The United States armed the allies fighting fascists through the conclusion of the war. We may honor Roosevelt's legacy by supporting Ukraine against Russia and Taiwan against the People's Republic of China (PRC).

Unfortunately, the United States also serves as the arsenal of narco-warlords. The Mexican people have every right to expect that, if they stand with us against Sinaloa, we will stand with them. The United States must commit to prevent weapons from arming those who defend the fentanyl epidemic. There are multiple tactics that could be employed to stymie the flow of guns going south. Obviously, we can enhance search and seizure of vehicles traveling south. CBP and ATF can increase targeted searches backed by intelligence from the new Gallant Phoenix Mexico where ATF and CBP agents will be stationed. Also, we must increase ATF presence at gun shows and at weapons dealers in border communities.

There are only two possible scenarios by which Sinaloa is acquiring weapons: either a weapons dealer is illegally selling weapons to Sinaloa henchmen, or a weapons broker is legally acquiring guns and illegally distributing them to Sinaloa militiamen. Further, the Second Amendment does not apply to Mexican citizens; we can seize any weapon crossing the border to Mexico.[19]

Investigating crimes like these is ATF's bread and butter. ATF just requires appropriate funding to focus on those cases where guns are headed to Mexico. Today ATF and CBP spend miniscule amounts of their time and resources to curb weapons moving south. This is understandable as we are undergoing a firearm homicide crisis in the United States. So ATF and CBP are, rightly, resourced to address our problems first. Curbing weapons flowing south, however, will assist our efforts to stop fentanyl moving north. Thus, we should appropriate new budget allocations for ATF and CBP to interdict weapons destined for Mexico. Undoubtedly if CBP makes a dent in land-based southbound weapons shipping, Sinaloa's logistician managers will take to the water. To date, the U.S. Coast Guard (USCG) is not funded or directed to prioritize weapons bound for Mexico. Along with ATF and CBP, the USCG will need resources to step up efforts in this arena.

This should be a highly visible line of effort in the counterfentanyl campaign. As mentioned in chapter 4, the effort should feature press conferences in border towns nearly every week of the campaign against Sinaloa. The press events should showcase mountains of seized guns, ammunition, grenades, and any other devices American merchants of death proffer to gangster warlords. Most crucially, we should empower Mexican officials to claim political credit for the seizures. Few issues poll better with Mexican voters than keeping American-made weapons out of cartel hands.[20] Allowing a Mexican governor or senator to stand in front of a cache of seized weapons for a photo op costs us nothing but buys us goodwill from the Mexican people and the political leaders we allow to share the credit.

Allowing Mexican government leaders to take credit for the seizures will provide them political space to act. The Mexican people do not want to live through another narco-war like the one in the 2000s that claimed nearly thirty thousand souls each year since 2018.[21] Thousands of the dead were bystanders. Further, many of the narcos killed were small-time errand boys and housekeepers. They were not murderers. These poor manual laborers treated the job as a side hustle and certainly did not deserve to be mowed down in gangland hits. Most important, all of the thirty thousand per year felled in the narco-wars were the children, siblings, and grandchildren of someone. Any political leader who proposes Mexico return to the days when Juárez had the highest murder rate in the world and many other Mexican cities were not far behind[22] will quickly be ushered out of office by voters. Voters will immediately install leaders who commit to end the violence by calling a truce with the cartels. Once that happens, fentanyl will resume its unabated flow to the United States, devoid of consequences for the narcos.

But we can provide political leaders a narrative backed up by action from the United States. That narrative may convince voters to provide political leaders the space to act. The narrative would read as, "We are going after the cartel's fentanyl operations once and for all. It will be a bloody fight. But in exchange for our support, the Americans have committed to dramatically step up their efforts to keep weapons out of the hands of these gangsters. Then we can defang this parasite for good. This offer from the Americans likely won't come again in our lifetime, so we should partner with them to make Mexico safer for generations to come."

Mexican voters are just as cynical as their American counterparts. This is why the ongoing series of press conferences is crucial. After political leaders in Mexico propose this effort, it must be backed up by tangible results from the United States. Once a week we should facilitate a press conference in rotating media markets across northern Mexico. There are roughly nine media markets on the northern border of Mexico. We can organize a press conference with a mountain of seized weapons and ammunition as a backdrop for the speakers once a week. If we rotate the media markets, we could hit each one about five times a year—essentially every other month. Additionally, CBP already pays for advertising in Mexico encouraging would-be migrants to stay put. Some of those funds could be used to push clips of the press events on social media across Mexico so that voters see political leaders ensuring the gringos live up to their end of the bargain. These press conferences and social media advertising buys will be crucial to contrast with the inevitable headlines of rising death tolls as SEMAR and the TCIUs attack the gangster militias. This fight requires we win the hearts and minds of the Mexican people. Demonstrating we are serious about keeping American guns out of the hands of the Sinaloa militiamen is our best shot.

5. Digital Warfare

We must put our cyberwarriors in the game. Sinaloa boasts a multibillion-dollar-a-year organization. It may not have installed the IT infrastructure of a legitimate Fortune 50 company. Yet thousands of cartel members leverage technology every day. Further, vast empires of homes, cars, bank accounts, and licit and illicit companies obfuscate the dons' wealth. All those assets require technology. Millions of payments are executed via cryptocurrency. Corporate financial management of that scale interacts with global digital infrastructure somewhere. Communications among the Sinaloa C-Suite, and the tens of thousands of suppliers, subcontractors, and brokers, are conducted over the licit communications infrastructure. All that infrastructure should be hacked relentlessly.

As discussed previously in multiple chapters, Sinaloa's capos are not ideologically motivated but exclusively motivated by profit. So Cyber Command (CyberCom) should aim its powerful but limited resources at clawing back bloodstained profits from the cartel. CyberCom will argue in response to this request, "We can do that, but which group of our elite hackers do you recommend we reassign from hacking Russia and China to put them on these low-tech criminals?" The answer should be "none." Instead, DHS should be funded to do this work at CyberCom via the USCG. The U.S. Coast Guard is both a military organization and under the management of the world's largest law enforcement organization, DHS. As both a law enforcement and military organization, the USCG is perfectly positioned to pack the most cyber punch. USCG can leverage CyberCom military authorities and its own law enforcement authorities when hacking Sinaloa. Further, CyberCom will be more comfortable with another military organization operating on its platform. Thus, USCG should gain access to the world's most sophisticated cyber weapons to hack Sinaloa. It could menace Sinaloa in cyberspace day in and day out. This effort should be funded through dedicated appropriations to both USCG's and CyberCom's budget.

The USCG option has been explored and discarded largely because USCG does not have the infrastructure or authorities to execute this mission itself. Instead, the infrastructure and some of the authorities lie with CyberCom. But USCG "coasties" should be assigned to CyberCom. They can operate under its authorities and on its infrastructure while adding their law enforcement authorities to the operation. USCG would maintain both military and law enforcement authorities as well as access to the most exquisite hacking technology the United States has to offer. Thus, the coasties on duty can serve as both a cyberwarrior and cybercop depending on the task at hand. That combination of authorities and exquisite tech would make USCG a force to be reckoned with in cyberspace. Further, Sinaloa is a relatively low-tech organization. It doesn't have anything approaching the cybersecurity of a Fortune 500 company, much less a nation-state. Thus, in short order, the coastie hackers quickly would burrow so deep into Sinaloa's networks. Soon they could switch the Chapitos' home refrigerator off and on at will.

While we ultimately won the war on terror, the war against fentanyl has to be won much more quickly given the number of lives at stake. We could empower some new or existing agency with both military and domestic law enforcement authority via legislation, funding, and hiring. However, we already have an agency in the USCG that, in partnering with CyberCom, can do everything we need and more. We do not need a new agency to supplement CyberCom; we already have the capability, personnel, and some of the authorities in USCG. By partnering with CyberCom, USCG can acquire the tools and authorities it doesn't have already. This is the fastest way to begin hacking Sinaloa without taking the military's eye off the ball in China or Russia.

Also, HSI and other law enforcement agencies must exploit more aggressively their authorities in cyberspace. HSI, DEA, and other law enforcement organizations have the authority to operate undercover in cyberspace, like HSI did in the Silk Road investigation.[23] Just as undercover agents create fake personas in the real world, they can do the same in the digital world. They can also infiltrate the real personas of the dons, their henchmen, and corrupt government officials. Using fake personas and by taking over the accounts of real mobsters, they can execute information operations against the narco-empire.

These undercover operations can sow discord among the dons and henchmen alike. Our undercover cyberagents can start feuds. They can sow distrust between the organization and its vendors by sending fake messages pitting one narco against another. They can degrade corporate command structure. They can engender conflict between corrupt government officials over bribes or investigations. Undercover agents in cyberspace could send fake messages to corrupt government officials claiming bribe payments will cease or that they are under investigation by authorities. By undermining confidence from government officials in the cartel, we can begin to hack away at the Sinaloa C-Suite's most important asset: the corruption racket protecting the narco-tycoons.

Coastie cyberwarriors can wield CyberCom weapons to hack cartel infrastructure and steal information about assets, shipments, and individuals for law enforcement to target. Agencies like HSI and DEA can spread discord in cyberspace among cartel leadership and corrupt government officials providing a veil of protection. This tag-team approach will have Sinaloa chasing its tail in cyberspace in perpetuity. It will also provide targets and intelligence for real-world disruption operations.

These are high-impact actions that are comparatively less expensive to execute than real-world disruption. For example, to maximize impact during the Blue Lotus Operation, we had to pay for five hundred personnel and their travel, housing, and equipment to round up gangsters and seize fentanyl. These cyber operations could be executed with a few dozen coastie hackers and HSI undercover agents. The low cost and high impact make a concentrated cyber assault on Sinaloa a no-brainer.

6. Three Hundred Chemical Brothers

Finally, we cannot let the Chinese chemical companies off the hook. As Attorney General Alejandro Gertz Manero pointed out, once the raw materials for fentanyl—like precursor chemicals and the pill presses that deviously make the poison look like real medicine—arrive in a cartel chemist's hands, we have already lost. Further, the list of Chinese chemical companies engaged in the fentanyl precursor trade is only around three hundred companies. With nearly seven thousand agents at HSI, we could assign a small team to each company. Since U.S.-China relations are at a low point, we cannot arrest and extradite Chinese nationals for this offence. There is, however, a laundry list of tactics we can employ to dissuade chemical companies from supplying fentanyl precursors to Sinaloa. First, HSI or other law enforcement agencies can threaten the companies' investors. HSI can notify the investors they are engaged in a criminal enterprise killing hundreds of thousands of Americans. Investigators tell me that this tactic will terrify investors. It will compel them to dump the stock and thus crash the stock price of the company. Investors may also force corporate board and C-Suite changes and bring in leadership who will quash sales to Sinaloa.

Additionally, most of the revenue from these companies is not generated by Sinaloa but, rather, from legitimate organizations. These corporations range from manufacturers of everything like paint to swimming pool cleaners to pharmaceutical company suppliers. HSI can also threaten these customers with a message mimicking one delivered to investors. Many of these customers will surely drop the Chinese firm like a bad habit. Just as important, delivering messages like these to customers and investors does not require a conviction in advance. The messages can be disseminated and deliver impact far more quickly than achieving a conviction.

CBP can also detain shipments from the company to customers in ports. It can seize nearly every shipment from the firm for further scrutiny until almost none of their products make it to customers in a timely fashion. On top of HSI's messages, CBP could notify investors and customers declaring shipments are delayed because any products from that company require extra scrutiny due to their involvement in chemicals provided to Sinaloa.

This would further launch customers and investors into a frenzy. As a result, the chemical company's corporate board and C-Suite will institute extensive "know your customer" (KYC) policies. These policies are standard in other industries like finance where bankers are required by regulators to keep narcos and terrorists off their books.[24] KYC policies are well known by corporate governance executives. A key role of a corporate board or C-Suite executive is to mitigate risk for the company. KYC programs are standard tactics board members and executives use to mitigate risk. Obviously alerts of illegal activity from HSI and CBP will be considered as increased risk for the company. This pressure from HSI and CBP would undoubtedly trigger corporate leadership to institute extensive KYC policies to CYA. Those policies alone should stem the flow of precursors to a trickle for the dons of Sinaloa.

The Treasury Department sanctioning a company obviously will be even more impactful. Implementing sanctions on a chemical company is like bringing a bazooka to a knife fight. Sanctions will certainly have the intended effect. However, unlike a letter from HSI or CBP that is comparatively simple to secure approval for, sanctions require mountains of justification, paperwork, and approvals. We should immediately pursue Treasury sanctions against all three hundred companies. Sanctions, however, will take much longer and should be considered a final step after CBP and HSI put the fear of Uncle Sam into the chemical corporate board rooms.

Surely, Sinaloa will go elsewhere for its chemicals like India, where it already sources some precursors. But this playbook can be repeated with any company in any country. Also, the United States maintains much better relations with most countries than China. Thus, local law enforcement agencies in other countries collaborate more closely with the United States. Additionally, most other countries are not home to robust chemical manufacturing industries. So, any country to which Sinaloa shifts its chemical supply chain will create even more difficulties to evade our law enforcement.

Taken together, these tactics, among others, would cripple the companies in question. Corporate leadership could either clamp down on all sales legitimate or illegitimate or be driven out of business.

Conclusion

Implementing these recommendations along with extending the massive operations the Biden administration implemented in 2022 and 2023 should help ensure the unpresented drop in the death rate from fentanyl witnessed in

2024 continues to at the same pace. We should approach the menace with a counternetwork strategy much like we did the war on terror. However, we cannot allow this operation to drag on as long as the war on terror did. Fentanyl causes fifty times more fatalities annually than did 9/11. Consequently, we should set out to accomplish this task much faster than we won the war on terror. Congress should provide the resources to attack Sinaloa and the fentanyl supply chain network with the ferocity we did for ISIS. With the appropriate resources and a clearly defined and executed strategic campaign plan, we should seek to achieve our goal in fewer than four years. We should set out a bold plan to drive fentanyl deaths down from one hundred thousand to below five thousand a year by 2029. Our communities should expect nothing less from their government.

Notes

1 "Overdose Deaths Decline, Fentanyl Threat Looms." Drug Enforcement Administration, December 16, 2024. https://www.dea.gov/press-releases/2024/12/16/overdose-deaths-decline-fentanyl-threat-looms.

2 Mann, Brian. "The Pipeline of Deadly Fentanyl into the U.S. May Be Drying up, Experts Say." NPR, October 1, 2024. https://www.npr.org/2024/09/30/nx-s1-5124997/fentanyl-overdose-opioid-btmps-drug-cartel-xylazine-tranq-mexico-china.

3 "Drug Seizure Statistics." U.S. Customs and Border Protection, n.d. https://www.cbp.gov/newsroom/stats/drug-seizure-statistics.

4 Cunningham, Robert. "New Border Tunnel Discovery Reveals Escalating Drug Cartel Operations in Arizona." Capitalism Institute, January 6, 2025. https://capitalisminstitute.org/new-border-tunnel-discovery-reveals-escalating-drug-cartel-operations-in-arizona/.

5 Jeong, Helen. "Mexican Cartels Team up with Chinese Nationals in Los Angeles to Launder Money, DOJ Says." NBC Los Angeles, June 18, 2024. https://www.nbclosangeles.com/news/local/mexican-cartels-chinese-nationals-los-angeles-launder-drug-money/3439504/.

6 Including 9/11, the total number of noncombat Americans killed by Islamic terrorism since 2001 is 3,920. "American Deaths in Terrorist Attacks, 1995–2019." START, n.d. https://www.start.umd.edu/publication/american-deaths-terrorist-attacks-1995-2019.

7 Since 2018, roughly 70 percent of fentanyl deaths have occurred among people aged thirty-five and older. "Who Is Overdosing on Fentanyl?" USAFacts, May 29, 2024. https://usafacts.org/articles/who-is-overdosing-on-fentanyl/?utm_source=chatgpt.com.

8 "Overdose Prevention." Office of Addiction Services and Supports, n.d. https://oasas
.ny.gov/prevent-overdose.

9 "Statement of Matthew Millhollin, Assistant Director, Homeland Security
Investigations, for a Hearing on Combatting Transnational Organizations and the
Trafficking of Humans, Narcotics and Firearms." Homeland Security Investigations,
May 3, 2023, 9. https://www.ice.gov/doclib/news/library/speeches/230503Millhollin
.pdf.

10 Caserta, Salvatore. *International Courts in Latin America and the Caribbean.* Oxford:
Oxford University Press, 2020. E-book. https://doi.org/10.1093/oso/9780198867999
.001.0001.

11 Stempel, Jonathan. "After Two Escapes, 'El Chapo' May Go to 'Supermax' Prison
to Avoid a Third." Reuters, July 17, 2019. https://www.reuters.com/article/world
/after-two-escapes-el-chapo-may-go-to-supermax-prison-to-avoid-a-third
-idUSKCN1UC142/.

12 Yamin, Tughral. "Pakistan's Role in the Global War on Terror: 2001–2005." Institute of
Strategic Studies Islamabad, May 2016. https://www.issi.org.pk/wp-content/uploads
/2016/05/Tughral-Yamin-35-No.2.pdf.

13 Shah, Syed Muhammad Ali. "Pakistan and the War against Terrorism." *Pakistan
Horizon* 60, no. 2 (2007): 85–107. https://www.jstor.org/stable/41500065.

14 "US Threatened to Bomb Pakistan after 9/11: Musharraf Says He Acted Responsibly."
Dawn, September 21, 2006. https://www.dawn.com/news/211502/us-threatened-to
-bomb-pakistan-after-9-11-musharraf-says-he-acted-responsibly.

15 Rediker, Douglas A. "The Consequences of Trump's Tariff Threats." Brookings,
December 11, 2024. https://www.brookings.edu/articles/the-consequences-of-trumps
-tariff-threats/.

16 "Strong U.S. Labor Market Drives Record Remittances to Mexico." Federal Reserve
Bank of Dallas, n.d. https://www.dallasfed.org/research/swe/2023/swe2310.

17 "US Has Given $591mn to Mexican NGOs in the Past Three Years." *Mexico News
Daily*, June 1, 2021. https://mexiconewsdaily.com/news/us-has-given-591mn-to
-mexican-ngos-in-the-past-three-years/.

18 Stevenson, Mark. "Mexican President to US: Fentanyl Is Your Problem." AP News,
March 9, 2023. https://apnews.com/article/mexico-fentanyl-epidemic-overdoses-26f
735a54ee0ba075c394ce85aef03d0.

19 "22 U.S. Code § 2778—Control of Arms Exports and Imports." Legal Information
Institute, n.d. https://www.law.cornell.edu/uscode/text/22/2778.

20 Carpenter, Ted Galen. "U.S. Gun Laws: Mexico's Favorite Scapegoat for Drug
Violence." Cato Institute, June 18, 2022. https://www.cato.org/commentary/us-gun
-laws-mexicos-favorite-scapegoat-drug-violence.

21 "Criminal Violence in Mexico | Global Conflict Tracker." Center for Preventive Action | Council on Foreign Relations, n.d. https://www.cfr.org/global-conflict-tracker/ conflict/criminal-violence-mexico.

22 "Cities in Mexico Dominate Global Violence Rankings." Cure Violence Global, January 16, 2024. https://cvg.org/2023-global-violence-rankings/.

23 For example, HSI already coordinates oversight of cyber activities with a dedicated center: "Cyber Crimes Center (C3)." U.S. Department of Homeland Security, n.d. https://www.dhs.gov/hsi/centers-and-labs/c3. DEA includes a specific line item budget request for extensive ongoing cyber activities: "DOJ FY2021 Budget Request for Drug Enforcement Administration." U.S. Department of Justice, 2021. https://www .justice.gov/doj/page/file/1246676/dl.

24 "Why Know Your Customer (KYC)—for Organizations." U.S. Bank, December 21, 2023. https://www.usbank.com/financialiq/improve-your-operations/minimize-risk/ Why-KYC-for-organizations.html.

Index

Note: Page locators followed by 'n.' refer to notes.

Abrams, J. J.   183
Adderall   134
Afghan(s)   9–11, 13, 17
    Airbnb   19
    army   1, 9
    biometric scanning   11, 12
    government   11
    job   18
    national force   1
    refugees   16
    resettlement crisis   18
    in United States   16
    to U.S. military   12
Afghanistan   1, 2, 9, 11, 15, 17, 20, 34,
        149, 164, 177, 178, 182
Airbnb   19
Air Force G5   217
alcohol prohibition   102
al-Qaeda   54, 94, 150, 173, 180, 182,
        193, 214, 241, 246
Amazon   18, 33, 168–9
American temperance movement
        102
April Anvil   35–6
Arellano Félix, Benjamin   110
Aristotle   82
"Arsenal of Democracy" speech   34
Asian immigrants   100
asylum seekers   7
Atlantic City   203, 207
Avilés Pérez, Pedro   104

bad-guy stuff   55
A Beautiful Mind (film)   162
Belsasso, Bibiana   72, 73
Ben'Ary, Michael   156, 233
be on the lookout (BOLO)   164
Bezos, Jeff   33, 168, 169, 172
Biden, Joe   16, 37, 49, 56, 57, 64, 86, 144,
        151, 213, 218, 233, 234
Biden administration   vii, 8, 29, 84, 90,
        94, 239, 257
big data analytics   160
bin Al-Hussein, Abdullah II   180
bin Laden, Osama   129, 162, 182
biometric scanning   11–12
Bitcoin   171
Black Hawk Down (film)   93
Blue Lotus Operation   228, 229, 235, 255
Boeing 727   107, 108
Bonilla Lara, Rodrigo   106
Border Patrol   6, 7, 27
Borgata Hotel   207
Brodman, Mathew   153–6, 228
Brooklyn   154, 195, 202
Bush, George H. W.   86, 124, 125, 153,
        246
Bush administration   148, 150, 246, 247
business-to-business (B2B)   123

C-17 military transport   9, 13
Canada   26, 126, 213, 244
Cancun   52

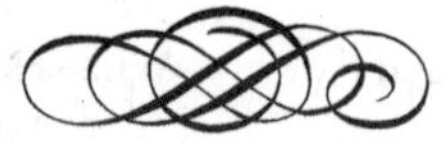

About the Author

Jake Braun was at the center of the U.S. government's plan to combat fentanyl. He served as the acting principal deputy national cyber director in the White House where one of the five top missions of the White House cyber strategy is to disrupt transnational criminal organizations like the cartels who traffic fentanyl. Before serving in the White House, Braun was senior counselor to the secretary of homeland security where he helped lead the team that established and oversaw the counterfentanyl strategy for the Department of Homeland Security (DHS). As such, he was also part of the White House / National Security Council (NSC) interagency group that developed the administration's government-wide strategic plan for combating fentanyl. The NSC strategy was the first of its kind for any administration. As part of these efforts, he engaged with counterparts at the highest levels of the Mexican government. While Braun spent a lot of time engaged with his colleagues in the White House and leadership in key national security agencies like DHS, the Department of Justice (DOJ), Department of Defense (DOD), State Department (State), National Security Agency (NSA), and Central Intelligence Agency (CIA), part of his role was also to roll up his sleeves with field agents and data analysts pursuing these cases on the ground or online in the United States, Mexico, and China. So, he gained both a bird's-eye and a worm's-eye view of the epidemic and the effort to combat it.

Braun has worked at the intersection of politics, national security, and foreign policy for more than two decades. President Obama appointed Braun as White House liaison to the Department of Homeland Security. There Braun was assigned to the highest-profile issues at DHS such as migration surges, counterterrorism, and cybersecurity. After he left the administration, Braun produced several award-winning reports on one of the hot-button issues of our time: election security. He and a few well-known hackers set out to prove voting equipment was hackable at DEF CON, the largest hacker conference in the world. Later Braun wrote an academic book on that topic, *Democracy in Danger: How Hackers and Activists Exposed Fatal Flaws in the Election System* (Rowman & Littlefield, 2019). Upon returning to Chicago, he established the Cyber Policy Initiative for the Harris School of Public Policy at the University of Chicago. Concurrently, he cofounded a national security consulting firm with partners from the Bush, Trump, Obama, and Biden administrations and served as a consultant to the seniormost levels of DOD, State, and DHS. The firm has operated in more than forty countries. Jake lives in Chicago with his family and has resigned himself to the pain and mental anguish caused by the Bears, Bulls, Cubs, and White Sox.